# Introduction to Production

*Introduction to Production: Creating Theatre Onstage, Backstage, & Offstage* defines the collaborative art of making theatre and the various job positions that go into realizing a production. Beginning with an overview of the art and industry of theatre, the book shows how theatre has evolved through history. The book then breaks down the nuts and bolts of the industry by looking at each professional role within it: from the topmost position of the producer down to the gopher, or production assistant. Each position is defined along with its respective duties, rules, and resources that figure in obtaining the job. Each chapter offers exercises, links to videos and websites, review quizzes, and suggested readings to learn more about the creation and production of theatre.

**Robert I. Sutherland-Cohen** is an Associate Professor Emeritus of Stage Management and Production Manager at Brooklyn College. He has been production stage manager for numerous Broadway and regional productions, as well as the New York City Opera. His diverse career in live performance presentations includes: Entertainment Operations Manager for the Tropicana in Atlantic City, Production Coordinator for Lincoln Center Festivals, and Associate Producer/ Writer for Westinghouse TV. He served on the Executive Board of the Stage Managers' Association, of which he was a founding member and former chairperson. He has taught at both Emerson College and Stockton State College, and has delivered guest lectures at Yale University, SUNY Purchase, and West Chester University. His most recent book is *Tesla for Beginners*.

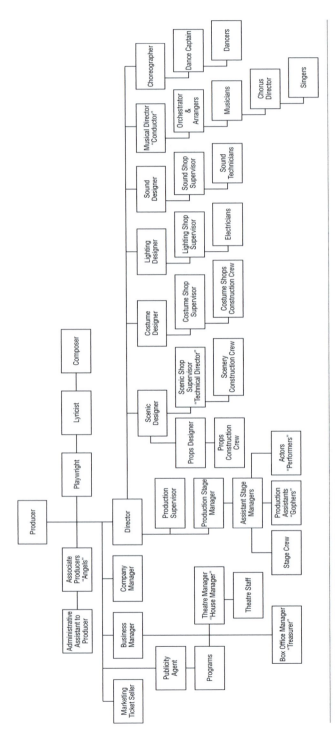

**Figure 0.1** Theatre Production Organization Chart

# Introduction to Production

Creating Theatre Onstage,
Backstage, & Offstage

*Robert I. Sutherland-Cohen*

*With a Foreword by Peter Lawrence,*
*Tony Award-Winning Stage Manager*

Routledge
Taylor & Francis Group

NEW YORK AND LONDON

First published 2018
by Routledge
711 Third Avenue, New York, NY 10017

and by Routledge
2 Park Square, Milton Park, Abingdon, Oxon OX14 4RN

Routledge is an imprint of the Taylor & Francis Group, an informa business

Library of Congress Cataloging in Publication Data
A catalog record for this book has been requested

ISBN: 978-1-138-65056-5 (hbk)
ISBN: 978-1-138-65777-9 (pbk)
ISBN: 978-1-315-61871-5 (ebk)

Typeset in Helvetica Neue and Times New Roman
by Servis Filmsetting Ltd, Stockport, Cheshire

Visit the e-resources at www.routledge.com/9781138657779

To my wife Patricia

. . . The Most Beautiful Star in All My Productions

# Table of Contents

# Acknowledgments

Theatre production by its very nature is a collaboration of many hands, and this book about theatre production follows that model. If I were to call upon all my collaborators to take a bow upon publication for their contributions, they would fill a stage larger than any historic grand amphitheater. My career began in college and continued across national and international stages, wonderfully concluding as professor emeritus in college. I am gratefully indebted to all my teachers and professional colleagues for their patience, expertise, and creative energy. We worked together to make every production the best possible. Without their support, knowledge, and inspiration this book would never have seen the light of day. My students too have taught me so much, and I hope now with this book we will reach many other students and colleagues.

Behind the scenes, but always in the forefront of my theatrical thoughts, many deserve to share the spotlight with me. These include my mentors at Northeastern University and Boston University, my colleagues at the Chateau De Ville Dinner Theatres, the hundreds of professionals Off- and On-Broadway, those dedicated artists across regional and international theatres, the specialists at the Tropicana Casino and Resorts, and the top-flight experts at Lincoln Center and the New York City Opera, as well as fellow professors and staff at Brooklyn College.

I specifically extend my thanks to: Jay Adler, Michael Anania, Joe Burkard, Vinnette Carroll, Rich Costabile, Andy Feigen, Beth Greenberg, Michael Hairston, Haejin Han, John Higbee, Larry Higbee, Marjorie Horne, Abe Jacob, Sarah Johnston, Paul King, Bill Lacey, Peter H. Lawrence, Steve Leber, David Leveaux, Emily Mann, Rose Mula, Ron Ostertag, Jenniper Pacheco, Joshua D. Reid, Bruce Richey, Ira Rosenbaum, Shuhei Seo, Jackie Smerling, Justin Townsend, David Wheeler, Susan Whelan, Diane Wondisford, and every member of the Stage Managers' Association. There are many individuals, actually too numerous to mention; but if you have helped me, I gratefully thank you.

Special thanks goes to Stacey Walker, Acquisitions Editor at Focal Press, for her faith, commitment, and passion for undertaking this project, and to Meredith Darnell, Editorial Assistant, who has devoted many painstaking hours to fielding questions. Thanks also to the production team and editors in the United Kingdom, including Carrie Bell and Maria Anson, for bringing this book to fruition.

Family always bears the greatest weight of living through the trials and tribulations of a professional stage manager. For their continual support and joyous "Oh, Daddy," I am grateful to be blessed with two loving daughters, Shana and Alyssa.

And, to my wife Patricia: without her eagerness for my success, always shining the spotlight on my endeavors, welcoming my return from rehearsals, performances, and repeated touring with rapturous laughter—as well as the repeated encouragement to persevere with all my undertakings—the journey to this book and through a theatrical career would have been impossible. In a word, her love has provided the most gratifying sustenance.

# Foreword

## Peter Lawrence, Tony Honor for Excellence in the Theatre – Stage Manager and Production Supervisor

The theatre is a chaotic place. It can often seem that disorganization rules – scripts change, music is re-written, set pieces are cut or added, actors are re-assigned roles, budgets expand. But this seeming chaos is really just part of a process. And it's an entirely creative process, whether one is a producer, an actor, a general manager, a designer, an actor or a stage manager. Each player in this process is lending his or her expertise to the shifting needs of a theatrical production.

Mike Nichols always said, "Everyone serves the production. And if you can't serve it, get out of the way."

But serving the production means different things to different professionals. For the General Manager, serving the production may mean putting it on a sound financial basis that will allow it to run and employ hundreds of people. For the stage manager, it may mean keep the production on schedule so as to be ready for the first preview. For the director, serving the production may mean working out a concept, no matter what the cost or difficulties. For the designers and technicians, it may mean collaborating to bring all the physical elements of the production to the stage in a seamless, unified fashion. For the actor, it may mean exploring his/her character with enough detail to make the performance both fully performed and real. And these competing goals are often in conflict and must be resolved.

It is from this very tumult, this clash of competing goals – and often of competing egos – that the theatre is born. It is collaborative in the best sense of the word – a group of professionals corralled together to accomplish a single goal. To tell a story in the clearest, most entertaining way possible – and, in the commercial theatre, to have it run long enough to make a profit. This sounds simple enough, but it is one of the most difficult processes in all the arts. If it were easy, all shows would succeed. But approximately 75% of commercial productions fail. And they fail because some of the members of the production team didn't "serve the production."

Either through artistic failure, financial restriction or sheer inattention, some parts of the show were let down.

Robert Sutherland-Cohen's book details what is the responsibility of each of the many professionals who must grapple a production to Opening Night. The book is an excellent guide for anyone trying to figure out how to bring order to the apparent chaos of the theatre. And his organization charts are a very handy way to visualize this process.

Robert has worked extensively in the Broadway and regional theatre, and is an Emeritus Professor at Brooklyn College. And so he has a unique perspective on how both the commercial and non-commercial theatres are organized and how they operate. He has the teaching skill to lay out this chaotic process in a logical way which students wanting to enter the professional theatre can understand.

As a long-time professional stage manager, I found Mr. Sutherland-Cohen's book to be an excellent refresher course on theatrical organization. And I particularly appreciated his "Fast/ Good/Cheap" triangle – a basic tenet of any business, but especially of the theatre.

It is often said that, "The theatre is no fit place for an adult." Well, Robert Sutherland-Cohen's book is written by an adult for adults.

# Preface

Our initial interest in theatre might have been sparked by witnessing an outstanding performance. However, there is much more that occurs onstage and behind the scenes that is worth explaining. Such work is carried out by a host of contributors other than actors for the creation of a theatrical event.

This book is intended for the person who in all truth and honesty wishes to learn about the collaborative support team that exists behind every performance. It is for a reader who desires to explore the multitude of opportunities and job possibilities that might lead to a fulfilling career in theatre. The serious person who embarks on this journey and expects to succeed will look beyond the excitement of opening nights and resounding applause. Theatre can be a rewarding career that combines almost single-minded dedication with much sacrifice. The fulfillment of successful collaboration, a necessity in all forms of theatre, is practically its own reward. Notice that we do not mention a monetary reward initially. With time, doors for more potential creative opportunities and a variety of employment paths could possibly open to the talented, the trained, and the skilled practitioner.

Theatre is part of that world we call "show business" for a reason: the "show" and the "business." There is an element of glamour to each of them. Yes, you can gain entry as a single actor performing your own, self-written, one-person play on a street corner or webcam, and solicit applause as well as donations from others. Yet these actions hardly sustain a career, or attract an audience on a consistent basis.

Bitten by the theatrical bug, inevitably many of you who thought about presenting a play in one fashion or another quickly realize that eventual success does not come from performing on a street corner. Perhaps this same street-corner actor has written a play that could be potentially performed in a space with a specific playing schedule, garnering positive reviews, and returning a monetary award to our performer. In order to gain this measure of reward it is highly unlikely the individual would have been able to do it alone. Understandably this solo performer had to collaborate with a number of individuals and assume a number of roles that are common to all theatrical productions before being justly rewarded: producer, theatre owner, publicist, ticket seller, and a paying audience to name a few.

All this seems straightforward. But wait, our performer's enthusiasm is getting ahead of reality. There are many practical steps along the way and many more opportunities for possible realistic success in theatre.

It is here that we begin our exploration of these many opportunities. Let's start with a look at an organization chart for a large-scale musical (see Figure 0.1). Typically, this same chart could serve for any amateur, community, not-for-profit, or commercial production. A number of the chart's job positions may be consolidated or eliminated depending on the varied skills required of the personnel engaged for the production. For instance, a quick look at the chart would reveal in all probability that a musical director and the attendant staff could be eliminated for a non-musical. In addition, the scale of the production could also be determined by economic factors. For a presentation in a very tiny theatre the entire management staff might be consolidated into one person who sells tickets, performs the duties of usher, and cleans the building. In essence the organizational chart will serve as a guide to the many and varied job positions that this book will present for someone who wants to get into theatre as a potential career.

There are many in-depth books and specialty courses on how to become a playwright, a producer, a general manager, a director, an actor, a scenic designer, a costume designer, a lighting designer, or other specialty designers, as well as guides to the various technical positions that comprise theatre production. This is not one of those books. This is a book about responsibilities and certain decisions that a theatre specialist has to undertake in order to contribute to the potential success of a production. In short, this is a book that endeavors to present a broad overview of theatre organization, lines of responsibility, and process.

One key element that is integral for everyone involved in a production is to read the play. How this becomes of major importance for practically every job position will be elaborated upon in the course of your reading this book.

Readers may find beginning inspiration in their initial reading of the book. There will be many forms, charts, drawings, illustrations, and exercises that are sprinkled throughout the book as supportive figures related to the text. Just reading this book may enlighten many. However, greater enrichment for learning about the theatrical production process will be gained by thoroughly engaging with the many exercises, activities, e-resource hyperlinks, and additional suggested resource materials. In particular, these include:

- **LEARN MORE**: Text box callouts for this book's e-resource (at www.routledge.com/ 9781138657779) provide hyperlinks for additional material and videos, as well as suggested exercises that bear directly on the text as you are reading it.

- **RELATED EXERCISES**: Opportunities for the reader to stretch their imagination and begin thinking about the decisions that a person in one of the positions on the organization chart must make in order to successfully complete their job.

- **FURTHER DISCUSSIONS**: Suggested participation with classmates and teachers on topics relevant to each of the chapters.

- **WHAT DID YOU LEARN?**: A few questions and answers that conclude certain chapters and serve as self-guides to essential material contained in those chapters.

- **ADDITIONAL RESOURCES**: Provided at the conclusion of each chapter for additional research material in print form as well as web resources in order to advance in-depth knowledge on the past, present, and perhaps future specific to the subject covered in that chapter.

Hopefully this book will spark your interest and lead you to embark upon a glorious theatre career. The greatest reward will come from getting out and seeing "live theatre." Enjoy and attend with an open eye!

# Production and Backstage Organization

## Production is a collaborative dream fulfilled

## DEFINING THEATRE PRODUCTION

A quick glance at the production organization chart (Figure 0.1) at the beginning of this book demonstrates how a theatre production is structured, in its relationships and responsibilities, much like virtually any corporation. Indeed, Nike, Coca-Cola, Ford Motors, or British Airways all have an organization chart. In our case the chart could relate to a specific production, such as the *Phantom of the Opera* or *Hamlet*. The positions relate to the different jobs that comprise the making of a theatrical production.

Take this opportunity to glance at the organizational chart and think back to any theatre production that you may have attended. It need not be a large-scale musical performed on Broadway or in the West End. It may not even have been a musical at all. In fact, it might have been a play specifically for children, or any piece staged in a high school, a church basement, a community hall, a local professional theatre, or even your own college drama auditorium—which we will touch upon in the pages ahead. It took many people holding different job **positions** while working in **collaboration** to realize the **production** that you attended.

Our organizational chart stands as an example of the many different kinds of job positions it might take to reasonably present a truly large musical production. As it happens, some of the positions may have had their duties combined or eliminated if music were not a component of the production. Many lines of reportage change as a production moves from inception to performance, as we shall see in the coming pages.

For those of you new to theatre many of the job positions on the organizational chart may be unfamiliar. Those of you who have had some exposure to live theatre may have already developed some ideas regarding what each of the positions attempts to accomplish. Hopefully the novice theatregoer and those that have attended live theatre with some frequency will come to appreciate the time, effort, talent, and money it takes to put on a show as you read further.

In the succeeding chapters we will elaborate on how the different positions (jobs) work in collaboration with one another in order to realize a successful production (the live theatrical presentation in a particular space), for it is the production that is the resultant dream which the many positions on the organizational chart working in collaboration hope to successfully realize.

It should be noted at this point that the term "production" is used interchangeably to define the process of making live theatre and to describe the fully staged event. For the moment let us look at the three major divisions of job positions for those who participate in the process of making a theatre production. These three divisions of responsibility are: **management** (business), **creative** (talent), and **technical** (construction and running crews). Figure 1.1 delineates the job positions for each division. Of special note is the position of stage manager, which invariably straddles all three divisions throughout the production process. This unique position will be discussed fully in a later chapter.

During the production process any one position may have to consider not only the execution of their own job, but also how they affect others to effectively perform their own respective tasks. Invariably, what someone on the management side of production does may affect how someone creatively produces their work, as well as how a technical person performs the job. This type of interdependence among everyone within the organization signals the need for everyone to be part of the collaborative process; awareness of this is intrinsic to possible success in the theatre. It is the process and the decision making undergone by each position within these three divisions that we will be examining in the pages ahead.

## A LITTLE BIT OF THEATRE HISTORY

Remember that sole street-corner actor we started with in the Preface? In essence that actor is not that far removed from the very first actor, Thespis, who stepped out of the chorus before a gathered Greek audience numbering in the thousands around the 6th century BC. Thespis not only recited; he also portrayed a character through movement, possible vocal changes, and perhaps had interactive spoken exchanges with the chorus. The chorus was a group of people

| PRODUCTION DIVISIONS | | |
| --- | --- | --- |
| MANAGEMENT (Business) | CREATIVE (Talent) | TECHNICAL (Construction & Performance Crews) |
| Producer | Playwright | Production Supervisor |
| Associate Producers | Lyricist | Scene Shop Supervisor |
| Administrative Assistant | Composer | Technical Director |
| Company Manager | Director | Scenery Construction Crew |
| Business Manager | Scenic Designer | Props Construction Crew |
| Theatre Manager | Costume Designer | Costume Shop Supervisor |
| House Manager | Lighting Designer | Costume Construction Crew |
| Box Office Manager | Sound Designer | Lighting Shop Supervisor |
| Theatre Staff | Prop Designer | Electricians |
| Publicity Agent | Musical Director | Sound Shop Supervisor |
| Programs | Conductor | Sound Technicians |
| Marketing Ticket Sales | Chorus Director | Stage Crew |
| | Singers | Gopher |
| | Choreographer | |
| | Dance Captain | |
| | Dancers | |
| | Actors | |
| Production Stage Manager | | |
| Assistant Stage Managers | | |

**Figure 1.1**   Production Divisions

## LEARN MORE: THE MAKING OF A BROADWAY MUSICAL

This might be a nice place for a video pause. Take a few minutes and jump ahead to the RELATED EXERCISES at the end of this chapter.

Follow the suggestions for viewing the DVD *Show Business: The Road to Broadway*. Within the video are ideas that apply to any level of production that will enhance your continued reading of this book.

that typically served to formulate, express, and comment on the moral issues raised by the dramatic action or to express an emotion appropriate to each stage of the dramatic conflict in a tragedy. The chorus was usually fully integrated into the action of the play and contributed to the unity of the plot, according to the Greek philosopher Aristotle.

It would not be long before costume elements would be introduced by a "lead actor" such as Thespis. This lead actor might portray a god and would be distinguished by wearing a ***chiton*** (a long flowing robe dyed in special colors and heavily padded to give the actor a grander look than the simply mortal members of the chorus). The actor would be elevated with thick-soled platform shoes called ***cothurni***. In addition, the actor donned a mask with thick, protruding lips that not only defined the actor as a god, but also aided in vocal projection in the large outdoor performance space or **amphitheater**.

The *chiton*, the *cothurni*, and the mask could easily be considered some of the earliest examples resulting from the work of a costume designer, although such a person would be hard to ascertain from historical records. However, the actor or someone else had to fulfill the position of costume designer and give some thought as how to design, fit, and functionally construct these costume pieces.

Similar thought must have gone into the layout and utilization of the space where Thespis and the chorus performed. We know from the ruins of ancient Greek theatres that the performance space was separated from the audience's seating area. This playing area was defined by a ground-level circular area (the orchestra) that contained a stone elevation or altar (Figure 1.2). In the background was the ***skene*** (a columned building) through which

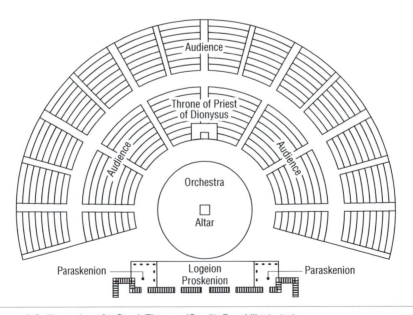

**Figure 1.2** Illustration of a Greek Theatre. (Credit: Focal Illustrator)

the actors possibly entered and exited. The *skene* also provided different levels for acting. In addition, an **ekkyklema** (a low platform that rolled on wheels) could be pushed onstage from the *skene* or revolved on an axis to reveal an interior or some offstage scene. Notice how the Greek word *skene* closely resembles the word "scene." Hence we arrive at the position of scene designer. With ideas taken into consideration by a scene designer, the Greek *ekkyklema* could be considered a forerunner of modern turntables and other revolving mechanisms (Figure 1.3).

This snapshot look at ancient Greek theatre production gives rise not only to today's production specialists such as the costume designer and the scenic designer, but also hints at antecedents to many more job positions on our production organization chart (Figure 0.1). Think about this for a moment as you reference the chart:

- Who might have written the play that the actor and chorus performed?
- Who might have decided to put on the play?
- How did people find out where and when the performance would take place?
- Did someone tell the performers where to enter, when to speak, how to interact, how loud to speak so that an audience numbering in the thousands could hear and understand them, etc.?
- Was someone responsible for leading the chorus?

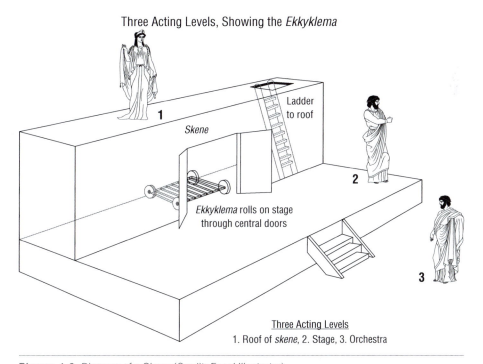

Three Acting Levels, Showing the *Ekkyklema*

1

*Skene*

Ladder to roof

2

*Ekkyklema* rolls on stage through central doors

3

Three Acting Levels
1. Roof of *skene*, 2. Stage, 3. Orchestra

**Figure 1.3** Diagram of a *Skene* (Credit: Focal Illustrator)

- Who moved the *ekkyklema*?
- Which technician turned the lights on?

Ooops! Caught you on that last one. There was no electricity during the 6th century BC. However, it becomes more apparent over time that there had to be some form of collaboration in order to realize theatrical productions for the previous thousands of years.

# THEATRE CONFIGURATIONS

As noted with the ancient Greeks, we have encountered what is recognized architecturally as the first performance space for putting on plays. Where an audience sits or stands in relation to a performance dictates the configuration or style of a theatre. There are generally six configurations within which an audience can view a live theatrical event. As you read about each of these configurations consider the advantages and disadvantages that each presents for a viewing audience.

## 1) AMPHITHEATER

Within an amphitheater the seating is arranged in a semi-circular fashion and the audience faces the performance space (see Figure 1.2). Notice once again the orchestra area and the *skene*. As you examine the *skene* there are two projecting side additions to it, alternatively called the *paraskenion* or *proskenion*. These one- or two-story wings framing the *skene* could be ornamented with columns or pillars topped by a frieze. It is from the word *proskenion* that we derive today's most common configuration for viewing a production: the proscenium theatre.

## 2) PROSCENIUM

The proscenium that had antecedents in the *proskenion*, those side portions in the *skene*, continues overhead today to form the proscenium arch. In this configuration the audience is seated to face a stage in which the proscenium forms an opening that separates them from the stage. This arrangement is such as if the audience were watching a play through a picture frame (Figure 1.4).

## 3) THRUST STAGE OR ¾ STAGE

A thrust stage or ¾ stage indicates that the audience is seated on three sides of a playing area or platform. The 4th side of the platform could be backed by a wall, a door unit, or any scenic arrangement that separates the remaining portion of the platform from the audience seated around the other three sides (Figure 1.5).

Another variant of the thrust stage or ¾ stage could be a platform that juts out of a proscenium opening (Figure 1.6). On the proscenium stage large pieces of scenery that form different backgrounds might be able to be interchanged readily. For instance a door unit might form the background for one interior scene and then be replaced by an exterior mountain that the actors could possibly scale. However, the audience remains seated on the three sides of the thrust stage.

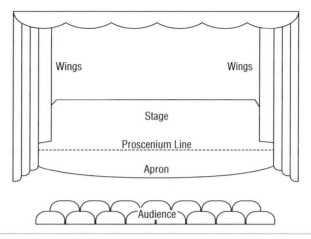

**Figure 1.4** Diagram of a Proscenium Stage (Credit: Focal Illustrator)

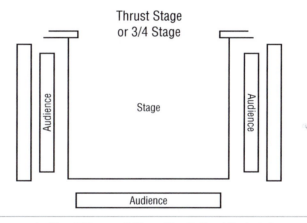

**Figure 1.5** Diagram of a Thrust Stage or ¾ Stage (Credit: Focal Illustrator)

## 4) THEATRE-IN-THE-ROUND OR ARENA THEATRE

For a theatre-in-the-round or arena theatre configuration audience seating encircles a playing area that typically might be floor level or on a raised circular or rectangular platform (Figure 1.7).

## 5) BLACK BOX

A black box theatre, as the name implies, is a box-shaped theatre that could start out with all four walls, ceiling, and floor painted black. A distinguishing feature of the black box theatre is that the audience seating area need not be in a fixed configuration. That is to say the audience may be seated in a thrust pattern, a circular pattern, or a random pattern for viewing a

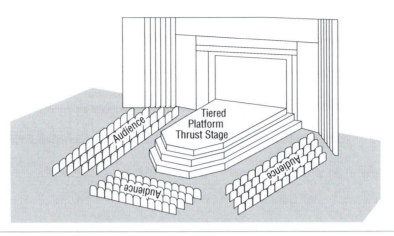

**Figure 1.6** Variant of a Thrust Stage or ¾ Stage (Credit: Focal Illustrator)

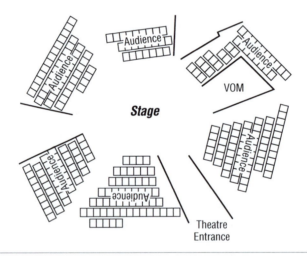

**Figure 1.7** Illustration of a Theatre-in-the-Round or Arena (Credit: Focal Illustrator)

particular staged event within the black box. The entire audience may be seated on the floor, or in non-permanent seats, or even on seats affixed to platforms of various heights. In short, the black box theatre affords flexible seating and a myriad of arrangements for staging a play in a theatre that need not always be painted black. This arrangement potentially presents infinite options for both staging a play and seating an audience.

## 6) SITE-SPECIFIC THEATRE

The locale for each site-specific theatre presentation is dictated by the subject matter of the performance. The audience could attend a religious play that utilizes an actual church for its performance, or wander through a series of rooms in a building for each respective scene portrayed; go from building to building in a designated area; be ushered though the cars on a moving train; or even be transported to different cities as the performance unfolds. The audience might sit or stand in each of these places. One of the most famous site-specific plays—one that has been conducted for over twenty-five years in Monroeville, Alabama—is a production based on Harper Lee's immensely popular novel *To Kill a Mockingbird*.

## STYLE ADVANTAGES AND DISADVANTAGES

Figure 1.8 summarizes some of the advantages and disadvantages of proscenium and thrust stage productions. Try filling in more advantages and disadvantages for these and the remaining styles listed in this chart.

| STYLE OF THEATRE | ADVANTAGES | DISADVANTAGES |
|---|---|---|
| Amphitheater | | |
| Proscenium | Entire audience is able to view the same stage picture<br><br>Large pieces of scenery may be brought onstage from above, below, and the sides<br><br>Allows for surprise entrance of actors | Less intimate as audience becomes seated further from the stage<br><br>Since large pieces of scenery can be utilized, costs can get very high<br><br>Maintaining such a theatre increases costs |
| Thrust or ¾ Stage | Intimate seating for viewing and hearing actors<br><br>Lower costs for minimal scenery<br><br>Generally smaller than a proscenium, and thus has lower maintenance costs | Viewing orientation and audibility changes as actors move about the stage, so an actor's back will always be to someone in the audience<br><br>Any large furniture would block audience's ability to always see the actors<br><br>Moving scenery on and offstage can be expensive if motorization is introduced |
| Theatre-in-the-Round or Arena Theatre | | |
| Black Box | | |
| Site-Specific | | |

**Figure 1.8** Styles of Theatre: Advantages and Disadvantages

Once you have successfully completed your chart, you might want to undertake RELATED EXERCISE #2 at the end of this chapter, which challenges you to research style configurations for some well-known theatres.

# THEATRE FACILITY LAYOUT

Up to this point the six styles or configurations for staging plays have been detailed. Not only do these configurations pose their own individual advantages or disadvantages; a number of the configurations also take on other considerations when they are included in a larger facility or other institutions, as you may have noticed in your research for the nine suggested theatres.

Refer once again to the organizational chart (Figure 0.1) and remind yourself of the many job positions that potentially need to function in an actual performance space today. Think about why many of these 21st-century positions were absent in the classical Greek theatre. Historically, the structure was a huge amphitheater with a stark performance space in which performers simply entered and exited to deliver their lines to the audience. However, thousands of years later advances in technology led to more elaborate and complex theatre facilities. Staffing these facilities and increasing the number of different jobs related to the production takes on added significance when situated in a larger modern facility. In Figure 1.9 the architectural floor plan locates the proscenium of Oregon's Camelot Theatre in such a facility.

In addition to an entire audience orientated in the same direction to face the stage, there is a whole network of spaces that function to support productions within the larger whole complex—in this case the Camelot Theatre. However, the ancient Greek theatre only had to serve two groups of people: the audience and the performers. Primarily the audience gathered for the actors to perform a play that reasonably relied on the simplistic technology of the day. In today's theatre both the audience and the performers place higher demands on the facility, and continually stretch the boundaries for greater technology.

From our production organization chart it is easy to deduce that there are in the neighborhood of forty different defined job positions for mounting a large musical. Depending upon the size of the theatre, the production, and the production budget, some of these positions may be combined. This does not necessarily mean certain work is eliminated. It only translates into the fact that fewer people have to take on more responsibility in order to produce a play.

Broadway and Off-Broadway in New York or the West End and Off-West End (i.e. the Fringe) in London may be considered the centers of commercial theatre. In such situations a larger variety of job positions than are represented on the organizational chart possibly exist. However outside of this theatre nexus throughout the United States and the United Kingdom there is a hotbed of all kinds of regional theatres. From your own theatregoing experience you may have noticed productions occurring in storefronts, schools, religious buildings, downtown theatres, or complexes such as the Camelot Theatre, New York's Public Theatre, London's National Theatre, or the Lowry in Greater Manchester, England. As mentioned above, certain

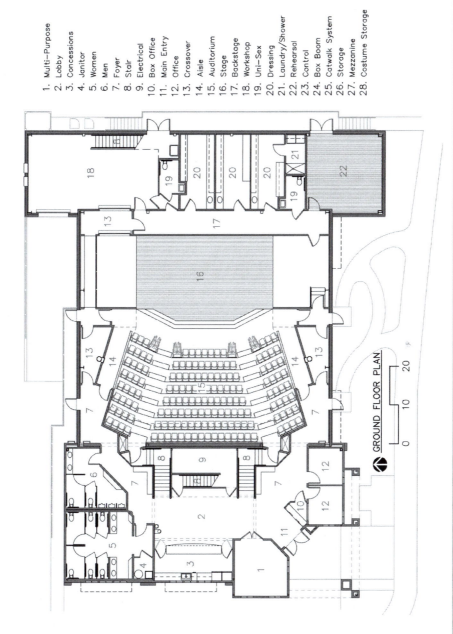

1. Multi-Purpose
2. Lobby
3. Concessions
4. Janitor
5. Women
6. Men
7. Foyer
8. Stair
9. Electrical
10. Box Office
11. Main Entry
12. Office
13. Crossover
14. Aisle
15. Auditorium
16. Stage
17. Backstage
18. Workshop
19. Uni-Sex
20. Dressing
21. Laundry/Shower
22. Rehearsal
23. Control
24. Box Boom
25. Catwalk System
26. Storage
27. Mezzanine
28. Costume Storage

GROUND FLOOR PLAN

0    10    20

**Figure 1.9** Camelot Theatre Ground-Floor Plan (Credit: Drawing by Bruce W. Richey, Architect, AIA, State of Oregon)

jobs may not exist in every theatre, responsibilities might vary, and duties might be combined to suit the particular needs of specific theatres.

# UNDERSTANDING THEATRE FACILITY LAYOUT: THE CAMELOT THEATRE

Although Broadway and the West End may be considered the major center of theatres in New York and London respectively, theatres are constructed throughout the United States and the United Kingdom with the intention of serving regional communities. Many have floor plans that bear similarities to the Camelot Theatre, which we will now examine.

In addition to supporting the audience and the performers, a theatrical complex very often takes on the responsibility for providing possible spaces for everyone on the production team to execute their jobs. This has to be accomplished in such a fashion that everyone who utilizes space within the complex has to fit into a seamless flow as they establish their presence and movement within the work spaces.

Looking at the ground-floor plan of the Camelot Theatre (Figure 1.9) you will notice that there are four distinct locations: the lobby, the audience seating area, the stage, and the backstage spaces. An economic balance has to be achieved in designing such complexes. This balance has to address how much space would be feasible for productions and how much should be allocated for an audience to realistically support such productions. Within the Camelot complex it was determined that close to 60 percent would be given over to audience services and the remaining 40 percent would support the performance.

In further designing such a complex, how space becomes allocated within the just-mentioned proportions also has to be determined. Certain spaces become designated for specific needs. Work areas, shops, dressing rooms, restrooms, lounges, etc. are allocated. Some areas become mixed usage. This can be seen upon closer examination of the lobby, where a few spaces possibly serve the production: the offices and the control/electrical space. Within the audience seating area there are also a couple of storage spaces that might serve this purpose. Suffice to say the audience is well served by the various amenities delineated in the ground-floor plan. Later in the book we will discuss front of house and address audience needs.

Now, from what you might guess or know about what each member of the production team has to accomplish in order to produce a *musical* (note the emphasis on musical), you need to begin to ask yourself how to make this work in the Camelot Theatre configuration. Since the proposed show is a musical this dictates live musicians (unless the music is pre-recorded) as well as rehearsals with singers and/or dancers prior to performance. Is there enough rehearsal space to conduct music, dance, or other kinds of rehearsals simultaneously? Where would the orchestra be located in order to save off-site rental costs?

Possible quick answers are that spaces below or above the theatre, or even the lobby could be utilized. Is there easy access from backstage to onstage? Is there sufficient space in the wings for scenery to be stored, as well as moved easily on- or offstage? Could scenery construction be conducted in the workroom without construction noises intruding upon a performance? Is there sufficient access to the facility for loading scenery built off-premises? How will costumes flow from a costume shop to dressing rooms, then to the stage for possible quick changes? Given the need for various people on the management side of the chart, is there sufficient office space for them? Remember these are only hypothetical questions that you might apply to any theatre. How many other questions can you come up with as you continue to search for the best fit for the show you are about to embark upon the role of producing? The next chapter on producing theatre will help you formulate answers to these questions and the role of the producer.

## WHAT DID YOU LEARN?

1. Who was reputed to be the first actor in the ancient Greek theater?

2. What are two styles of theatre configuration that provide the most intimate seating?

3. What are three major divisions of responsibility on a production organization chart?

4. What three present-day theatre terms derive their meaning from the Greek terms *ekkyklema*, *skene*, and *proskenion*?

5. How does theatre layout affect a production?

### ANSWERS

1) Thespis; 2) thrust stage or ¾ stage and theatre-in-the-round or arena theatre; 3) management (business), creative (talent), and technical (construction/performance); 4) turntable, scene, and proscenium; 5) provide possible spaces for everyone on the production team to do their jobs seamlessly as they establish their presence and movement within the complex.

## RELATED EXERCISES

1. With the production organization chart (Figure 0.1) in hand as you view the opening 20 minutes of the DVD *Show Business: The Road to Broadway*, make a list of each different job (other than actor) represented by the on-screen personalities. You should easily come up with at least a dozen. Kudos if you discover more—you are truly interested in learning how theatre is made.

2. Enjoy the challenge of researching and reading further on the style configuration for each of the theatres listed in Figure 1.10 and filling in your answers along with the theatre location.

| THEATRE | CONFIGURATION | LOCATION |
|---|---|---|
| Madison Square Garden | Arena | New York, NY |
| Donmar Warehouse | | |
| Theatre Royal Drury Lane | | |
| Opéra Bastille | | |
| BCA Plaza Theatre | | |
| *The Railway Children* | | |
| The Lost Colony | | |
| Radio City Music Hall | | |
| *Sleep No More* | | |

## ANSWERS

Donmar Warehouse, ¾ stage, London, England; Theatre Royal Drury Lane, proscenium, London; Opéra Bastille, proscenium, Paris, France; BCA Plaza, black box, Boston, MA; *The Railway Children*, site-specific, Waterloo Station, London; The Lost Colony, amphitheater, Roanoke, VA; Radio City Music Hall, proscenium, New York, NY; *Sleep No More*, site-specific, New York, NY

**Figure 1.10**  Style Configurations for Well-Known Theatres

# ADDITIONAL RESOURCES

## BOOKS

Oscar G. Brockett and Franklin J. Hildy, *History of Theatre*, 10th ed. (New York: Pearson), 2007.

J. Michael Dalton, *The Greek Sense of Theatre: Tragedy and Comedy Reviewed* (New York: Routledge), 2015.

Mira Felner and Claudia Orenstein, *The World of Theatre: Tradition and Innovation* (Boston: Pearson), 2006.

Thomas S. Hischak, *Theatre as Human Action: An Introduction to Theatre Arts* (Lanham, MD: Rowman & Littlefield), 2006.

## WEB RESOURCES

Throughout the book, where specific dates are not given, all websites were accessed and active as of January 2017.

Neil Genzlinger, "You Could Call It Theater of the Absurd: 'Take Me Home' Is for 3 in a Taxi, in Real Time," *New York Times*, February 2, 2014, www.nytimes.com/2014/02/03/theater/take-me-home-is-for-3-in-a-taxi-in-real-time.html

Additional illustrations for theatre layouts can be found at: www.bing.com/images/search?q=theatre+layouts&qpvt=Theatre+layouts&qpvt=Theatre+layouts&FORM=IGRE

# Producing Theatre

*The Producer latches onto a dream and assembles the best team possible to realize that dream*

## THE ROLE OF THE PRODUCER

Up to this point we have presented an overview of various venues and configurations where theatre may be produced. Why these locations and how theatre is made in them are different matters. In the course of theatrical history productions grew out of various purposes such as religious gatherings, rituals, instructive presentations, playwrights' troupes, and court entertainment at the behest of royalty. Shakespeare and Molière spring to mind when we consider playwrights whose work was under the patronage of a king, a queen, or other wealthy patrons.

In the 19th century, particularly with Western theatrical history, plays began to be mounted for commercial gain. The brainchild of such an endeavor could have been an entrepreneur or producer who chose the project (the production or play) for what might have been initially a dream in the producer's mind. In modern times along the way to the realization of this dream, the producer (sometimes called "presenter") will have to secure the licensing rights to the play (commonly known as the "property"), compile a budget, choose the location for presentation, and assemble a staff in order to execute the project.

As straightforward as this might sound, the role of the producer is one of the more difficult to define, since it means many things to many people. Some producers might be the face of a production, relentlessly "pitching" their project to the public. Others might work quietly in the background, tirelessly shepherding their dream to the stage. Still others may anonymously go about their business in the employ of such recognizable corporate institutions as Walt Disney Productions, Sony, the Really Useful Group, the National Theatre, or the now defunct Live Entertainment Corporation of Canada, Inc. (also known as Livent Productions). However, most shows today may be mounted by a **not-for-profit theatre organization** (one which is legally bound to do good for the public sector) or by **commercial producers** (who solely attempt to gain profit). In all instances producers have to operate within the bounds of strict legal constraints.

No matter the producer, the role initially breaks down to three major tasks: **securing or licensing the property**, **budgeting and financing a production**, and **assembling a team** that will be responsible for bringing the production from inception to successful performance onstage. How all this is realized will be discussed throughout the course of this book. However, before a producer embarks upon the actual tasks of producing, they may sift through hundreds of proposals or read through as many scripts for the *one dream play*. The eventual choice would be one that arouses unyielding passion in a producer's mind, body, and soul to devote tireless energy to bring the dream to fruition.

## READ THE PLAY: FIVE KEY ELEMENTS

"Read the play" seems like a self-evident bit of advice for a producer. Ideally it is a suggestion that everyone on the production team should heed before embarking on a production. The journey from inception through performance requires great commitment of time, energy, and money. Not everyone on the team need share the producer's passion for the play. Moreover, a thorough understanding of the play by all members of the team is intrinsic to the eventual success of the venture.

The understanding of a play need not be the literary analysis of grasping the thematic meaning or message of a play, or being able to explain the plot. For immediate production purposes Five Key Elements: Who, What, Where, When, Why (How) need to be sought from reading the play. In this first reading you should seek out just the elements indicated by the playwright, without trying to impose your own ideas. Creativity will be elaborated upon by the director and the team of collaborators.

Once a producer determines the Five Key Elements he or she will examine them from a budgetary point of view. In this regard:

- The Who might lead a producer to realize how many actors would have to be paid.
- Potentially the What could provide insight into the age range for each of the roles, whether the characters could easily be cast, or whether a star would be required.
- The Where could indicate the number of sets or the type of scenery required.
- The When might determine the time and period, or how lavish the scenery might be.

- Finally, the <u>Why</u> or <u>How</u> could provide the impetus for tackling such a production, or whether such a play would attract an audience.

All <u>Five Key Elements</u> govern cost factors, as the producer realizes a prospective budget.

As an initial exercise, determine the <u>Five Key Elements: Who, What, Where, When, Why (How)</u> for a play you know. It might be *The Glass Menagerie* by Tennessee Williams, as depicted in Figure 2.1. <u>Note that the entries for each element are only those indicated in the script by the playwright for Scene 1</u>. As you read through a play the contents for each <u>Key Element</u> might change over the course of the play. Try continuing this exercise for the remaining six scenes in *The Glass Menagerie*. Changes may also occur during the rehearsal process as the play evolves toward performance.

Naturally, each member of the production team will have the tendency to read a play from the perspective of their assigned position in the organization chart (see Figure 0.1). As an example, a costume designer might begin the read with a narrow focus on visualizing the clothing for each character. Before making such choices the costume designer must make many informed decisions while determining the <u>Five Key Elements: Who, What, Where, When, Why (How)</u> with early readings of the play. With further readings and guidance by the director, a costume designer's initial impressions could possibly change due to different choices the director might impose upon the play. Many of these governing factors will be elaborated upon as we look at costume design later in the book.

Meanwhile, the producer has to cast a wider net not only over the play but also in considering all the variables that affect the bottom line for realizing a budget, both before and after opening night. As we discuss budgeting and financing the production below, we will see how the <u>Five Key Elements</u> expand into the different production areas.

<u>FIVE KEY ELEMENTS</u>

*THE GLASS MENAGERIE*
by TENNESSEE WILLIAMS

Scene 1

| WHO | WHAT | WHERE | WHEN | WHY (HOW) |
|---|---|---|---|---|
| Amanda Wingfield | The Mother | An alley in St. Louis & the interior of the Wingfield apartment | Now and in the past | A "Memory Play" dealing with reality and illusion |
| Tom Wingfield | The Narrator & her Son | | | |
| Laura Wingfield | Her Daughter | | | |

**Figure 2.1** Five Key Elements for *The Glass Menagerie*, Scene 1

# SECURING OR LICENSING THE PROPERTY

Perhaps you have found a play that truly excites you and can't wait to present it to the world. "So you want to be a producer" is a phrase that has crept into the vernacular legend of many Hollywood films, and is a glib phrase that might be leveled at anyone who demonstrates the slightest inclination to "put on a play." Before a producer can even begin to go about the business of producing a play, the producer has to secure the rights to or license a play. The play is the intellectual property of the playwright, belongs to the playwright, and is protected by copyright laws. Therefore a producer is required to acquire legal permission to present a play.

If the producer is also the author of the play and funds the entire production solely out of personal money this simplifies matters and no further permissions need be sought. This is rarely the case for commercial success. Established producers or production organizations might receive scripts from authors, agents, friends, publishers, or even through unsolicited submissions. Possibly a producer might commission a work on a particular subject from a well-known playwright. More commonly the producer might attend a reading by an author with a group of people who read the play aloud in a living room, a rented space, or even an empty theatre. There also exists the opportunity to see a workshop production either staged by the playwright and the playwright's friends or self-produced by a playwright and staged as part of a festival.

In all these cases the play remains the property of the playwright. The exception are plays in the public domain; that is, plays whose intellectual property rights have expired, have been forfeited, or are no longer applicable. Examples would be plays by Shakespeare or Molière. Understandably, they are long deceased and copyright laws do not apply to them. However, this does not mean that all deceased playwrights have renounced their rights upon death. It is wise to check the writers' estates since the rights may be passed onto heirs. For example, a newly discovered play by dead playwrights Samuel Beckett or Bertolt Brecht may surface. Should a producer wish to produce such a play, the estates of these authors hold a tight grip on all licenses for any of their work intended for production.

The next step for a potential producer is a crucial part of the legal process. The producer takes out an **option** to produce the play. Within the option are various written agreements between the producer and the playwright, or the playwright's estate. Options tend to be low risk and may include a certain amount of money, a time limit (generally one year) for the producer to determine whether producing the play is economically feasible, perhaps to raise enough money in order to commit to producing the play, and to generate enough interest to attract top creative people to participate in the project.

During the defined option period the playwright agrees not to solicit the work for production by any other means. As mentioned, the author may also receive outright monetary compensation or monies against **royalties** should the play be eventually produced. Royalties are a percentage of any money a play earns once a production is mounted and running. The structuring and percentages of royalties vary depending upon the size of a production, where it is produced, and other governing factors that will be explained throughout this book. Suffice to say at the moment that the playwright is only one member of the **royalty pool** in addition to other members of the production organization who are entitled to royalties through union affiliations and/or contract negotiations who work on the development, creation, and execution of a production.

## BUDGETING FOR AND FINANCING A PRODUCTION

Concurrent with licensing the play, the producer would have to begin developing a budget in order to finance the eventual production. Finances might come from the **sole proprietorship** of the producer or investors in a theatrical company that the producer organizes to produce the play. Theatrical companies may take the form of:

- a **general partnership** (a group of people gathered to produce a play);

- a **limited partnership** (the most common means of producing commercial theatre, which requires at least one general partner and one limited partner, along with a great deal of federal, state, and tax paperwork);

- a **for-profit corporation** (underwrites the production following the applicable laws and tax regulations associated with a corporation); and

- the previously mentioned **not-for-profit theatre organization** (which finances its productions through grants, foundations, donors, and government agencies that are all accountable to a Board of Directors or the specific funding sources).

It follows that under a sole proprietorship, or even a general partnership, a producer would stand to make the most money, as well as lose the most money. The limited partnership offers more control to the general partner. The limited partners are considered 100 percent passive investors or shareholders (not involved in the business operations of the production company) and stand to gain or lose their investment in the theatre company.

For the formation of a limited partnership in the United States an offering prospectus is drawn up that has to strictly comply with the regulations of the Securities and Exchange Commission (**SEC**), as well as **"blue sky laws"** (security regulations designed to protect investors, which differ state by state). The offering prospectus is then filed with the SEC and/or a State's Attorney General, and is dependent upon many legal restrictions that exceed the purview of this book. However, it is important to note that the offering prospectus prominently warns the potential investor that there is an extremely high degree of risk, and investing should only be undertaken by persons who have no need for liquidity of their assets. In other words, the investors should be able to withstand losing all of their investment money without forfeiting their homes, emptying their bank accounts, or going into bankruptcy.

## PRODUCTION BUDGET

As part of the offering plan to attract investors (sometimes called **"angels"**) the producer would prepare two budgets: the **production budget** (all projected costs through opening night) and an **operating budget** (weekly operational costs and royalties paid out of weekly profits). In addition, there might be a third budget called a **recoupment schedule** (a statistical plan that shows investors variables such as potential gross sales for a number of weeks required to recoup (regain) their investments.

Recoupment schedules are as varied as the number of commercial plays proposed for production. In general though, they may include group sales projections for a specialized target audience: for example, if the play concerns civil liberties, there may be special sales efforts to attract lawyers or law-enforcement officials; similarly, a play that emphasizes the hip-hop generation might attempt to reach a youth audience. Depending upon demographics and how large a particular audience is, the producer might want to project that it would take a certain number of performances and particular advertising angles or marketing strategies to attract the optimal audience in order to recoup the investment.

Figure 2.2 presents a hypothetical look at the various budget allocations that might be included in an offering prospectus. However, this budget only reflects the amount of money that the producer proposes to spend to get the show to the opening performance. Not to be overlooked are additional advances on royalties to all members of the royalty pool (playwright, composer, lyricist, director, choreographer, designers, etc.).

Borrowing from an oft-used advertising slogan—"Wait, there's more!"—a cautionary warning is issued to the producer who thinks that the $1,000,000 represented by the proposed budget illustrated in Figure 2.2 is actually enough money.

In reality there are the additional bonds (usually two weeks' worth of salaries) that have to be deposited with the various unions in case the producer closes the show without two weeks' notification and to prevent any attempt to abscond with the funds). The bonds are recoverable provided the producer has paid everyone on time. These deposits, along with a contingency fee to cover overheads generally, would add another 25 percent to the production budget. In our example this amounts to $250,000 that should be added to the $1,000,000. What started out as a $1,000,000 musical now stands at one costing $1,250,000—the figure the producer has to actually raise before the show can open. In the following chapter we will take a look at a general manager's actual budget, which provides more details for the proposed production *Shim Sham*.

## WEEKLY OPERATING BUDGET

The proposed $1,000,000 musical may be considered a modest production by Off-Broadway standards and have a weekly operating budget (or **"weekly nut"**) of close to $350,000. Figure 2.3 provides an indication of how much this production must earn weekly before there

| | |
|---|---|
| PRODUCTION | $275,000 |
| Carpentry<br>Electrics<br>Costumes<br>Props<br>Automation | |
| FEES (Upfront/Non-Weekly Salaried) | $175,000 |
| Director<br>Choreographer<br>Scenic Designer<br>Lighting Designer<br>Costume Designer<br>Assistant Designers<br>Additional Designers | |
| AUDITION & REHEARSAL | $25,000 |
| Rental of Spaces<br>Scripts<br>Duplication<br>Office Supplies<br>Miscellaneous | |
| REHEARSAL SALARIES (Weekly) | $175,000 |
| Actors<br>Stage Managers<br>Musicians<br>Production Assistants<br>General Manager<br>Company Manager<br>Miscellaneous Staff | |
| ADVERTISING & PUBLICITY | $300,000 |
| ADMINISTRATIVE | $50,000 |
| Legal Fees<br>Accounting Fees<br>Insurance<br>Payroll (Health Benefits, Pension Workman's<br>   Compensation)<br>Office Fees<br>Opening Night Party<br>Miscellaneous | |
| GRAND TOTAL | $1,000,000.00 |

Figure 2.2 The $1,000,000 Musical: Proposed Production Budget

| | |
|---|---|
| SALARIES | $135,000 |
| Performers<br>Stage managers<br>Running crew<br>Health & pension contributions | |
| EXPENSES (maintenance & miscellaneous) | $3,000 |
| Stage management<br>Scenic, lighting, costumes, etc.<br>Music department<br>Repairs | |
| ADVERTISING & PROMOTION | $100,000 |
| Television, radio, print, web, etc.<br>Publicity appearances | |
| THEATRE | $85,000 |
| Rental<br>Utilities<br>Front-of-house staff<br>Musicians (Musicians' Union Regulation)<br>House members of stage crew<br>Pensions, taxes, etc. | |
| FIXED FEES<br>Music contractor (hires musicians/subs)<br>Music arranger<br>Certain designers<br>Casting director | $5,000 |
| PRODUCTION OFFICE EXPENSES | $25,000 |
| Legal fees<br>Accounting fees<br>Insurance<br>Phone, copying, postage, etc.<br>Miscellaneous | |
| GRAND TOTAL | $353,000.00 |

**Figure 2.3** The $1,000,000 Musical: Proposed Weekly Operating Budget

is a net profit (total ticket sales minus weekly expenses equal net profit). Bear in mind that those members of the royalty pool will only be paid their pre-negotiated percentages from the weekly net profits. However, the weekly net profits are generally split, with about 35 percent allocated to the royalty pool and 65 percent to the investors.

On a weekly basis profits and losses fluctuate, and thus how much money may actually be paid to both participants in the royalty pool and investors varies, as do the many variables for possible recoupment. Sadly, most shows lose money and are forced to close. The only person who can close a show is the producer.

For other budgets from both ends of the financial spectrum you might want to look at two representative examples. The first is for *Just So Stories*, which was presented by the Red Table Theatre (a children's theatre) to the Directors Guild of Great Britain for approximately $1600. At the opposite end of the scale is that for *Spider-Man: Turn Off the Dark*, which was presented to New York's Attorney General's office. With the unaudited production costs running to $48,141,068.12, this production has been billed as quite possibly the most expensive and most controversial musical in Broadway history. Internet links to these budgets are provided in **WEB RESOURCES** at the end of this chapter.

## FINDING A THEATRE

Now that the producer has licensed, budgeted, and put the financing in place, securing a theatre and assembling the production team can begin. In Chapter 1 we looked at six configurations for theatres: amphitheater, proscenium, thrust stage or ¾ stage, theatre-in-the-round or arena theatre, black box, and site-specific. Notwithstanding what type of theatre is available, it follows that a number of factors are important in choosing a particular theatre. Three that immediately spring to mind are **budget**, **size**, and **suitability** for a particular production. As you read the following discussions for each of these considerations, notice that each factor does not exist in isolation. They are all dependent on one another.

### BUDGET

In all likelihood, the larger the theatre the more money it would take to produce a play in such a venue. Imagine how large a staff you would need to support an amphitheater that seats many thousands, such as a musical by today's standards. Security and ushers are just the tip of the iceberg. Try making a list of other personnel it would take to run the amphitheater. It will grow pretty exhaustive when you include box office staff, cleaning crew, and everything in between.

Then turn your attention to the production's needs. The amount of lighting, sound, and scenic equipment alone would be enormous. Before we get too deep into entertaining the idea of presenting a play in an amphitheater we are quick to realize that it would take a lot of money to do so. The chance of recoupment is improbable.

Still on the upper reaches of budget are the Broadway and West End theatres, which are generally proscenium theatres, or some variant thereof. By no means are they cheap. Think of them as big business, much like the top tier of professional sports.

The **Broadway League** includes over 700 producers, general managers, presenters, theatre owners and operators throughout North American cities. Its British counterpart is the **Society**

**of London Theatre** (SOLT). Productions presented under the auspices of the Broadway League and SOLT require large support staff for their major technical undertakings. It really is a roll of the dice for which statistics are highly stacked against a show succeeding or recouping in this stratum.

On a financial level below Broadway or the West End are the secondary tier of theatres, which might include variations of proscenium, thrust stage or ¾ stage, theatre-in-the-round or arena theatre, black box theatre, and perhaps a site-specific venue. Financing a production in any of these theatres by virtue of their size practically dictates a less daunting budget than the major leagues. This not to say they are necessarily cheap, as we can see from the budgets that we present for the $1,000,000 musical.

At the other extreme is the small, black box theatre that comes with low rental, possibly few support staff, and minimal technical requirements. Usually dependent on the number of seats, technical capabilities, and condition of a black box theatre there is wide latitude for rental figures. There some very elegant black box theatres and some which qualify as "a hole in the wall." If such a space is all that your budget is capable of meeting then this type of theatre warrants consideration as you decide on other factors for presenting the play.

## FURTHER DISCUSSION

Where would amphitheaters be located?

What are some of the economic factors that determine the location of the other types of theatre?

What city ordinances could be considered when budgeting for a theatre?

What are some budgeting considerations when choosing a site-specific venue?

How does a union theatre versus a non-union theatre affect the budget?

## SIZE

As we have just seen, considering a theatre for presentation is largely determined by what a producer budgets for or can afford. Once this figure is safely arrived at, the choice of theatre could be further governed by location, general look or appeal, seating capacity, accessibility for an audience, association with prior success (or even failure), lobby size, ancillary space for a bar or merchandise sales, as well as many other intangibles that might possibly contribute to recoupment. Ideally the more seats there are, the more revenue would stream from the sale of those seats. However, achieving full capacity for every performance would not be realistic thinking on the part of a producer. Few shows sell out. Budgeting for more moderate success might lengthen the run of a production, ultimately returning a profit.

In addition to the number of seats in a theatre the producer must consider the actual stage size allotted for a production. Our earlier exercise with the Camelot Theatre is worth reviewing as an example for determining the flow of traffic backstage, and whether a theatre under consideration is viable for the intended production. Will the actual dimensions of the stage (the **footprint**) be able to accommodate scenery onstage and offstage (if there are multiple sets), all the lighting and sound equipment and additional technical equipment, and be spacious enough for a large cast if necessary? Would the theatre be able to safely accommodate any special effects—such as actual fires, or the flying of actors, or live animals onstage, etc.—should the script call for them?

## FURTHER DISCUSSION

Describe some of the theatre facilities that you have attended in your city.

If you attended a Broadway or West End production, what were your impressions of the facility?

How does a well-appointed facility affect your theatregoing experience?

How does a not so well-appointed facility affect your theatre-going experience?

What safety concerns might you have when entering a theatre?

## SUITABILITY

Not all plays are equal to all theatres is something that we have been hinting at as we have thus far discussed budget and size of theatres. With the first reading of a play the producer formulates impressions either to take on a project or drop it. In all likelihood very positive feelings toward a work engenders a great degree of excitement for the producer. Part of this excitement might be attributed to the producer's ability to visualize the production in a particular theatrical configuration.

As an example, the producer might read a play with two to four characters that is set in a single living room that takes place over the course of a day or two, and contains intimate dialogue and ideas. Most likely producing such a play in an amphitheater can be immediately ruled out. One possible reason is economic necessity; there would be little potential to sell thousands of seats for this type of play staged in an amphitheater. In addition, given the sheer size of such a theatre, a great amount of technical support would be required to see and hear the actors.

A large Broadway or West End theatre might be subject to the same constraints. However, if it were a "star"-driven production with Meryl Streep or Benedict Cumberbatch in the cast, the budget and the technical needs for such a theatre might be balanced in order for a profit to be realized.

Failing the ability to cast "stars" for such a production, or even to capitalize on another angle to attract a large audience, the producer might elect to choose one of the smaller theatres that provide a degree of intimacy with proven actors. In all cases there still remains the element of risk for the commercial producer, and for that matter the not-for-profit producer who has to satisfy a certain constituency.

Similar considerations have to be undertaken with a large-scale musical. The sheer size and scope of *Spider-Man: Turn Off the Dark* or *The Lion King* mitigates staging in most thrust stages or ¾ stages or black box theatres. These types of theatre would not be able to accommodate the flying apparatus, the extensive amounts of scenery, or the large casts called for. Both productions have been staged in proscenium theatres. Quite possibly producers have entertained ideas of eventually staging these productions in large arenas, site-specific situations, or even amphitheaters. Time will tell for an adventurous producer.

Balancing a realistic budget and obtaining an adequate sized theatre, as well as one that is suitable for a given play, are some requisites for a successful producer. As an illustration of these combined forces let us look at an abbreviated production history of the Off-Broadway musical *Little Shop of Horrors*. Basing their musical on the original, low-budget 1960 film directed by Roger Corman, composer Alan Menken and writer Howard Ashman fashioned a workshop production that premiered in spring 1982 at the tiny Works Progress Administration (WPA) Theatre in New York City. Subsequently it attracted producers David Geffen, Cameron Mackintosh, and the Shubert Organization to join with the WPA to produce it Off-Broadway in New York's Orpheum Theatre, where it ran from July 1982 to November 1987.

So popular was the production that the Shubert Organization repeatedly urged Menken and Ashman during the course of the downtown run to move the production uptown. The reasoning was that in a larger Broadway theatre more people could see the show, and more profits would be realized. Ashman held firm to the belief that the Orpheum Theatre in the gritty East Village mirrored the downtown skid row location depicted in the musical, and predisposed the audience that the Orpheum was the ideal location to see the show.

Other possible considerations for Ashman were that if the production transferred uptown, ticket prices would have to increase. The increase could be attributed to the additional amount of scenery or larger orchestra that might be necessary for Broadway theatre. Also the budget would have to accommodate higher-paid union stagehands and perhaps a larger cast. And finally the show could close prematurely, since it would exhaust its potential audience sooner. This would become an important part of the reasoning in marketing strategy. The longer *Little Shop of Horrors* ran, the more the brand name was in the public eye. More people would want to come to New York and see the show, and the greater potential existed for subsequent productions both in the United States and abroad.

More importantly, Ashman's infinite wisdom dictated that with the transfer to a cavernous Broadway theatre the intimacy of the production would be lost, for at the core of the production was the thinking that each and every audience member was potential food for the flesh-eating plant center stage. This was a real threat as the play unfolded. In a surprise ending in the intimate Orpheum Theatre, the plant's tentacles dropped from hidden recesses in the ceiling, the leaves grazing most of the attendees and joyously shocking them out of their seats. It was an important culminating moment for this play-going experience.

The fact that this production of *Little Shop of Horrors* held a surprise ending contributed to its mystique and popularity as a "must-see" production. Replicating this rapturous moment was technologically impossible in the 1980s, and remained an obstacle until a mostly tepid production was mounted in 2003. For more on this bumpy ride to Broadway and the *New York Times* review follow the links in **WEB RESOURCES** at this end of this chapter. Perhaps in the final analysis Howard Ashman clung to the old Broadway adage "You can't make a living, but you can make a killing," and sticking to his principles, kept *Little Shop of Horrors* viable. By keeping the production running for over five years Off-Broadway, *Little Shop of Horrors* has instituted itself in the public mind. It has continued to earn royalties from thousands of community theatres, high schools, and countless revivals, as well as multiple media presentations to this very day.

## *FURTHER DISCUSSION*

What considerations would you undertake in transferring a production from a larger theatre to a smaller theatre?

*Little Shop of Horrors* is one example of a one-to-one attachment between audience members and the production. Describe other such possible attachments.

What would make a site-specific location suitable for a production that centered on the Nativity?

What budgets items would you consider for such a production?

# THE THEATRE TICKET

Combining business acumen and artistic vision is intrinsic to successful producing. With a play chosen and licensed, a budget determined, and a venue secured, the producer would then set out to assemble the production team. Up to this point we have presented various budget concerns for a producer and the overall organization of a production company. Before examining the various members of such a team let us take a moment to review what we have learned through an exercise, "Where Does the Money Go?" This is a question that many of us might magically entertain when we pay $100 for a Broadway production (Figure 2.4) or, similarly, £66 for a West End production.

**Figure 2.4**  The $100 Ticket

This exercise is suggested by the anecdotal articles "And the Stub Is All Yours" and "How Much Does It Cost to Buy a $110 Theater Ticket?" by Jesse McKinley and Cara Joy David respectively, and previously published in the *New York Times* (see **WEB RESOURCES**). Completion of this exercise at this moment will give the reader a better understanding of how the money gets divided.

Beside each position in Figure 2.5 you will need to reasonably rank which position receives the highest percentage of revenue from the sale of each ticket down to which position receives the lowest percentage of revenue. Figure 0.1, could possibly serve as a reference guide for your decisions depending upon where each position is in the hierarchy.

Although prices and wages have gone up since Jesse McKinley wrote his article based upon the 2002 ticket prices for the Broadway production of *Mamma Mia*, the percentages for each category have remained basically the same in the intervening years. A producer might have to shift the percentages a little bit in today's economy for each category in order to accommodate paying for fixed costs versus those categories that receive various royalty percentages of the gross income. Once you have completed the exercise compare your answers to the equivalent allocations back in 2002. Much to your surprise, those that are closer to the top of the organization chart will absorb a higher percentage of the revenue derived from each ticket sold. This is due to economics, statistics, mathematics, and the many contracts entwined in a commercial production.

Ironically, a ticket is itself a contract between the producer and the buyer. The contract (be it unwritten, for free, or at a set price) guarantees that a "show" will be performed for an audience. Also the ticket would state the name of the show that will take place in a certain theatre, on a particular date and time, with or without an assigned seat.

In our discussion thus far we have focused on a producer's initial undertakings: **securing or licensing the property**, **budgeting and financing a production**, and **assembling a team**. Opinions as to what constitutes a successful producer have been shaped by many historical personages. They might include mythic stories surrounding the entrepreneurial P.T. Barnum

## "Where Does the Money Go?"

Instructions: Rank each job position or category that receives a certain percentage of money from the sale of each ticket for **The $1,000,000 Musical**. You should rank each job position or category from 1 to 15: 1 being the highest percentage down to the lowest percentage allotted. Note: To get you started, four of the positions have been ranked. You have to figure out how to rank the remaining eleven.

| RANK | JOB POSITIONS OR CATEGORIES APPLICABLE TO THE WEEKLY RUNNING OF A PRODUCTION |
|---|---|
| | Cast salaries |
| | Crew salaries |
| | Musicians' salaries |
| | Rental of the theatre |
| | Other salaries/theatre staff |
| | Royalties |
| | Publicity |
| | Theatre personnel, electricity, misc. |
| | Group sales commissions |
| 14 | Insurance/accountants |
| 9 | Lighting, sound, and miscellaneous equipment rental |
| | Benefits: health insurance, vacation and sick pay, pensions |
| 13 | Maintenance of costumes, scenery, etc. |
| 15 | Theatre facility fee |
| | The investors (producers) |

### Answers

1) The Investors (Producers): 2) Royalties: 3) Publicity: 4) Benefits: Health Insurance, Vacation & Sick Pay, Pension; 5) Crew Salaries; 6) Rental of the Theatre: 7) Cast Salaries; 8) Theatre Personnel, Electricity, Misc.; 9) Lighting, Sound, and Miscellaneous Equipment Rental; 10) Group Sales Commissions; 11) Musician Salaries; 12) Other Salaries/Theatre Staff; 13) Maintenance of costumes, scenery, etc.; 14) Insurance/Accountants; 15) Theatre Facility Fee

**Figure 2.5** Where Does the Money Go?

of circus fame; a testament to Richard D'Oyly Carte, who nurtured dramatist/librettist W.S. Gilbert and composer Arthur Sullivan in developing comic operas; or the cigar-chomping, stereotyped producer boss from countless Hollywood movies. Significant producers include: David Merrick, Nelle Nugent, Hal Prince, Emanuel Azenberg, Sir Cameron Mackintosh, and Rosie O'Donnell, or a producing organization such as Woodie King Jr.'s New Federal Theater. Some of these names we may greet with familiarity and recognition for high-minded, serious drama and populist musicals, or for the failure of one production. At the end of this chapter in **ADDITIONAL RESOURCES** there are links to material on the successes and failures for some of these producers. Perhaps you could formulate your own opinion as to which producer might be most adept to fulfill a dream production.

However, the producer's role does not end here. Although a producer's function on the surface seems mainly monetary in nature, the role reaches into many aspects for the complete production. Some producers may act in a hands-off fashion and others may have their fingers in every aspect of production. In the forthcoming chapter we will examine how some of these issues affect the duties of the assembled management team. Remember though, no matter how well or how poorly a show is received or how effective a management team is, there is only one person who can close a show: the producer.

## WHAT DID YOU LEARN?

1. What do you call the type of production that is produced primarily from grants and donations?

2. What are royalties?

3. What three steps must a producer undergo prior to assembling a production team?

4. What are three important considerations that a producer has to take into account when choosing a theatre? Explain.

5. What are the Five Key Elements that one should determine when reading a play? Explain.

### ANSWERS

1) Not-for-profit theatre; 2) A percentage amount of money that a play earns once a production is mounted and running; 3) Securing or licensing the property, budgeting and financing a production, and assembling a team; 4) Budget, size of theatre, and suitability for a particular production; 5) Who, What, Where, When, Why (How)?

# ADDITIONAL RESOURCES

## PRODUCERS

Emanuel Azenberg. Internet Broadway Database (accessed November 5, 2015). http://ibdb. com/Person/View/21830

"Woodie King, Jr. and New Federal Theatre to be Honored with 2013 Edwin Booth Award, 5/6." Broadway World.com (accessed November 5, 2015). www.broadwayworld.com/ off-off-broadway/article/Woodie-King-Jr-and-New-Federal-Theatre-to-be-Honored-with-2013-Edwin-Booth-Award-56-20130429

Cameron Mackintosh. Broadway World.com (accessed November 5, 2015). www.broadway-world.com/people/Cameron-Mackintosh/

Nelle Nugent. Broadway World.com (accessed November 5, 2015). www.broadwayworld.com/ people/Nelle-Nugent/

Hal Prince. Internet Broadway Database (accessed November 5, 2015). http://ibdb.com/Person/ View/15921 (producer of *Fiddler on the Roof*)

Frank Rich, "David Merrick, 88, Showman Who Ruled Broadway, Dies," *New York Times*, April 27, 2000, www.nytimes.com/2000/04/27/theater/david-merrick-88-showman-who-ruled-broadway-dies.html

Stephen Silverman, "Rosie Pulls Plug on her Broadway Baby," *People*, January 14, 2004, www.people.com/people/article/0,,627443,00.html

Howard Taubman, "Theater: Mostel as Tevye in 'Fiddler on the Roof': Sholem Aleichem Tales Made into a Musical," *New York Times*, September 23, 1964, https://assets.documentcloud. org/documents/805563/original-review-fiddler-on-the-roof.pdf

## BOOKS

Glen Berger, *Song of Spider-Man: The Inside Story of the Most Controversial Musical in Broadway History* (New York: Simon & Schuster, 2013).

William J. Byrnes, *Management and the Arts*, 3rd edn (Burlington, MA: Focal Press, 2003).

Charles Grippo, *The Stage Producer's Business and Legal Guide* (New York: Allworth Press, 2002).

Tobie S. Stein and Jessica Bathurst, *Performing Arts Management: A Handbook of Professional Practices* (New York: Allworth Press, 2008).

## WEB RESOURCES

"A Look at the Finances of 'Spider-Man'," *New York Times*, June 23, 2011, www.nytimes.com/ interactive/2011/06/23/theater/23spider-documents.html?ref=theater&_r=0

Ben Brantley, "A Hungry Actor? Audrey II Is Back," *New York Times*, October 3, 2003, www. nytimes.com/2003/10/03/movies/theater-review-a-hungry-actor-audrey-ii-is-back.html

The Broadway League, www.broadwayleague.com. (This website also provides links to affiliated productions throughout the world.)

Cara Joy David, "How Much Does It Cost to Buy a $110 Theater Ticket?," *New York Times*, February 10, 2007, www.nytimes.com/2007/02/10/theater/10fees.html

Jesse McKinley, "Where Does the Money Go?," *New York Times*, May 19, 2002, www.nytimes. com/2002/05/19/arts/theater/19TICKET.html

Robin Pogrebin, "The Show That Ate the Original Cast," *New York Times*, October 20, 2003, www.nytimes.com/2003/10/20/theater/the-show-that-ate-the-original-cast.html

"Sample Budgets," Red Table Theatre, accessed November 23, 2015, http://redtabletheatre. com/open-book-theatre/sample-budgets/

Society of London Theatre, www.solt.co.uk/

# Management

*The Management Team sets the fiscal course and guides the production through the dream's journey*

## THE ROLE OF THE BUSINESS MANAGER AND/OR GENERAL MANAGER

At this point we have met the producer, who sits as the titular head of the production team, most notably in the commercial theatre. In meeting this producer, we have loosely defined some of the narrow duties such a person faces in the commercial theatre. However, in the many school theatres, community theatres, Off-Off Broadway, or Off-Off West End theatres producers take on many, many more responsibilities. Not only do these producers have to obtain the rights to a play, budget for its production, and secure a venue, they might also have to cast, direct, design, publicize, and sell tickets, as well as plan the opening night party. In all fairness, taking on these many jobs would be overwhelming for one person to perform in the arena of professional theatre and in the leading not-for-profit theatres. In these situations, managing increased budgets, dealing with a multiplicity of unions, and negotiating an array of contracts consumes vast amounts of time, energy, and specialized expertise. Wisely, within the commercial and not-for-profit sectors the delegation of various duties has become more compartmentalized, as borne out by our organizational chart (Figure 0.1), where the business manager and/or general manager heads up the management team situated just below the producer. When choosing such a person, the producer will need a business manager who is on the same page, and who will protect the producer's interests and control the money wisely.

Such a business manager would seem to befit the financial aspects of the position, although general manager would be a more apt term. This is because responsibilities extend to oversight

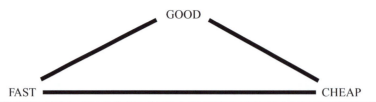

**Figure 3.1** Production Axiom: "Why Can't You Have All Three?"

of all marketing and organizational aspects for operating a successful production. With so many fiduciary decisions and approvals to execute, the astute general manager will ultimately consciously or unconsciously follow the **production axiom**, a truism depicted in the production axiom triangle shown in Figure 3.1.

When making a financial decision or otherwise, the general manager must weigh the benefits of having the outcome be good, fast, or cheap. According to the production axiom, only two out of the three options are possible. It is impossible to obtain all three outcomes. Therefore, the general manager has to decide whether a product can be obtained by doing it fast and good, then it will be expensive (not cheap). Similarly, if the general manager applies good and cheap for a result, then it will be a slow finish (not fast). Finally, when applying fast and cheap the production will lack quality (not good).

## READ THE PLAY

Applying the production axiom to a thorough reading of the play, the general manager will need to ascertain the <u>Five Key Elements: Who, What, Where, When, Why (How)</u>. Along with input from the producer the general manager would be able to reapportion the producer's initial proposed budget and more accurately reflect figures for producing such a venture. This retooling of the budget is due to the general manager's broad knowledge regarding the current market, prevailing salaries, contract loopholes, tax laws, and any number of hidden costs.

What might have started out as a hypothetical proposal for a $1,000,000 musical in the previous chapter could morph into something closer to the reality of the general manager's budget for the aborted Off-Broadway 2009 musical *Shim Sham* referred to in Figure 3.2.

Notably absent from this budget are the fees and advances to Johnny Brandon—the author, composer, and lyricist who also served as the producer for the proposed musical. With further readings and discussions between the producer and general manager it became apparent that central to the musical were the shim sham tap dance routines attributed to Willie Bryant and Leonard Reed, Harlem tap dancers in the 1920s. So essential was this feature that a specialized acoustic tap dance floor and attendant scenery would have to be budgeted for at close to $100,000, or almost 10 percent of the budget. It is this type of juggling of numbers that points to an important part of the general manager's role in service to the producer.

## SHIM SHAM

### ESTIMATED PRODUCTION BUDGET ($)

| 1. | | REHEARSAL (5 WEEKS): | |
|---|---|---|---|
| Cast (AEA): | 3 @ 1,500 x 5 wks | 22,500 | |
| | 12 @ Average 1000 x 5 wks | 60,000 | |
| Understudies (AEA) | | 2,000 | |
| Stage Manager (AEA) @ 1,100 x 5 wks | | 5,500 | |
| Asst. SM (AEA) @ 960 x 5 wks | | 4,800 | |
| Prod. Asst. @ 500 x 5 wks | | 2,500 | |
| | SUB TOTAL: | | 97,300 |
| Musical Director/Vocal Arr. @ 1,500 | | 7,500 | |
| Asst. M.D./Dance Music @ 1,200 | | 6,000 | |
| Audition Pianist | | 500 | |
| Orchestra Rehearsal | | 800 | |
| General Manager @ 1,500 | | 7,500 | |
| Company Manager @ 1,100 | | 5,500 | |
| Press Agent @ 1,100 | | 5,500 | |
| Crew (Set Up/Get In) | | 5,000 | |
| | SUB TOTAL: | | 38,300 |
| **TOTAL 1:** | | | **135,600** |
| **2.** | **FEES:** | | |
| Author | | | |
| Composer | | | |
| Lyricist | | | |
| Director | 10,000 | | |
| Choreographer | 8,000 | | |
| Asst. to Dir/Chor. | 2,500 | | |
| Musical Dir/Vocal Arr. | 2,000 | | |
| Asst. to M.D.Dir/Dance Arr. | 1,000 | | |
| Costume Designer | 8,200 | | |
| Asst. Costume Designer | 5,000 | | |
| Set Designer | 11,000 | | |
| Asst. Set Designer | 5,000 | | |
| Lighting Designer | 7,500 | | |
| Asst. Lighting Designer | 5,000 | | |

Figure 3.2 *Shim Sham* Budget

| | |
|---|---|
| Sound Designer | 4,100 |
| General Manager | 15,000 |
| Casting Director | 10,000 |
| Technical Supervisor | 6,000 |
| Prop Shopper | 1,000 |
| **TOTAL 2:** | **101,300** |

| 3. | PHYSICAL: | |
|---|---|---|
| Scenery | 35,000 | |
| Acoustic Tap Floor | 60,000 | |
| Costumes, Shoes, Accessories | 25,000 | |
| Hair, Make-Up | 2,000 | |
| Props | 3,000 | |
| Wardrobe Set Up | 2,000 | |
| Electrics Prep (in Theater) | 5,000 | |
| Electrics/Perishables | 1,500 | |
| Sound Prep (in Theater) | 5,000 | |
| Sound/Perishables | 1,000 | |
| **TOTAL 3:** | | **139,500** |

NOTE: This production budget is predicated on union demands in a 499 seat Off-Broadway Theatre.

**Figure 3.2** Continued

# COLLECTIVE BARGAINING AGREEMENTS AND UNIONS

With the general manager in place, the hiring and contracting of all production personnel is the next order of business. Unless the producer has not already done so, the general manager will have to initially draw up a contract with the playwright or the playwright's agent, possibly working from a template provided by the Dramatists Guild of America **(DGA)**. The DGA, which also extends to Britain, is the professional association of playwrights, composers, lyricists, and librettists, and will be discussed further in Chapter 4: Creating Theatre. Similarly, the producer may have chosen the creative team: a director, a design team, and (if required) a composer and a lyricist, as well as a music director and a choreographer.

Once the creators' contracts are settled the general manager has to go about contracting the extended members of the management team: company manager, publicity agent, stage manager, and other such creative types as needed. Working on a Broadway production automatically means that practically every employee is covered by one labor union contract or another. Upper management, producers, and general managers (members of the Broadway League) are exempt by the very nature of their positions. As such it is the Broadway League (a multi-employer across many sectors) that enters into negotiations with different labor unions at various yearly intervals in order to reach **collective bargain agreements**. A collectively bargained agreement is said to be reached following negotiating sessions between one party of representatives from management (e.g. the Broadway League) and representatives of a union (e.g. the International Alliance of Theatrical Stage Employees, or **IATSE**). The collective bargain agreement results in a contract that governs the minimum salaries and working conditions that both management and union must adhere to for a fixed number of years, generally ranging from three to five years. Upon expiration of the contract, management and labor will need to renegotiate in order to continue working. This may not always be accomplished in a timely fashion. The contract may be extended for work to continue under the previously negotiated conditions. Once a new agreement can be collectively agreed upon, retroactive compensation might be achieved and cover the interval when work continued without a contract. Sometimes there is an impasse when management and labor are unable to reach an agreement. If neither party wishes to grant concessions or settle the agreement, the result may be a strike by labor, or management may call for a lockout (suspension of work). If the negotiations reach a hopeless deadlock an outside arbitrator (whose decision is binding) may be called in to adjudicate the contract.

In the United States and the United Kingdom there are many unions governing an assort-ment of jobs within the theatrical industry. Figure 3.3 delineates some of the more recognizable unions. Applicable to a number of personnel covered in this chapter are the Association of Theatrical Press Agents and Managers (**ATPAM**) in the United States and its United Kingdom counterpart, the Theatrical Management Association (**TMA**). These unions govern press agents, publicity and marketing specialists, company managers, and house and facilities man-agers. The remaining unions noted in Figure 3.3, as well as others, will be elaborated upon throughout this book.

# COMPANY MANAGER

As the general manager is revising production budgets, weekly operating budgets, and recoup-ment schedules, a company manager is hired to manage the daily operation of the production. Company managers on Broadway are members of ATPAM. In smaller theatre operations and regional theatres, the positions of general manager and company manager might be combined, and are unlikely to be under the jurisdiction of ATPAM. Membership of ATPAM may be gained through an apprenticeship program. For more about ATPAM you are encouraged to go to the **ATPAM** website listed in Figure 3.3.

Company managers' duties are primarily financial in nature. Topping the list is attending to the weekly payroll and acting as liaison between the performers, the crew, and manage-ment. Among other duties are reconciling and settling box office receipts for each evening's performance, petty-cash dispersals to stage management, paying for production supplies, deliveries, cleaning bills for costumes, as well as approving and issuing payment for overtime.

| U.S. Union | U.S. Website | U.K. Union | U.K. Website | Sector of Union Coverage |
|---|---|---|---|---|
| Association of Theatrical Press Agents and Managers (ATPAM) | www.atpam.com/ | Theatrical Management Association (TMA) | www.uktheatre.org | Press agents, publicity, and marketing specialists, company managers, and house and facilities managers |
| International Alliance of Theatrical Stage Employees, Moving Picture Technicians, Artists and Allied Crafts (IATSE) | http://iatse.net/ | Broadcasting, Entertainment, Cinematograph and Theatre Union (BECTU) | www.bectu.org.uk/home | Live theater, motion picture and television production, trade shows and exhibitions, television broadcasting, and concerts as well as the equipment and construction shops: behind-the-scenes workers in crafts ranging from motion picture animator to theater usher |
| United Scenic Artists, Local USA 829 (USA 829) | www.usa829.org/default.aspx | Society of British Theatre Designers (SBTD) | www.theatredesign.org.uk | Designers, Artists, and Craftspeople |
| American Federation of Musicians (AFM) | http://afm.org/ | Musicians' Union (MU) | www.musiciansunion.org.uk/ | Professional musicians |
| Actors' Equity Association (AEA) | http://actorsequity.org/ | Equity | www.equity.org.uk/home | Actors and Stage Managers |
| Stage Directors and Choreographers Society (SDC) | www.sdcweb.org/ | Stage Directors UK (SDUK) UK Theatre/Equity Choreographers | www.stagedirectorsuk.com/ www.uktheatre.org/ | Directors and Choreographers (United States); Directors (United Kingdom) Choreographers (United Kingdom) |

Figure 3.3 Representative Theatrical Unions

When a show travels to other locations the company manager makes housing arrangements for the touring company and oversees the transportation of cast, crew, and the physical production. Additionally, the company manager is charged with adhering to various contract **riders**, chief of which are those appended to a performer's contract. A rider is a written attachment to the original contract (i.e. a collectively bargained Actors' Equity Agreement) that avoids rewriting the original contract and includes additional negotiated stipulations. These might be the provision to provide an actor a limousine or other automobile; a personal assistant; specific housing arrangements over and above the minimum defined by the collectively bargained agreement; or first-class air tickets, their own star dressing room, etc.

## PUBLICITY AND/OR PRESS AGENT

As with any goods—such as an automobile, an electronic device, or a beverage—a theatrical production may be thought of as a product that must attract ticket buyers in order to be commercially successful. Hence, there is the need for publicists or press agents, members of ATPAM, who primarily create unpaid advertising for a production. In essence the press agent generates awareness through campaigns ranging from press releases to print outlets and various other media such as television or radio. The agent also arranges interviews for a show's stars or prominent directors, through Facebook, Twitter, or other electronic means, mall appearances or other publicity stunts, internet blasts, etc.

Intrinsic to a press agent's job is overseeing the creation of a definable image for the show. For example, one of the most universally recognizable images is the logo of two yellow feline eyes for the musical *Cats*. In essence the design captures the spirit of the play and has been reproduced in all sorts of media, print, theatrical programs, and the ubiquitous **window cards** employed to advertise the production. Window cards are those 1′2″ × 1′10″ stiff posters that are hung in store-front windows or in restaurants, etc.

As iconic as the image is now for *Cats*, reaching consensus on a single design is as varied as the number of productions for any given play. A short look at different graphic designs for some of Arthur Miller's plays can be found in Erik Piepenburg's article in the *New York Times* listed in **WEB RESOURCES** at the end of this chapter. When examining the designs, notice how artists reflect variations of thematic insight for different productions of *Death of a Salesman* or *All My Sons*.

## THE SANDBOX WINDOW CARD

Before embarking on a publicity campaign and overseeing the creation of a window card, the publicist not only has to read the play for all Five Key Elements: Who, What, Where, When, Why (How), but also has to gather all the names, job positions, and facts that relate to the production. Most window cards include these Five Key Elements: Who, What, Where, When, Why (How). Try your hand at filling in the possible missing elements from the window card in Figure 3.4. In order to start you off, the What is "The Sandbox," the title of the production, and the Why (or the How of the production) is "The Groundbreaking Musical." Further hints demonstrate more than one missing Who on the card. It is your job to enter the missing job position for each of these Whos (but you do not have to come up with actual names of people for the missing jobs). In total there are 12-missing entrants that you have to come up with. **Notice that this window card bears a similarity to many theatrical organization charts**.

**Billing**, or the positioning of correctly spelled names on window cards and all forms of advertising, is determined by prior contractual negotiations. The press agent would have to obtain this information, as well as details such as size of print, from the general manager.

When determining the Why or How of the production the press agent might include a **money quote**. The money quote may be an endorsement of the production by a famous critic or media personality, or a statement that sets the production apart historically from its predecessors. An example is "The Groundbreaking Musical," utilized to describe *The Sandbox* above. Ideally the quote is attention grabbing and signals interest for building an audience and selling tickets.

As a show proceeds through rehearsals the press agent has been soliciting various writers, editors, and media outlets to provide as much supportive coverage as possible during the production's march toward opening night. With opening night dates set, the press agent has to invite and field critics' requests for press nights. This can be a delicate operation as press kits and programs have to be prepared, optimal viewing seats have to be assigned, and personal attention expended to insure that each and every critic is comfortably treated and is in a positive frame of mind when the curtain goes up. Thereafter the press agent's hands-on approach ceases and critical opinion, whether it is favorable or negative, remains with the critic.

## PROGRAMS

The creation of theatre programs or playbills is an important function of the publicity department. In the United States the monthly magazine trademarked as *Playbill*® is distributed free of charge to Broadway patrons and to various theatregoers across the country. Information for each production is supplied to the magazine by the press agent. This includes listings of scenes, songs, performers, and photos of the cast along with their biographies, as well as biographies for the creative and producing personnel. In addition, the magazine would include listings of all personnel associated with the production, descriptive essays, intermissions, as well as particulars on the theatre.

In England various productions issue their own souvenir booklets for sale at West End theatres. These tend to be more lavish than *Playbill*®, on glossier paper, with production photos, and are seemingly intended as a keepsake.

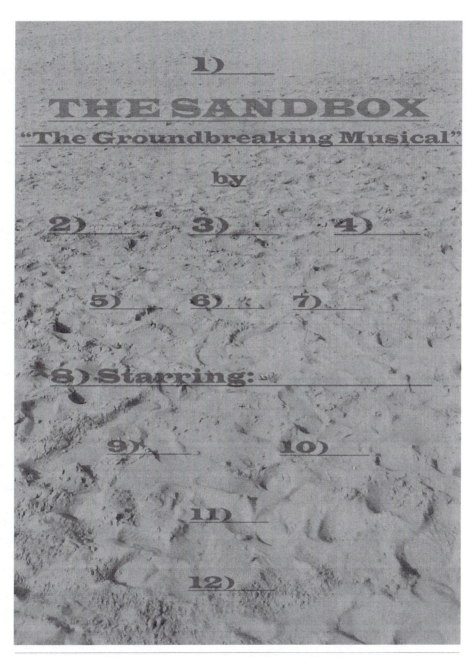

1) ___

# THE SANDBOX

## "The Groundbreaking Musical"

by

2) ___   3) ___   4) ___

5) ___   6) ___   7) ___

8) Starring: ___

9) ___   10) ___

11) ___

12) ___

**Figure 3.4** *The Sandbox* window card

# COMMERCIAL MARKETING AND TICKET SALES

## LEARN MORE: PROGRAM INFORMATION EXERCISE

You are invited to look at the *Playbill®* exercise on the e-resources for the Broadway musical *Hamilton*.

Search out the title page and note the arrangement of the information, beginning with the producers on top followed by the creative team, the performers, the designers, etc. The layout bears a striking resemblance to the hierarchy on a theatrical organization chart.

Now imagine yourself as a press agent and create a form for a production that you might be engaged in and that you could present to *Playbill®* or anyone else creating a program which not only lists the information that goes on the title page, but also includes subsequent pages for the song listings, the biographies and the page(s) that list all personnel associated with the production.

**"*Playbill®* Exercise"**

Marketing and ticket sales parallel the publicity director and press agent. However, one major difference is that the marketing department achieves ticket sales through paid advertising whereas the press agent, as previously mentioned, attracts patrons through unpaid advertising. In many theatrical organizations these positions may be consolidated into one job, much like general manager and company manager.

The marketing department concerns itself with direct sales: subscription brochures targeting specialized groups, and attracting patrons through diverse strategies. Arming itself with statistical analysis and demographic reports, an astute marketing department will target a range of groups through direct mail and online media campaigns. These might include certain religious denominations, schools, charities, special interest groups, and those that exhibited inclinations to attend theatre regularly with membership of such organizations as the Theatre Development Fund (**TDF**) and Audience Extras, or who have bought tickets through online agencies, as well as joining online groups.

The marketing department's reach extends to placing tickets for sale on a daily basis at the various discounted ticket booths in significant theatre centers. Half-price ticket booths (**TKTS**) are prominent in both New York City's Times Square and in London's Leicester Square. These two booths are under the aegis of the TDF and the Society of London Theatre respectively. Figure 3.5 lists representative ticketing agencies for the United States and the United Kingdom.

Additionally, group sales outreach includes travel organizations, both nationally and internationally. These theatre packages possibly encompass transportation, hotels, theatre tickets,

| United States | | |
| --- | --- | --- |
| | Ticketing Agency | Website |
| | Broadway.com | Broadway.com |
| | Playbill | Playbill.com |
| | Theatremania | www.theatermania.com/ |
| | Audience Extras | www.audienceextras.com/ |
| | Theatre Development Fund (**TDF**) | https://tdf.org/ |
| | TKTS NYC | http://tkts.org/ |
| United Kingdom | Broadway.com | http://london.broadway.com/ |
| | Official London Theatre | www.officiallondontheatre.co.uk/ |
| | The Audience Club | www.theaudienceclub.com/ |
| | Society of London Theatres | www.solt.co.uk/ |
| | TKTS London | www.TKTS.co.uk |

**Figure 3.5** Representative Ticketing Agencies

and special opportunities. Theatres in individual cities may offer a subscription series of plays. These may include shows produced at a particular theatre, others packaged as productions "direct from Broadway," or some combination of both.

Generating a fan base and audience development becomes a large part of marketing strategies. Reaching potential audience members through social media, creating a theatre buzz, and tailoring advertising to fans who regularly attend productions continues to spread the word for a particular show. In a relatively new angle, BroadwayCon, inspired by Comic Con-type events, has partnered with *Playbill*® to gather like-minded theatregoers to share and spread their enthusiasm for hit productions.

Tied in to marketing ticket sales has been the exponential increase in merchandise sales. In earlier years a hit musical might have issued an original cast recording or a special souvenir program as a keepsake of a show's popularity. Today, marketing departments are constantly dreaming up new ways to imprint a show's logo on a wide array of merchandise. Selling a show's brand on apparel, drinks cups, jewelry, souvenirs, and various media significantly increases profit.

# NOT-FOR-PROFIT MARKETING

As much as profit is the driving force behind a commercial production, monetary gains from ancillary means such as merchandising also benefits not-for-profit productions. Such rewards are poured back into a non-profit company and help underwrite future productions, educational programs, and community outreach.

Ongoing fundraising is an integral part of the not-for-profit sector. In addition to the various forms of ticket sales and merchandising, the not-for-profit theatres place great emphasis on hiring high-powered development directors. These directors oversee capital campaigns that bring improvements to the theatre plants and endowments, as well as a continuous influx of money for productions and programs for the public good. Many contributions come from large corporations seeking tax benefits. Therefore, the development director must also be well acquainted with the many tax regulations.

One concluding note before leaving publicity: "It costs money to make money." Without a hefty allocation for publicity in the budget few people would know about the production, and fewer would attend. Pinpointing an exact amount of money a producer should budget for advertising is not an exact science. However, if you examine budgets for advertising and/or publicity in Figure 3.2, Figure 2.3, and Figure 2.5 you will notice that this line item ranks high in dollar allocation: in the vicinity of 25–33 percent of the total overall budget for each of these examples. Working with the producer and general manager, the publicity director has to strike a balance between spending money on paid advertising and unpaid publicity. Similarly, development directors have to work with their theatres' producing directors, as well as a board of directors, to meet financial targets when soliciting donors.

## WHAT DID YOU LEARN?

1. What is collective bargaining? What are some reasons for it?

2. What is the production axiom and how is it applied to a production?

3. What is the difference between paid advertising and unpaid advertising? Explain.

4. What does the theatrical term "billing" mean and how is it applied to programs?

5. What are some of the different merchandising products associated with the hit musicals *Cats* or *Hamilton* that you might have seen branded with the show's logo?

## ANSWERS

1) An agreement reached following negotiations between management representatives. It results in a contract that governs minimum salaries and the working conditions that management and labor union(s) must adhere to for a fixed number of years, generally three to five. 2) A production can be good, fast, or cheap. According to the axiom, only two out of three options are possible; it is impossible to obtain all three outcomes. 3) Paid advertising must be paid for (e.g. newspaper ads or television commercials); unpaid advertising is free (e.g. public appearances or interviews). 4) Billing or positioning of correctly spelled names on window cards, in advertising and in programs that is determined by prior contractual negotiations. 5) Original cast recordings, t-shirts, mugs, key chains, throw pillows, etc.

# ADDITIONAL RESOURCES

## VIDEO

*Moon Over Broadway*, a film by Chris Hegedus and D.A. Pennebaker (1997; Los Angeles, CA: New Video, 2000), DVD.

## BOOKS

Steven Adler, *On Broadway: Art and Commerce on the Great White* Way (Carbondale, IL: Southern University Press), 2004.

Suzanne Carmack Celentano and Kevin Marshall, *Theatre Management: A Successful Guide to Producing Plays on Commercial and Non-profit Stages* (Studio City, CA: Players Press), 1998.

Robert Cohen, *Working Together in Theatre: Collaboration and Leadership* (Basingstoke: Palgrave Macmillan), 2011.

L. Peter Edles, *Fundraising: Hands-On Tactics for Nonprofit Groups* (New York: McGraw-Hill), 1993.

Lisa Mulcahy, *Building the Successful Theater Company* (New York: Allworth Press), 2002.

## WEB RESOURCES

**General Manager:** Albert Poland in Conversations with William M. Hoffman, Lehman College, www.bing.com/videos/search?q=videos+on+general+managing+theatre&&view=detail&mid=57D00B3A8773C262715C57D00B3A8773C262715C&FORM=VRDGAR

**Poster Design:** Erik Piepenburg, "Designing Arthur Miller: Simple Gestures, Big Ideas," *New York Times*, November 11, 2015, www.nytimes.com/2015/11/11/theater/designing-arthur-miller-simple-gestures-big-ideas.html?ref=topics&_r=0

**Producing Broadway:** Working in the Theatre #367, www.bing.com/videos/search?q=videos+on+producing+theatre&view=detail&mid=8B0BED7514B5B8923DE88B0BED7514B5B8923DE8&FORM=VIRE7

**Publicity:** BroadwayCon, www.broadwaycon.com

# Creating Theatre

*The Creators articulate a dream*

## THE ROLE OF THE PLAYWRIGHT

Temporarily putting aside the business side of organizing a production, it is necessary to begin considering the artistic components. A production in the theatre emanates from a play, a play script, a concept, or a **devised work** for the theatre (from which a script may ultimately issue through collaborative or improvisatory work by a group of people, rather than from a writer or writers). Our focus now shifts to the primary artist, the playwright. It is their written script or theatrical conception that a producer secures for possible performance. Within the script the playwright sets down the dialogue that is to be spoken by the actors performing the various roles. It is also true that playwrights might include lengthy descriptions of scenery, costumes, lighting, sound, and other technical necessities, such as stage directions, as well as detailed characteristics for each role. However, theatre itself is ephemeral. Drawings, photographs, and video recordings might survive from a production that provides some indication of what the actual theatrical event looked like. Yet, through the ages, the script remains the one constant that theatrical practitioners rely upon for creating a production. For this reason, we look to the playwright's recorded words throughout history when embarking upon a production.

## A SHORT REVIEW OF PLAYWRITING

When we think of playwrights working in the Western tradition it is safe to say that anyone reading this book may have heard of such classical playwrights as Aeschylus, Sophocles, and Euripides (spanning c. 525–407 BC). The earliest plays may have evolved out of ritual, and, in the case of the classicists, moral tragedies were written to celebrate the god Dionysus coming to Athens in an effort to maintain moral order. Tragedies were rigid and in a strict form that defined theme, roles, and staging. In writing his *Poetics*, Aristotle derived his theories primarily from Sophocles' *Oedipus Rex*, and thus laid the foundation for defining tragedy. On the other hand, examples of comedy arose with Aristophanes (c. 448–380 BC), who satirized society's disintegration in the hope of restoring order.

Moving ahead hundreds of years, two of the most famous playwrights that might spring to mind are William Shakespeare (1564–1616) in England and Molière (1622–1673) in France. Unlike the classicists, their plays were written less along the formal precepts of tragedy and comedy. Their works would include elements of each form to suit the purpose and situations encountered as the play developed.

Other notable European playwrights that you might have encountered are Beaumarchais, a writer of French comedies in the 18th century, and 19th-century tragedians such as the Russian Anton Chekhov or the Norwegian Henrik Ibsen. When you arrive at the early 20th century, George Bernard Shaw's works are difficult to compartmentalize as either tragedy or comedy, since so many of his plays are concerned with a battle of ideas.

At this point it is important to pause to once again bring up the issue of copyright and licensing discussed in Chapter 2. Ironically, Shaw provides a bridge between those earlier playwrights mentioned above, whose works fall into the public domain and thus may be more freely produced. There are certain caveats, especially concerning licensing restrictions for the work of Shaw, who may or may not be produced so easily.

A conundrum exists between Canada and almost everywhere else in the world. Canadian law holds that copyright expires fifty years following an author's death, whereas outside of Canada copyright expires seventy years after the author's death. Therefore, at the time of writing, Shaw's works would be in the public domain in Canada, since he died in 1950, but not necessarily elsewhere. Therefore, in Canada royalties would have to be paid to Shaw's estate until 2020 in order to license his productions elsewhere, including the United States and the United Kingdom. Similarly, royalties would have to be paid to more recently deceased playwrights as Samuel Beckett, Harold Pinter, Brian Friel, etc.

As we continue our short review of playwriting, you might want to familiarize yourself with other 20th-century writers such as Lorraine Hansberry, Arthur Miller, Eugene O'Neill, Joe Orton, J.B. Priestley, and Tennessee Williams. Notably bridging this past century and successfully writing into the 21st century are Edward Albee, Caryl Churchill, Nilo Cruz, David Hare, Suzan-Lori Parks, Neil Simon, Tom Stoppard, and August Wilson. This list of playwrights throughout history is not meant to be exhaustive, as these names are just a tiny fraction of a selection that conceivably runs into the thousands. What stands out among them is certain name recognition with the general public. In the case of the 20th- and 21st-century playwrights, they have achieved major awards in American and/or British theatres.

## PLAYWRITING AWARDS

At international level, the Nobel Prize in Literature has been awarded to playwrights such as Eugene O'Neill, Samuel Beckett, and Harold Pinter. The most recognizable awards in the United States and the United Kingdom are for the Broadway and London stages respectively. They include Broadway's Tony Award for Best Play and London's Laurence Olivier Awards for Best New Comedy and Best New Play. Another prestigious award for literary success in the United States is the Pulitzer Prize for Drama (which currently has no equivalent in the United Kingdom).

Very few playwrights rise to the ranks of the above awardees, or achieve similar levels of fame (and possible wealth). Playwriting for the commercial theatre is a very risky proposition, and getting a play read by a potential producer is extremely rare. Few producers, if any, accept unsolicited manuscripts. For the most part, plays for consideration are submitted through agents with successful track records or via highly trusted associates. Time to read thousands of submissions and the sheer economics of producing on Broadway and the West End dictate against the risk of producing an unknown playwright's work. These factors govern producing at almost every commercial level as well.

However, all hope is not lost. Any number of not-for-profit theatres have play-reading personnel seeking works that fulfill their legal obligation to do good for the public sector and fit the demographics of their audience. These theatres may still only invite submissions via agents, but also may sponsor grants and playwriting contests with specific restrictions that tailor scripts to their particular mission statement.

Other opportunities for playwrights to have their work read and perhaps produced exist through community groups and numerous festivals. However, while production in these cases may not bring instant wealth or fame, they do bring all-important opportunities for playwrights to hear their words spoken, see their plays enacted, evaluate what works or does not work, and perhaps strike a receptive chord in some producer's mind to give the play another chance of monetary gain. You are encouraged to search for "playwriting festivals" and "playwriting contests" on the internet and go to **WEB RESOURCES** at the end of this chapter for further information.

## THE DRAMATISTS GUILD AND ROYALTIES

Many years of toiling, scraping for grants and entering playwriting contests is hardly enough to sustain a career. Those fortunate enough might attract an interested producer for their work and gain a production. Conceivably, at this point the playwright might be in line to earn money, as well as future royalties on a subsequent production of the play. For this undertaking the playwright would be best served by approaching the Dramatists Guild, which, according to its website, is "the only professional association which advances the interests of playwrights, composers, lyricists, and librettists writing for the living stage." Members of the Dramatists Guild may obtain model contracts for use as templates to begin negotiations for licensing a work for commercial and/or non-commercial production. Typical examples of such contracts are: "Form of Licensing Agreement," "Small Theater Contract—National Premiere," "Form of Option Underlying Rights (Plays/Musicals)," "Form of Commission Agreement (Plays/ Musicals)," and "Approved Production Contract for Musicals." There was an almost immediate need for an "Approved Production Contract for Musicals" in one of the rarest of situations for the creators of the musical *Urinetown*, which made a fast leap from the New York City Fringe Festival to Off-Broadway (May 6–June 25, 2001) and then opened on Broadway (September 20, 2001). Remember that the more likely scenario for a play's journey to possible success is through readings, perhaps a series of grants, workshops, festivals, and maybe a commercial run in a small theatre or a not-for-profit production.

Continuing along this spectrum, once a play achieves a successful commercial run—or for that matter, a number of performances in a notable not-for-profit theatre—there exists the possibility that other producing entities would subsequently desire to produce the play as well. Rather than negotiate with each individual theatre the playwright and/or their agent will nego- tiate a contract with a **play-licensing** and theatrical publishing **agency** to secure publication of the play for residual amateur rights. Figure 4.1 shows an example of licensing instructions as published in the Samuel French edition of *The 39 Steps* by Patrick Barlow. Similar pages appear in the front of every published playscript. The instructions should be read thoroughly and adhered to by anyone who wishes to produce any particular play. The licensed play is the means by which a playwright earns their royalties. Some of the well-established licensing publishers and agencies are listed in Figure 4.2.

## THE DRAMATURG AND PLAYWRIGHT IN REHEARSAL

Theatre is the only performance medium in which the writer retains the rights. This is not the case with writers for film or television. However, the thought of solitary ownership ceases when a playwright engages the play for production. Now the playwright has to participate in a collaborative effort with a score of creative artists.

If it can be loosely said that the playwright, in giving birth to a play, is the mother, then the director who shapes the play into a production is the father. With a living playwright in the rehearsal room it can be a symbiotic relationship that may not always go smoothly. In the middle of this same relationship there also exists the possibility of a **dramaturg**, or a midwife.

Although the appointment of a dramaturg is a more recent phenomenon over the past few decades in the United States and the United Kingdom, the role has existed since 1767–1769. During that time Gotthold Ephraim Lessing—a German playwright, philosopher, art critic, and publicist—was hired to form an identity for the productions of the Hamburg National Theatre.

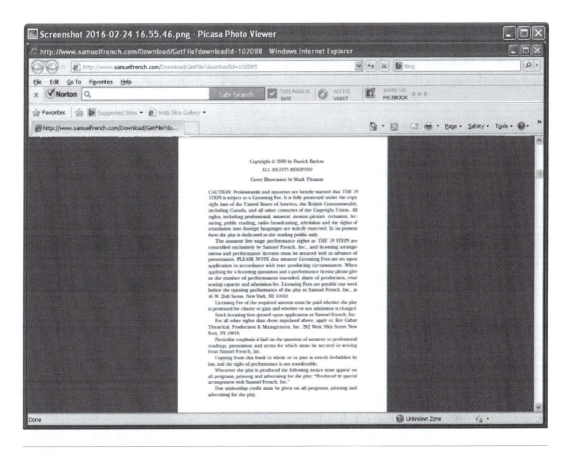

**Figure 4.1** A Screen Shot of the Licensing Page from *The 39 Steps*

| Bloomsbury Publishing | www.bloomsbury.com/us/academic/academic-subjects/drama-and-performance-studies/ |
| --- | --- |
| Dramatists Play Service | www.dramatists.com/ |
| Samuel French | www.samuelfrench.com/ |
| Theatre Communications Group | www.tcg.org/publications/books/index.cfm |

**Figure 4.2** Representative Play Publishers and Licensing Agencies

By his own identification, Lessing credits himself as the first dramaturg. In this role he wrote essays on the acting and literary merits of theatre productions as a means of enlightening the Hamburg National's audiences.

For today's audiences, especially those in regional theatres, a dramaturg is more commonplace, though virtually unseen by the public. The dramaturg assists with advice on a range of such diverse subjects as historical accuracy, research, etymology, script analysis, editing, design input, acting style, pronunciation, preparing study guides, stimulating outreach programs, etc. If the play originated in another language, the dramaturg may also serve as translator if one had not been engaged to collaborate with the playwright.

In the rehearsal room the playwright is able to hear his or her words repeatedly spoken by actors, as well as see many of the movements dictated by the script. What seemed plausible to the writer when creating the play may not always ring true in the rehearsal process. This is the opportune time for rewrites and changes. One of the best services that an exceptional dramaturg can provide the playwright and director during this period, particularly as rewrites occur, is to insure that continuity, consistency, and accuracy are maintained for all production aspects. All of this input is invaluable to the playwright and director as the dramaturg offers constructive advice and helps shepherd the play from page to stage. When the curtain goes up or the lights come on at the beginning of a performance the audience is disposed to greet the play with a willingness to suspend disbelief. If the playwright, the director, and the dramaturg interrupt this disbelief by inserting a production element that disrupts the consistent belief, then the audience might be disengaged from their intellectual and emotional involvement with the performance. This is a surefire signal for a play's failure.

## MUSICAL THEATRE CREATORS: LIBRETTIST, COMPOSER, AND LYRICIST

Whereas a play might have been the creation of one writer or a group of writers, a musical production opens the door to a set of three distinct creators. These include the **librettist** (the book or story writer), the **composer** (the music writer), and the **lyricist** (the writer of the words that accompany the music). In some instances, the creators may wear one, two, or even three hats whereby the composer and lyricist might be the same person—such as Stephen Sondheim for the musical *Sweeney Todd* or Lin-Manuel Miranda, who is the librettist, composer, and lyricist of *Hamilton*.

In a musical it is the librettist who writes the dialogue for all the characters, fashions the book, and plots where the characters might carry the story through song and/or dance. Although there are many original musicals, seemingly more often than not they are adaptations of other sources, and may be inspired by various stories, non-fiction material, plays, movies, or even a body of hit songs. These popular songs are shaped into what has been commonly called a **jukebox musical**, which might combine one artist's hit releases or music of a particular time period into an evening of theatre. Test yourself on what provided the source material for the musicals referenced in Figure 4.3.

Similar to the playwright, a musical's creative team will be in line to have their work published and represented by a licensing agent upon a successful production, as depicted in Figure 4.4.

| PRODUCTION | SOURCE MATERIAL |
|---|---|
| *West Side Story* | 1) |
| *Saturday Night Fever* | 2) |
| *Mamma Mia!* | 3) |
| *Cats* | 4) |
| *Wicked* | 5) |
| *Fun Home* | 6) |
| *We Will Rock You* | 7) |
| *Cabaret* | 8) |
| *Big River* | 9) |
| *Kiss Me Kate* | 10) |

## ANSWERS

1) *Romeo and Juliet* by William Shakespeare; 2) Bee Gees hit songs; 3) ABBA hit songs; 4) *Old Possum's Book of Practical Cats* by T.S. Eliot; 5) *Wicked* by Gregory Maguire; 6) *Fun Home*, the graphic memoir by Alison Bechdel; 7) Queen hit songs; 8) *The Berlin Stories* by Christopher Isherwood; 9) *The Adventures of Huckleberry Finn* by Mark Twain; 10) *The Taming of the Shrew* by William Shakespeare.

**Figure 4.3** Sources for Musical Theatre Productions

| | |
|---|---|
| Josef Weinberger Ltd. | www.josef-weinberger.com/ |
| Music Theatre International | mtishows.com/ |
| Rodgers & Hammerstein | www.rnh.com/ |
| Tams-Witmark | www.tamswitmark.com/ |

**Figure 4.4** Representative Musical Publishers and Licensing Agencies

With the librettist's script fashioned, fellow creative collaborators such as the composer and lyricist can begin their examination of the book's <u>Five Key Elements: Who, What, Where, When, Why (How)</u> prior to engaging with the director, etc. While doing so the relationship between composer and lyricist becomes symbiotic. In many instances the relationship is so entwined that oftentimes (as mentioned above) the composer and lyricist are the same person. As an illustration, when examining the <u>Who</u> from the list of characters, the composer and lyricist would determine all the principal characters, subsidiary roles, and the various chorus parts. Closer examination would follow the <u>What</u>, or whether a character might be a parent, a teenager, a lover, a villain, a civil servant, a teacher, a laborer, etc.

Much like the playwright, the librettist would have to include certain types of dialogue that match that character's personality and method of speaking. In turn, the lyricist would have to match the style of dialogue within the lyrics. Similarly, the music would have to support the lyrics as well as the story's situation at any given moment, i.e. the <u>Where</u> and <u>When</u>. An example could be the farmhand Curly singing "Oh, What a Beautiful Morning" in the groundbreaking musical *Oklahoma!* (1943). That show would insert a song and/or dance to further the plot and tell the story. The first song's up-tempo melody and lyrics as sung by Curly exalted the beauty of the morning and the meadow, and captured his powerful masculinity, or the <u>Why (How)</u> as he greeted a new day. "Oh, What a Beautiful Morning" immediately set the tone for a feel-good musical, and popularized the lush orchestrations of the day.

Befitting the style of a more current musical, Lin-Manuel Miranda—*Hamilton*'s librettist, composer, and lyricist—has chosen to employ rap music for the successful show's opening number. Not only does he introduce the title character along with other major characters, he also majestically unleashes the show's premise and sets up the powerful thrust of the story about to unfold. In relating the story of one of America's major revolutionary authors, Miranda matched the production with rap music, fast-paced riposte, and intellectually infused lyrics. Like his predecessors on *Oklahoma!*—Richard Rodgers, who wrote the book, and Oscar Hammerstein II, the composer and lyricist—in his threefold creative capacity Miranda outlined for himself the <u>Five Key Elements: Who, What, Where, When, Why (How)</u>. This all continued as he worked through the rehearsal process with the director and all the other collaborators.

Ironically, with such a production (steeped in fact and historical accuracy) Miranda may not have had a dramaturg present. However, he did consult Jeremy McCarter, a cultural critic and theatre artist who was involved in the development of the project from its earliest stages. Also, he was fortunate to have had Ron Chernow, author of the biography *Alexander Hamilton* that the musical was based on, for additional feedback. Back in 1943, when dramaturgy had not yet risen to today's prominence, Rodgers and Hammerstein had distant input from Lynn Riggs, whose earlier play *Green Grow the Lilacs* (1931) was the basis for *Oklahoma!*

## REHEARSALS

No script, musical score, or set of lyrics that arrives on the first day of rehearsal predictably will survive in its entirety by the time opening night occurs. As previously mentioned regarding the playwright who is present for rehearsals of a new play, the composer and lyricist face similar fates, for it is in the very nature of rehearsals—when musical passages are played and songs are sung by actors—that the perspectives the composer and lyricist had when creating the work may be significantly altered. For instance, what might have seemed the perfect love ballad when the composer and lyricist were hammering out the number around a piano in their own studio or apartment might not ring true when the leading man and his leading lady sing it to each other in rehearsal. This could be for any number of musical reasons—such as the tempo, vocal range, rhythm, and rhyming scheme of the lyrics not fitting the moment or the singers' ability to interpret the song in that particular situation. As written, the song might not work.

In this process of discovery, the composer and/or lyricist might have to make changes to their material, as well as create a new musical number, delete it altogether, or perhaps shift it to another section of the musical. Other alternatives would be to assign the song to another character, or augment it with choral parts. Maybe the song need not even be sung, but rather interpreted through dance.

In short, putting together a musical could be seen as one big jigsaw puzzle in which book sections, songs, and musical passages might be created in the moment, jettisoned altogether, or reordered. The librettist, the composer, and the lyricist must pay careful attention to the Five Key Elements: Who, What, Where, When, Why (How) as they go about the restructuring.

For the moment, think of this process as analogous to painting. Stephen Sondheim, one of theatre's greatest composers and lyricists, aptly captures such artistic struggles in the song "Putting It Together" which he composed for the musical *Sunday in the Park with George* (1986). Lyrically it would be "Bit by bit . . . note by note."

## LEARN MORE: ARTISTIC STRUGGLES

Follow the construction of George's work of art and the many insights into his character that Sondheim reveals with the song's progression in the YouTube video on our e-resources with the following link:

**"Putting It Together"**

Undergoing this process in the rehearsal room is only one part of the equation. Once a production moves to the stage for technical rehearsals, and actual moving scenery is introduced, the composer and lyricist will potentially face another set of situations not previously encountered. Such circumstances will be discussed in Chapter 9: Production Crews.

# ASCAP, BMI, SESAC, AND ROYALTIES

Earlier we presented lists of publishing and licensing agencies for playwrights and the creators of a musical (see Figure 4.1 and Figure 4.4). These agencies primarily serve the creators of

| ORGANIZATION | MEMBERS | COVERAGE | MEMBERSHIP |
|---|---|---|---|
| ASCAP (American Society of Composers, Authors, and Publishers) www.ascap.com | Composers Lyricists Songwriters Music Publishers | United States | Open |
| BMI (Broadcast Music Inc.) www.bmi.com | Composers Songwriters Music Publishers | United States United Kingdom | Open |
| SESAC (Society of European Stage Authors and Composers) www.sesac.com | Composers Songwriters Music Publishers | United States United Kingdom | Invitation Only |

**Figure 4.5** Performing Rights Organizations

dramatic presentations. Composers and lyricists may also earn public performance royalties (i.e. those collected from businesses and organizations such as the recording industry, television, etc. that want to play their music publicly). These additional royalties are issued by one of three organizations, as depicted in Figure 4.5.

## RELATING TO THE OTHER MEMBERS ON THE ORGANIZATIONAL CHART

The rehearsal period, as previously noted, is potentially full of change and adjustment. Not only do playwrights, composers, and lyricists have to interact with a dramaturg; they might also be subject to many suggestions from the producer, as well as from the director, the choreographer, or a member of the musical director's team. The performers very often voice contributions, and stage managers sometimes have constructive advice regarding the technical feasibility for a particular staging. The music and dance departments will also have an impact on how the finished product will shape up. All of this input has to be filtered by these creative artists: to accept it, reject it, or figure out an artistic means that improve upon the eventual outcome. In the next chapter we will encounter the creative team and how they add to the dynamics of the playwright, composer, and lyricist.

## CAN YOU MATCH THE PLAYWRIGHT?

Figure 4.6 provides a list of playwrights and plays. You are required to match each playwright to the correct play. Try your hand at naming additional plays written by these playwrights.

| PLAYWRIGHTS | PLAYS |
|---|---|
| 1) William Shakespeare | A. *Fences* <br> *The Piano Lesson* |
| 2) Harold Pinter | B. *The Coast of Utopia* <br> *Rosencrantz & Guildenstern Are Dead* |
| 3) Lillian Hellman | C. *A Moon for the Misbegotten* <br> *Long Day's Journey Into Night* |
| 4) August Wilson | D. *American Buffalo* <br> *Glengarry Glen Ross* |
| 5) Oscar Hammerstein II | E. *Death of a Salesman* <br> *The Crucible* |
| 6) Neil Simon | F. *They're Playing Our Song* <br> *Brighton Beach Memoirs* |
| 7) Wendy Wasserstein | G. *Romeo and Juliet* <br> *Julius Caesar* |
| 8) Sam Shepard | H. *The Room* <br> *The Homecoming* |
| 9) Arthur Miller | I. *Fool for Love* <br> *A Lie of the Mind* |
| 10) Eugene O'Neill | J. *The Heidi Chronicles* <br> *The Sisters Rosensweig* |
| 11) David Mamet | K. *Oklahoma!* <br> *Carousel* |
| 12) Tom Stoppard | L. *Little Foxes* <br> *The Children's Hour* |

**ANSWERS**

1-G; 2-H; 3-L; 4-A; 5-K; 6-F; 7-J; 8-I; 9-E; 10-C; 11-D; 12-B

**Figure 4.6** Match the Playwright

# WHAT DID YOU LEARN?

1. Who are the three main artists responsible for creating a musical before it begins rehearsal, and what are their contributions?

2. What is dramaturgy, and who is considered the first dramaturg?

3. What is a devised work for theatre? Explain.

4. Why are George Bernard Shaw's plays not allowed to be performed outside of Canada without a license? How does this case serve as an example for securing a license of a deceased playwright?

5. Name the four representative play publishers and licensing agencies that were listed in this chapter. In addition, list three representative musical publishers and licensing agencies.

## ANSWERS

responses.

If you are unsure of the remaining answers, please review the chapter for the correct

was considered the first.

preparing study guides, stimulating outreach programs, etc. Gotthold Ephraim Lessing

on, e.g., historical accuracy, script analysis, editing, design, acting style, pronunciation,

sung words. 2) The theory and practice of dramatic composition. The dramaturg advises

1) Librettist (playwright) writes the dialogue; composer writes the music; lyricist writes the

# ADDITIONAL RESOURCES

### BOOKS: PLAYWRITING

Toby Cole, *Playwrights on Playwriting: From Ibsen to Ionesco* (New York: Cooper Square Press), 2001.

Steven Gooch, *Writing a Play* (London: A & C Black), 2004.

Jeffrey Hatcher, *The Art and Craft of Playwriting* (Cincinnati, OH: Story Press), 1996.

David Letwin, Joe Stockdale, and Robin Stockdale, *Architecture of Drama: Plot, Character, Theme, Genre, and Style* (Plymouth, UK: Scarecrow), 2008.

David Savran, *In Their Own Words: Contemporary American Playwrights* (New York: Theatre Communications Group, Inc.), 1989.

Stuart Spencer, *The Playwright's Guidebook* (New York and London: Faber & Faber), 2002.

Walter Wager (ed.), *The Playwrights Speak* (New York: Delacorte Press), 1967.

### BOOKS: MUSICAL THEATRE

Marty Bell, *Broadway Stories: A Backstage Journey Through the Musical Theatre* (New York: Limelight Editions), 1993.

Lin-Manuel Miranda and Jeremy McCarter, *Hamilton: The Revolution* (New York: Grand Central Publishing), 2016.

Michael Riedel, *Razzle Dazzle: The Battle for Broadway* (New York: Simon & Schuster), 2015.

Stephen Sondheim, *Finishing the Hat: Collected Lyrics (1954–1981) with Attendant Comments, Principles, Heresies, Grudges, Whines, and Anecdotes* (New York: Alfred A. Knopf), 2010.

Stephen Sondheim, *Look, I Made a Hat: Collected Lyrics (1981–2011) with Attendant Comments, Amplifications, Dogmas, Harangues, Digressions, Anecdotes and Miscellany* (New York: Alfred A. Knopf), 2010.

Jack Viertel, *The Secret Life of the American Musical* (New York: Sarah Crichton Books/Farrar, Straus & Giroux), 2016.

Max Wilk, *OK!: The Story of Oklahoma!* (New York: Grove Press), 1993.


## WEB RESOURCES

**George Bernard Shaw Copyright Issue**: Jennifer Kavur, "George Bernard Shaw Plays Sidestep Copyright Headaches," *IT World Canada*, April 15, 2009, www.itworldcanada.com/article/george-bernard-shaw-plays-sidestep-copyright-headaches/11375#ixzz40e1vPZuU

*Playwriting Awards*

www.nobelprize.org/nobel_prizes/literature/laureates/

www.olivierawards.com/

www.pulitzer.org/

www.tonyawards.com/index.html

*Playwriting Festivals and Contests*

The Bruntwood Prize for Playwriting, www.writeaplay.co.uk/

Edinburgh Festival Fringe, www.edfringe.com/participants

The Eugene O'Neill Theatre Center, www.theoneill.org/summer-conferences/npc/

Fringe Festivals, http://fringefestivals.com/fringe-festivals/

Fringe New York City, http://fringenyc.org/

Hedgebrook Women Playwrights Festival™ (HWPF), www.hedgebrook.org/women-playwrights-festival/

Playwriting Contests, http://plays.about.com/od/playwritingcontests/

# The Creative Team

*Shaping the Dream*

## THE ROLE OF THE DIRECTOR

With licensing rights to the play and/or musical secured by the producing team, it is time to bring on board the creative team that will breathe life into the product. First and foremost would be the hiring of a director, who is situated at the center of the organizational chart (Figure 0.1). A musical director and choreographer would follow for a musical production. On occasion the director and choreographer might be the same person. Occupying these three positions are the major personnel who will set the course for bringing a playscript and/or musical to life, for it is the director who interprets the <u>Five Key Elements: Who, What, Where, When, Why (How)</u> of a script for an audience by presenting actors on stage utilizing dramatic action and sound to convey the writer's emotional and intellectual concepts. This person is ultimately in charge of everyone and everything that appears onstage.

## A BRIEF OVERVIEW OF DIRECTING

Prior to the mid-1800s what we commonly think of as directing was a helter-skelter affair. At best actors would dress in their own clothes, and memorize and speak their lines as they saw fit, as well as moving about the stage to where they deemed was a suitable position to be heard. Scenery, if any, would consist of what was at hand. The few props utilized were primarily chosen for functionality. Rehearsals were non-existent, since what passed for staging was handed down through the years as prescribed convention. Any organization for a production was brought about by the actors or actor/manager. In short there was little unification of vision, concept, or adherence to historical accuracy.

This began to change under **Georg II, Duke of Saxe-Meiningen** (1826–1914), who had a background in the visual arts and was head of his own small German theatre. In practice he unified the many elements of his productions, composing stage pictures with the actors arranged on multi-levels for crowd scenes which all looked to be of the same place, time period, and were fittingly costumed. This unification extended to other technical elements as well, such as scenery and lighting. By touring his visually unified productions to many European cities, Georg had far-reaching influence on many of the day's leading playwrights. These included Henrik Ibsen, August Strindberg, and Anton Chekov, who would go on to incorporate thematic unity in their psychological plays. By the time Georg's company disbanded in 1890 his pictorial methods impacted younger European stage directors such as Frenchman André Antoine, who founded the first theatre of **naturalism** (Théâtre-Libre, Paris, 1887), and the Russian director Konstantin Stanislavsky (Moscow Art Theatre, 1898), who emphasized psychological **realism** in his productions, as covered below.

## STAGING A PERFORMANCE

In Chapter 1 we considered six theatre configurations for a live presentation: theatre-in-the-round or arena, amphitheater, thrust stage or ¾ stage, black box, proscenium, and site-specific. Within these configurations various styles of staging might be possible. By staging we mean how the actors perform within the confines of scenery located in relationship to an audience; specifically, how the scenery is defined and how the actors relate to it, as well as how the audience perceives this interaction. In the earliest of formats, arena theatre, performances might have been viewed as folkloric dances, or certain rituals performed in a space with no scenery, with the audience surrounding the event. If the audience were to perceive any scenery it would only be a figment of their imagination, something that the actors described in their dialogue. We could call this **arena staging**.

With further development of theatre and staging in an amphitheater, we previously learned that the performers were generally arranged in certain patterns to face the audience. Any scenery was fairly neutral: a few stairs, perhaps a platform or two, a wall for the *skene*, and maybe a higher elevated space for the gods. For the most part location was not defined by the scenery. The performances tended to be mostly declarative, delivered facing front on to the audience, in an arrangement that we might describe as **formal staging**.

Around the 13th century in Europe, to coincide with the development of mystery, miracle, and morality plays (i.e. biblical or religious works, and plays extolling certain ethical lessons respectively), the actors would perform in front of a series of panels or scenic backgrounds. Some productions in France and Italy might take place on stages up to 100 feet wide. An actor traversing the production space might play out earthly scenes in the middle of the stage and travel to heaven or hell represented by scenic backdrops at either end of the stage. As the actors moved across the stage these backgrounds would give the sense of passing from one location to the next in what we would term **simultaneous staging**. In the process of simultaneous staging the actors would also use real props, bludgeon one another, use fire effects, and strive for a physical reality, all in an effort to deliver moral lessons that we might view as unsophisticated today.

Eventually theatre began to develop as an entertainment vehicle. Thereafter, various personalities stepped to the forefront to take charge and implement their ideas. These included writers, actors, actor-managers, and even tradesmen to build scenery. All these individuals were instrumental in devising methods for staging plays.

With the rise of the Elizabethan theatre (late 1500s) spaces were built to accommodate the plays of William Shakespeare and Christopher Marlowe, among others. Two of the most renowned buildings were the Swan and the Globe, built out of wood and eventually destroyed by fire.

## LEARN MORE: THE SWAN AND GLOBE THEATRES

For further insight into the staging areas of these Elizabethan theatres see a surviving sketch of the Swan Theatre from 1595 and a drawing for the reconstructed Globe from 1997 on the e-resources at the following links:

*"Swan Theatre"/"Globe Theatre"*

Within the structures of these theatres any number of playing areas were utilized, such as: a raised platform stage, doorways, balconies, windows that opened off the balconies, the large area below the stage (forestage) where the groundlings (the audience) stood, galleries, side stages, and even a towering structure constructed behind and above the stage. Items such as tables, chairs, thrones, or constructed bushes might be carried into place.

Unlike simultaneous staging, the actors would move throughout the theatre's structure in a **multiple staging** fashion. Through their dialogue they might define their location—a palace chamber, a forest, or a balcony (as for a love scene played out by Romeo and Juliet)—in order to indicate where they performed in different locations in the theatre. By their design these theatres brought the actors into close proximity with their audiences. One result was that the acting could be more intimate and tended to be more believable than with the previous conventions utilized in arena, formal, and simultaneous staging. A drawback, however, was that shifts between locales could take considerable time and would interrupt the continuity of a play.

During the Italian Renaissance (14–16th centuries) and the Restoration (17th–18th centuries) in England, as well as in other 18th-century theatres, artists addressed the situation by depicting specific locations painted on scenic backdrops that would be employed in proscenium theatres. With actors performing in front of the scenery, locations could be changed more rapidly, referential dialogue could be eliminated, and continuity could be streamlined. By its very nature this type of staging in which the audience observes the artificiality that is taking place before their eyes has often been described as **theatrical staging**. The sense of believable setting held audiences in awe for the next 200 years.

Transitional romantic plays were penned, and the rise of **romantic staging** evolved through the work of the English actor-manager of the Theatre Royal, Drury Lane, David Garrick (1717–1779). Although he abandoned what was conventional dress of the day for leading characters and clothed them in wardrobe more appropriate for their particular role, Garrick did not bring that unity to the remainder of the actors. The plays would be plot-driven, idealizations, staged with acting that still relied upon stock conventions and poses—such as a hand to the head to indicate surprise or shock, or a hand to the heart to illustrate swooning or being touched by love. Although the backgrounds signified location, actors still performed loudly, softly, coarsely, broadly, intimately, dignifiedly, or in whatever style they felt would be necessary to garner an audience's admiration. Actors remained the center of attention. Believability in a character was really not the goal of actors. They performed to receive accolades and please audiences. There was no one of strong hand to instruct them otherwise.

The delineation of the various methods of staging up to this point in history is significant to our understanding of modern directing. What followed was the truly groundbreaking work of the aforementioned directors André Antoine (**naturalism**) and Konstantin Stanislavsky (**realism**). Under the strong influence of Georg II, Duke of Saxe-Meiningen, Antoine began to direct with a somewhat scientific approach. Taking his cue from the French novelist, essayist, and playwright Émile Zola, who collected his criticisms in "Le Naturalisme au théâtre," Antoine's plays would be examined as if under a microscope. He would stage his productions with naturalism: a fashion that was realistic, action that grew out of situation, and motivations that were grounded in the environment, as if they were "slices of life." Performing behind the proscenium, the idea was that the "fourth wall" was removed. Audiences would be peering at the action through a non-existent wall. Instead of the painted backdrops for exterior scenes, Antoine would present plays that predominately had interior environments that could be reproduced with indoor, three-dimensional accuracy in all detail on a stage. He would reject the conventions of previous acting styles in an attempt to have his actors behave naturally within their stage settings, although it was obvious that the actors were still playing to the audience. The aim was to present theatrical works that were a perfect illusion of reality. A typical example could be a play that was set in a kitchen or a barn. Antoine might have included actual cooking smells, or live animals and hay to heighten the illusion.

Stanislavsky, who spent the summer of 1888 studying in Paris and attending Antoine's performances, went one step further in his approach to directing. Not only did he absorb the external trappings of naturalism; he also set about developing a method that unified the internal psychological and external aspects of acting. Now commonly called the Method, actors are trained in body, voice, and movement to completely embody the character being played, as well as to physically react to their stage environment as if everything was being performed in a unified whole.

Much of Stanislavsky's teachings is still practiced today and is central to all directors' work with actors, as well as to the unification of an entire production. It is because this unity now rests with one person, the director, that it is all the more important for a producer to hire a director who shares an equal passion for the property and is in line with the author's conception of the play. That is to say, all three positions have to be thoroughly invested and in harmony with one another in order to attain a successful production. They need to share a common vision.

## THE DIRECTOR'S VISION: CONCEPT AND STYLE

Drawing upon our discussion of staging styles, we can now approach a director's vision and how it combines concept and style. The common vision that the hired director has struck with the producer and playwright (or the creators of a musical) is a result of repeated readings of the work (and perhaps a thorough listening of a piano score in the case of a musical). Carefully analyzing, visualizing, and interpreting the script through the lens of the Five Key Elements: Who, What, Where, When, Why (How), the director would arrive at a concept and a style for the production.

### CONCEPT

Different directors are attracted to different works for many reasons. Chief among them is that the director has to connect with the work. Some directors inherently gravitate toward works by Shakespeare and other historical plays, or those that have themes which resonate with contemporary ideas that deal with abortion rights, jurisprudence, civil rights, mysteries, generational divide, gender issues, or a host of other concerns or genres. Other directors may be attracted to similar themes, yet find they prefer to express their vision by directing musicals. While developing a concept the director will determine the most important of the many images, ideas, and emotions that will be shared with the designers and actors, as well as with the entire production team. Hopefully the concept will be shaped into a production that will translate the director's vision into a successful viewing experience for vast audiences.

In addition to a director's track record with plays that illustrate particular concepts, consideration for being hired may depend on many other factors. A few of these may include a director's simpatico relationship with the playwright, a strong leadership and team approach, an ability to work with stars or temperamental actors, and being able to unify the work of all the designers while at the same time adhering to budget constraints.

The concept might arise simply from the play as written. For instance, Arthur Miller's *A View from the Bridge*, which was set on the 1955 Brooklyn waterfront in New York, was written to depict the main character, Eddie, driven to near insanity by his repressed desire for his niece Catherine, who wants to marry the illegal immigrant Rodolpho. In order to prevent the marriage, Eddie betrays Rodolpho to the immigration authorities. Vengeful Marco, Rodolpho's brother, kills Eddie. In a straightforward concept, the murder of Eddie onstage can be seen as just retribution for not preventing the deportation of the brothers.

However, taking another approach, the Belgian director Ivo van Hove, with the London's Young Vic and the subsequent 2015 Broadway production of *A View from the Bridge*, moves beyond Miller's elaborate instructions included in the script. Instead of faithfully examining the play with the Five Key Elements: Who, What, Where, When, Why (How) and adhering to Miller's indications, van Hove chose to examine the play as if its characters were pitted against each other in a brutal, moral battle that paralleled violent myths of antiquity. By arriving at unexpected insights into Miller's characters, and thinking of them as doing battle in an arena—a much different locale than the script's indicated street and the skeletal front of a tenement building that included actual rooms—van Hove arrived at what we would call a **high-concept** approach to directing. By taking a familiar play and adding his own interpretation, the director has made the audience look at it in an astonishing and surprisingly different fashion. Simply put, high concept might mean a play staged in a different period than originally intended.

There are many directors who have ascribed to investing their productions with high concept. Besides the productions of Ivo van Hove, the reader is encouraged to research some of the notable productions associated with the directors indicated in Figure 5.1 by exploring some of their more successful productions. The list begins with Peter Brook, the British director who most famously and almost single-handedly started the high-concept bandwagon with his legendary 1970 production of Shakespeare's production of *A Midsummer Night's Dream*.

## LEARN MORE: PETER BROOK'S CONCEPT

It is worth seeking out a video of the stark, practically all-white production of *A Midsummer Night's Dream*, replete with actors on stilts and trapezes in the YouTube video on the e-resources with the following link:

*"Brook, Midsummer 1970"*

### STYLE

In order to complete his vision for directing *A View from the Bridge*, Ivo van Hove would have to translate his concept into a physical production style—**style** being the manner

| MATCH THE DIRECTORS TO THEIR HIGH-CONCEPT PRODUCTIONS | |
|---|---|
| DIRECTORS | PRODUCTIONS |
| 1) Peter Brook | A. *A Midsummer Night's Dream* |
| 2) Rupert Goold | B. *Sweeney Todd* |
| 3) Mary Zimmerman | C. *Pippin* |
| 4) Ivo van Hove | D. *Cabaret* |
| 5) Lee Breuer | E. *Krapp's Last Tape* |
| 6) Sam Mendes | F. *The Lion King* |
| 7) Diane Paulus | G. *Mabou Mines DollHouse* |
| 8) Robert Wilson | H. *Macbeth* |
| 9) John Doyle | I. *Metamorphoses* |
| 10) Julie Taymor | J. *The Crucible* |

**ANSWERS**

1-A, 2-H, 3-I, 4-J, 5-G, 6-D, 7-C, 8-E, 9-B, 10-F

**Figure 5.1** High Concept Directors

(or the How) in which a play is performed. To match his concept of the characters pitted against one another in battle, van Hove chose to have the actors display all of their emotions at fever pitch. They made rapid entrances, and characteristically the action was loud, raw, and reminiscent of imagery initially conceived in his collaboration with the design team. Thus a portion of the style was an outgrowth of the concept. Van Hove has presented iconoclastic takes on other classics such as Miller's *The Crucible*; Eugene O'Neill's *More Stately Mansions*; and, a seeming favorite of deconstructionists, Tennessee Williams's *A Streetcar Named Desire*, in which the character Stanley appeared shockingly nude in a bathtub.

Joining the *Streetcar* parade was Australian director Benedict Andrews, who originated his production at London's Young Vic. Andrews's decision was to dispense with the picaresque but squalid French Quarter of New Orleans. Instead he would update the production to the present and situate the action in a newlywed's first apartment, fitted out with stark, seemingly self-assembled furniture. To heighten the brutal battle portrayed by the characters, ear-splitting electronic music filled the theatre between scenes. Also, the alleys outside the Kowalski apartment teemed with people engaged in animalistic fury. How unity in concept and style are further achieved between the director and the remaining members of the creative team will be discussed in Chapter 6: The Creative Artists.

## BASICS OF DIRECTING

As mentioned earlier, it is the goal of modern directors to unify all elements in their productions, something that van Hove and Andrews among others accomplished. Although we briefly touched on the acting style in these previous examples, our primary concern in this book is to elaborate on the tangible manifestations of production. Therefore, material that springs from a director's emotional and intellectual being, as well as an actor's, are left to the many fine books and courses on those subjects. What follows here are the physical basics of directing demonstrating a director's vision, and therefore contributing to an audience's understanding of a play or musical. In large measure, how a director executes these basics will ultimately affect the bottom line of a production budget—in particular scenic, costume, lighting, and the many other technical elements.

Once a scenic design is decided upon that will fit the director's vision, the director will have to cast and rehearse the actors in such a fashion that the basics of directing are consistently applied to reveal the play in a unified production. Alexander Dean and Lawrence Carr isolated these basics as the "Five Fundamentals of Directing" in their landmark study, first published in 1941. These fundamentals are composition, picturization, movement, rhythm, and pantomimic dramatization. Since Dean and Carr proposed their fundamentals, directors have been applying them in efforts to convey a production's intellectual and emotional concepts. Figure 5.2 offers a succinct summary of the means a director would apply in pictorial representations of each of these fundamentals.

**Composition:** This is the overall shape or form of a group onstage. However, it does not convey meaning. In Figure 5.2a, the rectangular shapes represent five characters in a straight line, perhaps on a bare stage. They could possibly indicate color, abundance, or form and express a mood or a feeling. However, they do not tell a story. Therefore, composition is the technique.

**Picturization**: Imagine if you would that the gray rectangle on the right were placed slightly apart from the other four as in Figure 5.2b. This arrangement, without any dialogue or movement, might suggest that the gray rectangle was leading the other figures on a marching field. Similarly, if the play called for five people arranged in a group, seated or standing in a living room in a given moment, and completely silent, their composition would also not reveal story. However, if a director were to arrive at a visual interpretation of each moment in the play, in other words a series of picturizations, the director might possibly be able to indicate the mental and emotional feelings of the characters toward one another. In doing so the dramatic nature of the situation would be revealed, and the audience would then be able to visually interpret the play in its entirety. Thus, picturization illustrates the concept.

**Movement:** Figure 5.2c demonstrates three changing picturizations moving in the direction of the arrows. Movement combines both the technique of composition and the concept of picturization. In other words, one could think of a series of compositions and pictures, much like a storyboard or the individual cells in film strips. Movement as it relates to areas of the stage will be elaborated on in the section on **blocking** below.

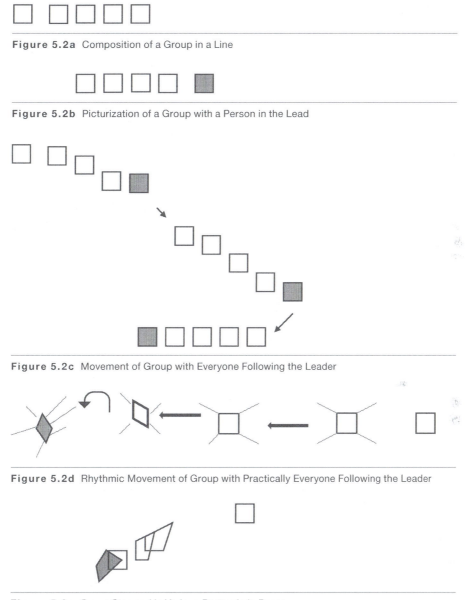

**Figure 5.2a**  Composition of a Group in a Line

**Figure 5.2b**  Picturization of a Group with a Person in the Lead

**Figure 5.2c**  Movement of Group with Everyone Following the Leader

**Figure 5.2d**  Rhythmic Movement of Group with Practically Everyone Following the Leader

**Figure 5.2e**  Group Stopped in Various Pantomimic Poses

**Rhythm**: Figure 5.2d not only portrays the group marching from right to left at different speeds, but also perhaps adopting different vocal cadences, or shaking motions. This is indicated by the lines radiating from the rectangles. The characters are seemingly out of step with one another as they twist and turn their shapes and direction. Lagging behind the group to the far right is a single unmoved rectangle, or character. How an audience perceives the disjointed movement and hears the various voices will impact the audience's emotions and physical feelings arising from the viewing of such a sequence of impressions. Not only would an audience receive their sole impression of the disjointed marching line, the actual stage surroundings also could be a contributing factor. If the rhythmic movement matched the locale, then the characters could also be said to be in rhythm with their environment.

**Pantomimic Dramatization:** Hypothetically, if our marching group were not in a field, and instead might be marching through a kitchen—tripping, or banging into pots and pans, and ending up bumping into each other such as in Figure 5.2e—their sequence of actions without words, such as movement, facial expressions, and body language, becomes pantomimic dramatization. The characters would provide a complete visualization performance. That is to say the characters combine composition, picturization, movement, rhythm, and pantomime to convey all the elements of the play without words.

## BLOCKING

During the ensuing rehearsal period the director—equipped with a vision, a chosen theatre, and a scenic design—will unify the concept and style for staging the performance. Notwithstanding all the other elements the director is in charge of, he or she will then apply their own variant of the directing fundamentals to a company of actors. Whether the director is dictatorial, loud, brash, humorous, gentle, receptive to suggestion, stubborn, well-organized, or a "let's see what happens" type of person (among the thousands of possible approaches), the major thing that a director has to achieve is blocking the play. Blocking constitutes all movement by the actors: not only where they move to, but also where they enter or exit, and how they move, as well as all properties they handle—basically all their action. Rather than say to an actor, "Move there," "Sit there," or "Enter from that side of the stage," a shorthand system of stage area designations simplifies the process. Figure 5.3 shows a **blocking key**, which provides the shorthand notation for each area and their respective longhand meaning (viewed from the actor's perspective).

You will notice that the letter "U" in the key refers to "up" or "upstage" and "D" to downstage. This has practical meaning and derives from the fact that, many years ago, particularly with proscenium style theatres, stages would be built so that they were inclined like a ramp, or **raked**. The top of the rake would be the furthest point from the audience, and an actor would be best seen and heard from this high point as they would be standing above (or higher than) the actors who were said to be downstage. As actors cross from the lowest point to a higher point, they are usually said to be crossing upstage, or away from the proscenium. Since an audience member's attention might be diverted to an actor at a higher point on the stage, that actor might also be said to be **upstaging** another actor. This can be very distracting if the real focus should be on the actor further downstage who might be speaking or engaged in integral business.

Figure 5.4 shows blocking for a small proscenium stage. Further refinements of this diagram for a larger stage are the designations in Figure 5.5. Both diagrams may also be utilized

| NOTATION | STAGE AREA (from actor's perspective, facing the audience) |
|----------|-----------------------------------------------------------|
| C | Center |
| D | Down |
| U | Up |
| R | Stage Right |
| L | Stage Left |
| RC | Right of Center Stage |
| DRC | Down Right of Center Stage |
| DR | Down Right |
| LC | Left of Center Stage |
| DLC | Down Left of Center Stage |
| DL | Down Left |
| ULC | Up Left of Center Stage |
| UL | Up Left |
| URC | Up Right of Center Stage |
| UR | Up Right |

**Figure 5.3** Blocking Key

| UR | UC | UL |
|----|----|----|
| R | C | L |
| DR | DC | DL |

**Figure 5.4** Blocking areas for a small proscenium stage

| 3 | UR | URC | UC | ULC | UL | 3 |
|---|----|----|----|----|----|---|
| 2 | R | RC | C | LC | L | 2 |
| 1 | DR | DRC | DC | DLC | DL | 1 |

**Figure 5.5** Blocking areas for a large proscenium stage

for a thrust stage or ¾ stage as long as one of the sides becomes the primary reference point for the actors.

With additional instructions an actor could be directed to cross from up right to downstage left, from stage left to stage right (or vice versa), or any other combination of moves. Also, actors may enter or exit the stage from the adjacent stage left wings or stage right wings (a series of tall suspended drapes) or **flats** (large muslin framed panels) that serve to **mask** (hide) the actor in an offstage area prior to an entrance or following an exit. Note the numbered areas off to the left and the right of the acting areas in Figure 5.5, which are the numbered wings, beginning with the most downstage wing (Number 1) and proceeding upstage to any additional remaining wings (in this case there are only two more, Numbers 2 and 3). A shorthand instruction to an actor entering or exiting Number 2 stage right would be, "Enter in-2, SR." Can you figure out how to give similar instructions to actors entering or exiting the remaining wings?

Additionally, actors may make their entrances or exits through any number of points (such as doors, windows, from behind boulders, from beneath the stage through **traps** (trapdoors), or even flown in on a vine such as in the musical *Tarzan*. All of this movement is left to the ingenuity of the director, and most often dictated by the script and the resultant scenery. Thus, when blocking a show a director has to make sure that moving the actors about the stage is done in a such a fashion that the audience is able to continually focus on the character who is speaking or performing related action, and not on someone who is likely to **steal focus** or upstage the other actors. All of this takes great skill as a director applies the fundamentals of directing.

The situation becomes a bit more problematic when directing in an arena situation. As you might remember, with an audience surrounding the acting area, one actor or another always has their back to someone in the audience. With this in mind, a director has to be very adroit in blocking actors in order to maintain balanced focus throughout the performance. Blocking notation for arena staging would take a different form than that for a proscenium or ¾ thrust as described above. Instead of looking at the stage as a rectangular grid, think of the arena stage as a combination of concentric circles. Whereas upstage, downstage, stage left, stage right, etc. are more common designations for the proscenium and ¾ thrust stages, the arena stage lends itself more easily to be thought of as a clock face, with hourly numbers serving as directional areas. Figure 5.6 provides an example of such notation.

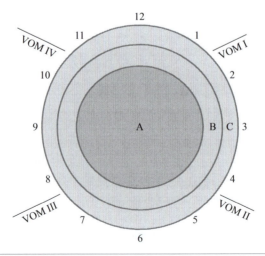

**Figure 5.6** Blocking Areas for an Arena Stage

Instead of entering or exiting from wings as in the proscenium or ¾ thrust configurations, actors often do so through the aisles that are sometimes designated VOM I, VOM II, VOM III, VOM IV, etc. According to legend, gluttonous attendees viewing the gory proceedings in the ancient Roman Coliseum would lean over the vomitoriums and vomit their meals; technically though these *vomitoria* were passageways that actually disgorged patrons to their seats.

Where an actor might have been directed to cross from UL to DR on a proscenium stage, a director might say to an actor positioned in the outer circle 'C' at 1 o'clock on an arena stage, "Please move to 'A' at 7 o'clock." "Oh," the director might add, "Please then exit thru VOM III." Similarly, a director might have an actor enter from VOM II and cross to center stage.

- Can you figure out where this would be represented in Figure 5.6?
- How many other stage directions can you offer if you were directing actors on an arena stage?

## A MUSICAL PRODUCTION

Up to this point we have been discussing the direction of a non-musical and how a director applies the five fundamentals of directing—composition, picturization, movement, rhythm, and pantomimic dramatization—to such a production. This does not change with a musical production. When a musical director and a choreographer become part of the responsible triumvirate, their contributions help bring a production to fruition. However, they will have to subordinate their work to that of the director; otherwise the unity of vision would be violated, and the resulting production in all likelihood would prove unsuccessful.

## THE MUSIC DEPARTMENT

Within a non-musical production it is somewhat safe to say that the major creative energy emanates from the playwright and director. The shared driving force becomes even more divided on a musical with the creative musical triumvirate of the librettist, composer, and lyricist. Since it is called a musical it can be fairly assumed that the heart and soul of such a production is the music. However, music, libretto, and lyrics all have to be in accord with the director's vision. Chapter 4 examined the creators' contributions to the musical. Going a bit further, this chapter will begin with the people whose line of responsibility is traced back to the composer. These include the arrangers, the orchestrator, and the copyist, all of whom shape the composer's music into a score that is delivered to the music director, as depicted in Figure 5.7.

### THE MUSIC DIRECTOR

Before the final score is in the hands of the music director (part of the creative team), in charge of all things musical, many alterations will be made to the composer's music. Different

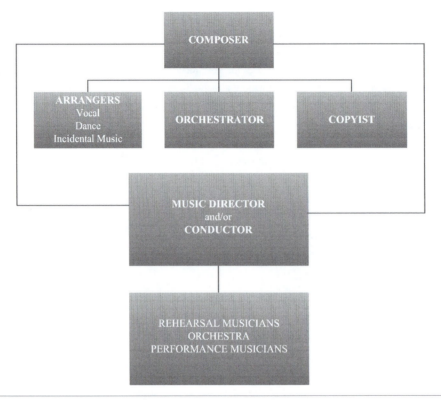

**Figure 5.7** The Music Department

composers work differently. Some may fully notate music. Some might play out their ideas on a piano or guitar, hum or sing into a recorder, or develop their material on a computer. No matter how the music is composed, it is likely an **arranger** will be engaged to write out all the sung parts, the music for dance, the incidental music that might be needed for overtures, music for the audience's exit following the performance, the music between acts (**entr'actes**), as well as scene change music. The arranger will write out much of this music so that it can be played by a pianist, a drummer, or a guitarist to accompany rehearsals because the cost of hiring a full orchestra for rehearsals is prohibitive.

Thereafter an **orchestrator** will take the arranger's score and determine the instrumentation and how many musicians will comprise the final orchestra for the production. A key factor in determining the size of an orchestra will need be reached in collaboration with the composer (who has in mind the eventual sound for the production) and the producer (who has to agree on a budget that will capably meet the composer's wishes). Cost considerations are not only how many musicians, but may also extend to which musicians double on certain instruments, as well as whether certain instruments can be reproduced by a computer. Once these decisions are made the orchestrator will then expand the rehearsal score for a full orchestra. Thereafter, the **copyist** will prepare individual scores for each of the musicians. That is to say, if there are five violinists in the orchestra, the copyist will prepare five individual violin scores to be placed on each of their music stands.

At this stage the score will arrive in the hands of the music director, who will then interpret the score through the Five Key Elements: Who, What, Where, When, Why (How). It is the music director, sometimes called a music supervisor who is the day-to-day person in the rehearsal room, much like the director and choreographer. The music director assigns who sings what, the tempo they sing it, where they might even be best positioned to sing (along with the director and choreographer's collaboration), when to phrase, breathe, how loud, how soft, or not to sing at all, etc. The music director might have an assortment of associates or assistants to function as rehearsal pianists, vocal and choral coaches, or to maintain changes in the score. Eventually, when the production moves from the rehearsal spaces to the theatre and the orchestra is brought on board, the music director might relinquish responsibility to the conductor—the person who actually waves the baton to lead the orchestra. In some instances, the music director and conductor might be one and the same person.

By now you might notice that the music department can be fairly large. The number of people in the music department expands to fill the needs as a production grows from a small community theatre production to the large scale of a Broadway or West End production. With a small production we often see many of the positions in the music department consolidated. A small production might start out with a composer writing out the entire score for a single piano, such as the long-running *The Fantasticks*; or it might be comprised of a 29-piece orchestra for the plush, rich-sounding 2015 revival of the Lincoln Center's *The King and I*. Within this production the music director oversaw a large chorus of children, adult singers, solo performers, and a multitude of dance numbers, as well as an exciting, exuberant orchestral sound.

## THE CHOREOGRAPHER

The choreographer is responsible for staging all of the dance numbers in a musical. Often the choreographer might also be called upon to stage large crowd scenes. Following the director's lead and working closely with the music director, the choreographer will have to interpret the dance numbers adhering to the Five Key Elements: Who, What, Where, When, Why (How). Compare all these elements in the scene between the King of Siam and the English tutor for the number "Shall We Dance?" from *The King and I*.

Not only did the music director have to match tempo to the variety of music, such as a waltz and a polka, as well as the vocalists' inflections or phrasing to character; the choreographer had to capture the movement of a Siamese king and a proper English woman, and radically alter an audience's expectations of the characters' stations in life. In addition, the choreographer had to note scenically where the dance took place and how it would grow from an intended awkward beginning to a rousing finish.

## LEARN MORE: CHOREOGRAPHER'S INTERPRETATION

It is worth noting the choreographer's adherence to the Five Elements in the scene between the King of Siam and the English tutor for the dance number "Shall We Dance?" from *The King and I* (with Lisa McCune and Teddy Tahu Rhodes) in the YouTube video on our e-resources with the following link:

*"Shall We Dance"*

## LEARN MORE: CHOREOGRAPHING THE HOW

Once you have viewed "Shall We Dance?," watch the film version of *The King and I*, with Marni Nixon (dubbing Deborah Kerr) and the Chorus singing "Getting to Know You." You may notice the rich variety of voices and accents of all performers, as well as the many gestures the children employ in marrying both music and dance to achieve the How during this musical number in the YouTube video on our e-resources with the following link:

*"Getting to Know You"*

The combination of choreography and musical direction in both of these clips captures the results of a unified director's vision that brings together the cross-cultural references which were called for with the libretto, the music, and the lyrics of *The King and I* in both the film and stage versions.

## CASTING BY THE CREATIVE TEAM

A major consideration for the director and other creative team members is who will be cast as the various characters in a play or musical. It has been said by various notable directors that "Directing is 80 to 90% casting." After a careful reading of the script to determine the Five Key Elements: Who, What, Where, When, Why (How) the team will need to decide what type of actors, singers, and dancers will fulfill the production's needs. Thereafter an audition process will be undertaken to choose actors of a certain look, age, gender, skill set, vocal quality and range, and dance capability, and a host of other qualities that could potentially fulfill the creative team's expectations that they would be able to develop through rehearsals for a successful production.

## THE CREATIVE TEAM IN REHEARSALS

The rehearsal processes for non-musicals and musicals differ considerably in their very nature and number of personnel involved. Generally, for a non-musical the actors rehearse under the aegis of the director along with a stage management staff in one rehearsal room (see Chapter 8). Additionally, often present will be the playwright, perhaps a dramaturg, and/or an assistant director, or perhaps a speech consultant in order to add changes, research, and instruction as necessary. On occasion members of the producing, management, or publicity staff will drop in, as well as any number of designers and their respective assistants. For the most part the director will spend most of the time analyzing the script with the actors and working through the fundamentals of staging the play, utilizing rehearsal props and furnishings or mock-ups of set-pieces as needed. The situation might occur whereby intricate blocking is required, such as for the many pratfalls included in the movement on a staircase for the farce *Noises Off*, or a boxing ring that is called for in the musical *Rocky*.

Rarely does a play rehearse on an actual set, since the cost to do so is prohibitive from the perspective of both the high cost of theatre rentals and the additional requirement for stage-hands to be present. In all likelihood, scenery is being constructed at offsite shop spaces while rehearsals are being conducted. This also has a practical side. For example, in the course of rehearsals certain stage business could dictate change, such as a dining table that has to be enlarged to accommodate additional actors. Such a piece of scenery could be built easily at the shop without disrupting rehearsals.

In the direction of a musical, similar situations might also occur for scenes involving the libretto, or book scenes. However, most musicals rehearse with additional rooms for music and dance. In the music room—for the most part with a pianist, guitarist, drummer, or other key instrumentalist present—the music director and the various assistants will go through the process of teaching the singers, chorus members, and dancers all the musical parts. In particular, such rehearsals will often have to be held before the dancers are able to learn their choreography. Often the music rehearsals begin a week or so before the cast is fully assembled to work with the director.

When the dancers have learned the music they can be turned over to the choreographer and the assistant choreographer and/or **dance captain** who support the director's vision. A dance captain would not only work on some of the choreography before actually teaching it or trying it out on the dancers; he or she would also be responsible for learning all of the finalized choreography, as well as maintaining it throughout the run of the production. More on this position will be covered as we discuss stage management.

The dances that the choreographer creates have to be shaped, molded, and executed by a dancer or dancers to fit the production's story and music. Since the success of *Oklahoma!* (1943), which integrated dance into the storyline, it has become commonplace that dance numbers should not be gratuitous and must further the story.

In the end the choreographer and the assistants are pretty much responsible for the movement of all performers, especially when music is involved. This might include entrances and

---

## LEARN MORE: FURTHERING THE STORY

One of the most memorable and quintessential numbers in musical theatre history "The Music and the Mirror," was created for the Pulitzer Prize-winning and long-running Broadway production *A Chorus Line*. While viewing the video of Charlotte d'Amboise performing the number from the 2006 Broadway revival, note the desperation of an aged dancer auditioning both in front of a casting director (as well as "us"—the live audience) while examining her past, present, and future abilities in the mirrors behind her. Maybe she is no longer able to kick as high, or her leg extensions are not as crisp as they once were. The subtext of the number is that dancers need to dance; they need a dancing job to truly live, as demonstrated in the YouTube video on our e-resources with the following link:

*"The Music and the Mirror"*

---

exits that have to be timed to musical cues, scenery movement, and curtain calls, etc. Can you think of other instances?

An expedient rehearsal situation that frequently occurs is that, simultaneously, in the morning the director works on book scenes, the music director is teaching the singers, and the choreographer is working with the dancers. After lunch everyone gathers in one rehearsal space to integrate a section that involves book, music, and dance. As you can well imagine, all this can take some thorny scheduling that has to be fully thought through by the director, the music director, the choreographer, and the stage managers.

However, everything does not always happen as planned. One would hope that the producer and general manager has hired all the correct people and that everyone gets along as they work toward a common goal. However, artistic differences can occur that might necessitate firings and/or replacements. No one is exempt, as you might have heard from legendary stories; possibly an overnight "star" is born as a result of these moments of friction.

Upon concluding our discussion on the major creators of a musical it might be worth noting their professional membership of various unions, as depicted in Figure 5.8. In the United States directors, conductors (not musical directors), and choreographers are able to join unions, whereas in the United Kingdom union affiliation is only available to directors and musical directors in West End theatres.

## ADDITIONAL CREATIVE TEAM MEMBERS

Very often a production calls for specialized skills that the director, musical director, or choreographer might not possess. In these instances, various experts are added to the creative team.

| ORGANIZATION | MEMBERS | COVERAGE | MEMBERSHIP |
|---|---|---|---|
| SDC (Stage Directors and Choreographers Society) http://sdcweb.org/ | Directors Choreographers | United States | Must provide proof of paid prior engagement for any theatrical production or companies organized under one of the performing arts unions: AEA, AGVA, AGMA, or SAG/AFTRA |
| AFM (American Federation of Musicians) www.afm.org/ | Conductors (does not cover Music Directors) | United States Canada | Open |
| SDUK (Stage Directors UK) www.stagedirectorsuk.com/ | Theatre Directors | United Kingdom | Provide proof of one paid production in front of a paying audience |
| Musicians' Union (MU) www.musiciansunion.org.uk/ Files/Rates/Theatre-Rates/ MU-SOLT-Agreement | Music Directors | London | Specific to West End Productions |

**Figure 5.8** Representative Creative Team Members' Unions

As previously noted, rehearsals might be conducted with mock-ups, or even with the actual scenery, in order to re-enact the stage business called for by the play or musical. See Figure 5.9 for examples of additional creative team personnel. Can you think of other such specialists and productions that require other expertise?

## HEALTH AND SAFETY

Perhaps you have heard the oft-repeated adage "The show must go on." For this reason, it is appropriate that we take a preliminary look at health and safety (H&S) in the theatre environment. As you might be aware, working in theatre poses many potential risks. By introducing the interaction of bodies in motion in this chapter, i.e. directors rehearsing with actors, some cautionary words would be worthwhile.

Rehearsals are a period of exploration between creative team members and performers. Not only does everyone work mentally on interpreting the script through the Five Elements and the fundamentals of directing; physically the process requires the expenditure of much energy, concentrated focus, and long hours. "Let's try this. Try that" are repeatedly echoed throughout the course of rehearsals by directors, choreographers, music directors, fight supervisors, etc. Naturally the actor wants to please, make the best move, hit the requested notes, or take the boldest leap. In order to oblige, the performer must remain

| PRODUCTION | CREATIVE MEMBER'S TITLE | PRODUCTION REQUIREMENT |
|---|---|---|
| *K2* (Broadway, 1983) | Climbing Instructor | Actors had to climb and rappelle off a scenic mountain |
| *Pippin* (Broadway, 2013) | Circus Creator | Performers had to perform various circus acts |
| *Ghost The Musical* (West End, 2011) | Illusionist | Optical magic and various tricks |
| *Rocky* (Broadway, 2013) | Fight Choreographer | Choreography of actors engaged in boxing |
| *War Horse* (West End, 2009) | Director of Movement and Horse Choreography<br><br>Puppet Fabrication and Direction | Performers had to manipulate and realistically move the large horses they were harnessed in |
| *Tarzan* (Broadway, 2006) | Aerial Design | Actor required to fly through the air |
| *Harry Potter and the Cursed Child* (West End, 2016) | Special Effects | Seeing will be believing |

**Figure 5.9** Additional Creative Team Members

healthy, and be well rested, alert, trained, and skilled for whatever they are called upon to execute. At the same time everyone must remain vigilant that conditions are safe for carrying out the attempts. This includes the entire creative team making the requests as well as the performers.

Sounds simple? Not always. Exhaustion, fatigue, slippery floors, rickety mock-ups, pressure to accomplish everything in a finite time, and perhaps improper training can lead to some awful mishaps. Therefore, it is important for theatre practitioners to incorporate safety precautions into whatever level of theatrical experience they are engaged in. The subject of safety will be revisited as a cautionary tale throughout the remainder of this book, in addition to the Five Elements.

## WHAT DID YOU LEARN?

1. Name the person who is generally credited with the role of directing as we know it today. What did this person achieve in order to deserve this recognition?

2. Today we are more apt to acknowledge this achievement as a director's (fill in the blank) which consists of (fill in the blank) and (fill in the blank).

3. What are the eight styles of staging described in this chapter? Explain each style.

4. What are considered to be the Five Fundamentals of Directing? Explain.

5. Try recreating your own diagram for blocking areas for a large proscenium stage.

6. Provide the titles of five different people or groups who comprise the music department and are responsible for interpreting the compositions for a musical theatre production.

7. What is the function of a dance captain in a musical theatre production?

8. What should all participants engaged in any production be aware of above all else?

## ANSWERS

1) Georg II, Duke of Saxe-Meiningen, who unified the many elements of his productions, arranging actors to look as if they were in the same place and time period, and suitably costumed within scenery and lighting that supported this unity; 2) Vision, concept, and style; 3) Arena, formal, simultaneous, multiple, theatrical, romantic, naturalism, and realism; 4) Composition, picturization, movement, rhythm, and pantomime dramatization; 5) See Figure 5.6; 6) Arrangers, orchestrator, copyist, music director or conductor, and orchestra (musicians); 7) Assists the choreographer, teaches dance to performers, and maintains the choreography throughout the production's run; 8) Safety

# ADDITIONAL RESOURCES

## BOOKS

Robert Berkson, *Musical Theater Choreography: A Practical Method for Preparing and Staging Dance in a Musical Show* (New York: Back Stage Books), 1990.

Anne Bogart, *Conversations with Anne: Twenty Four Interviews* (New York: Theatre Communications Group), 2012.

Barrett H. Clark, *European Theories of the Drama* (New York: Crown Publishers), 1918.

Joseph Church, *Music Direction for the Stage: A View from the Podium* (Oxford University Press: New York), 2015.

Toby Cole and Helen Krich Chinoy, *Directors on Directing: A Sourcebook of the Modern Theater* (New York: Bobbs-Merrill), 1963.

Alexander Dean and Lawrence Carr, *Fundamentals of Play Directing* (Long Grove, IL: Waveland Press), 2016 (first published 1941).

John E. Dietrich, *Play Direction* (Englewood Cliffs, NJ: Prentice-Hall), 1953.

Donald C. Faber and Robert Viagas, *The Amazing Story of The Fantasticks: America's Longest Running Play* (New York: Citadel Press), 1991.

John Gielgud, *Stage Directions* (New York: Capricorn Books), 1966.

Jan Kott, *Shakespeare our Contemporary* (New York: W.W. Norton), 1974.

Samuel L. Leiter, *The Great Stage Directors: 100 Distinguished Careers of the Theatre* (New York: Facts on File, Inc.), 1994.

Margot Sunderland, *Choreographing the Stage Musical* (London: Routledge), 1990.

## PLAYS

Michael Bennett, James Kirkwood, and Nicholas Dante, *A Chorus Line: The Complete Book of the Musical* (New York: Applause Books), 1995.

Tom Jones and Harvey Schmidt, *The Fantasticks 2 Celebration* (New York: Drama Book Specialists/Publishers), 1973.

Arthur Miller, *A View from the Bridge* (New York: Viking), 1960.

Stanley Richards (ed.), *Great Musicals of the American Theatre* (Vols. 1 and 2) (Radnor, PA: Chilton Book Company), 1973 and 1976.

# The Creative Artists

## *Designing the Dream*

## ADHERING TO THE DIRECTOR'S VISION

In the previous chapter, although we did not say it, we made the assumption that, in order for the director and choreographer to actually have begun their work with performers, all of the scenic designs were approved. This being the case, we can now look at how the designers go about adhering to the director's vision and realizing their respective designs.

Once the director's vision is accepted by the producer and creators, then the **general manager** begins the process of hiring the main designers (scenic, costume, lighting, and sound), as well as some of the specialty designers (special effects, flying, automation, etc.). As with the creative team of directors, choreographers, and musical directors there is a symbiotic path for designers to be hired. Inasmuch as playwrights and directors have to be on the same page, designers also have to be communicative and collaborative in realizing the director's vision. Each designer hired, for the most part: possesses a combination of previous familiar work that is respected by management and creators; is a potentially well-suited collaborator; and is capable of thoroughly understanding and realizing the director's vision with their respective designs. Generally speaking, in the high-stakes' environment of Broadway and the West End, hiring of seasoned professionals is practically the norm. It is only at the other end of the production spectrum that we are apt to see a chance taken on engaging someone lacking great experience or fresh out of a reputable college design program.

No matter the road to a design position, all designers have to quickly read the work and isolate the <u>Five Key Elements: Who, What, Where, When, Why (How)</u>. Although with subsequent readings they begin the process of examining the work from the perspective of their own respective discipline, the script might already contain extensive descriptions for scenery, costumes, and perhaps lighting—such as George Bernard Shaw or Eugene O'Neill were prone to do in their writing. Ultimately, the play is only words on a page. However, if the words elicit an emotional reaction comparable to one that might potentially grab an audience, then a designer may have an urge to embrace the project. Without such passion or excitement, then another designer might be better suited for the production. Therefore, the reading stimulates visual ideas and is a catalyst for the designer's imagination as to what the production might possibly look like onstage. In many cases the designers will draw sketches based upon this reading. Therefore this initial reading lays the groundwork for a designer's first meeting with the creators and creative team. A couple of overriding questions are: "How shall we do it? What could it look like?" In such meetings ideas are bantered back and forth. Thereafter, when the director's vision is effectively communicated and accepted by each designer, then the actual collaborative design process can commence.

## SCENIC DESIGN

One of the most influential directors of the 20th century, Peter Brook, famously said in his pioneering 1968 book *The Empty Space*, "A stage space has two rules: (1) Anything can happen and (2) Something must happen." It follows that without scenery there would be little for the actors to perform on or engage an audience with except a bare stage. Similarly, lighting and costumes can engross an audience. However once scenery is introduced then the other designers can bring a tangible focus to their respective creations.

Ideally each designer brings to the table a thorough understanding of the various styles of staging discussed in the previous chapter. A resultant scenic design may be a combination of the various staging styles as dictated by the director's vision. With the advent of two-dimensional scenery painted on drapery, large canvases, or even **flats** (painted canvases stretched over wooden frames), sets would be shifted in full view of an audience as the need for a change of location was called for in the performance. Many sorts of mechanical apparatus were developed to fly in scenery that was hidden behind the proscenium arch, rolled on from the sides of the stage (the left and right areas behind the framing portion of the proscenium arch, called the **wings**), or brought up from below on elevating platforms to stage level (through trap-doors, or **traps**) utilizing a system of winches, pulleys, and ropes.

Over the centuries, with the rise of realism and naturalism, newer technologies were developed to build and execute scenic changes. The early practice of constructing scenery out of wood and natural fabrics continues right to this day. However, when you add steel, aluminum, glass, plastics, polycarbonates, polyfibers, 3D modeling, cutting-edge engineering, etc., the opportunity potentially exists to build scenery and costumes that spring from a designer's mind-boggling imagination. Some of these extremes will be discussed in Chapter 8, which presents the role of the technical director and the decision process for constructing production elements.

For the moment, let us take a look at the collaborative nature of how designer and director arrive at a design that supports the director's concept. In the previous chapter we discussed Ivo van Hove's vision and concept for his Tony Award-winning version of *A View from the Bridge* in which he chose to examine the play as if its characters were pitted against each other in a brutal, moral battle that paralleled violent myths of antiquity. The collaborators took a visual cue provided by his set designer, Jan Versweyveld, of a large rock being lifted so that ants would be seen feverishly darting about. Van Hove imagined that the action should take place within a sparse arena-shaped stage. Not only would van Hove set his production in a different locale, with costumes and lighting that fit the change of style originally called for in the Miller script, but he also chose to display all of the characters' emotions at fever pitch. At the beginning of the performance a massive rock is lifted above the stage out of sight. In essence, Versweyveld chose the barest minimum of what was needed to convey van Hove's concept. The stage was uncluttered and so did not distract from the action. The actors made rapid entrances, and characteristically the action was loud, raw, and reminiscent of the ant imagery initially conceived by the designer and director.

With a different approach, another Tony Award-winning designer, John Lee Beatty, translates the emotional grasp a play has on him from his early readings of the script into his scenic designs. Reading plays like a director from the vantage of the <u>Five Key Elements: Who, What, Where, When, Why (How)</u>, Beatty embarks upon extensive homework and research. He seeks out the little things by walking a city or visiting an environment: for *Dinner at Eight* (2002) he wandered into a number of lobbies along New York's Park Avenue; and the gold tones and low light in the Dutch painter Vermeer's works inspired his look for *Tartuffe* (2003). Beatty's efforts provide him with ideas that would fit with the behavior of an actor's character while occupying the created world of the onstage scenery.

Now, let us take a look at some of the practical steps for developing a scenic design. Keeping in mind that a similar process is also undertaken by other designers we will meet later in this chapter, Figure 6.1 details the key steps that scenic designer Joseph Burkard undertook in developing his design for a production of *Middletown* by Will Eno.

It should be noted that design is the first of three major phases before scenery appears onstage, namely: **design**, **fabrication**, and **installation**. Fabrication (the actual building of the scenic elements) and installation (the assembling of the elements onstage) can only evolve from the primary process: design.

Within the design phase there are also many other areas in which the practicality of building such scenery, budgetary constraints, and technical construction drawings all contribute to the process. Once Burkard had read the play and determined the <u>Five Key Elements: Who, What, Where, When, Why (How)</u> for himself, he set about sketching ideas that he derived from this reading. At an initial meeting with the director and the other designers he was able to gain insight into the director's concept. Some considerations that arose from such a meeting would be to locate where walls, doors, windows, staircases, and the various placements for entrances and egresses should go. Thereafter Burkard would refine his sketches

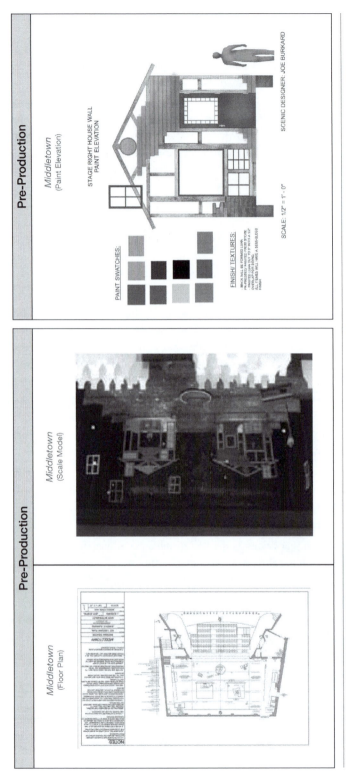

**Figures 6.1a** The Process of Scenic Designing *Middletown*. (Credit: Used with permission of joeburkarddesigns.com)

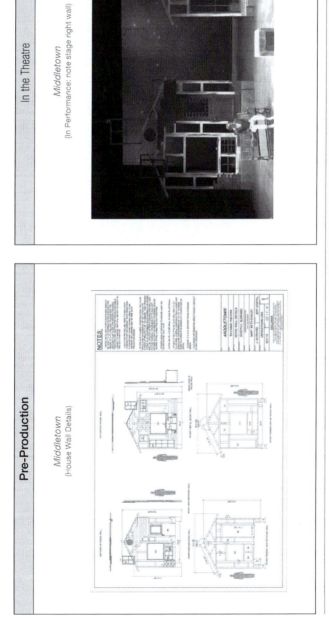

**Figures 6.1b** The Process of Scenic Designing *Middletown*. (Credit: Used with permission of joeburkarddesigns.com)

through subsequent meetings and present a color rendering for his proposed scenic design. Upon the director's approval the scenic designer would collaborate with assistant designers and the technical director to realize the actual dimensions of the proposed scenery. They then arrive at a scale blueprint or ground plan for all elements of scenery that touch the stage floor.

From the two previous examples of designer and director collaboration it might become apparent that the designer contributes immeasurably to telling the story through design. One way to measure this contribution is to strip away the dialogue (without actors present) and look at the stage picture of a successful design. It is highly probable that you would be able to determine the Five Key Elements: Who, What, Where, When, Why (How) for yourself.

Let's try such an exercise with a few scenic designs, bearing in mind every picture tells a story. From the picture of each offered scenic design, you have to arrive at factors that unify the five key elements for this design. We will include similar exercises for other designers throughout this chapter. All of these exercises will provide you with an opportunity to develop your imagination. Perhaps they may even spark a desire to pursue a career path in designing for the theatre.

## LEARN MORE: SCENIC DESIGN EXERCISE 1, INTRODUCTION

Let's begin the exercise with a play that you might be familiar with—Arthur Miller's *Death of a Salesman*—and its original Broadway scenic design by Jo Mielziner by viewing it on our e-resources at the following link:

**"Death of a Salesman"**

After viewing Jo Mielziner's design, examine Figure 6.2, which summarizes possible scenarios for each of the Five Key Elements: Who, What, Where, When, Why (How) that might be revealed upon viewing the scenic design for *Death of a Salesman*.

## A SHORT HISTORY OF COSTUME DESIGN

Of all the positions on the theatrical organizational chart (see Figure 0.1), the two that many of us can readily identify with are actor and costume designer. It is from earliest childhood that many of us were captivated by playing make-believe, and raided our parents' closets or attics for clothes and accessories to fit our fantasies. The allure of dressing up made instant costume designers of many of us. Each item or **fabric** we chose for its **color**, **texture**, or

| | DEATH of a SALESMAN<br>Scenic Design<br>Five Key Elements |
|---|---|
| WHO | Possibly a family occupies this space as indicated by the three beds. Perhaps two teenagers or young adults sleep upstairs in the single beds (most likely of the same sex) and the parents sleep in the double bed in the room SR. |
| WHAT | A representation of a small house with an upstairs bedroom, a SR bedroom, and a kitchen. It is representational since the frame of the house and the walls are skeletal. Only the barest of furnishing is present: beds, chairs, a table, a stove, and a refrigerator, etc. There is nothing ostentatious. The DS area might possibly be outside, in front of the house. |
| WHERE | It appears to be a single home in front of a looming tenement apartment building. Such a building, with fire escapes, indicates that the story takes place in a large city rather than a rural area. |
| WHEN | The major clue is in the refrigerator at center stage and the stove just right of it. They seem to be vintage 1930s' appliances. The chairs evoke a similar period. There is a gloominess to the apartment building of something past. Also there is an overall feeling that this is a house that has seen many years of occupancy. Seemingly, the appliances have not been replaced, but the children grew older, necessitating single beds. Therefore, the play quite possibly takes place in the latter 1940s.<br><br>From the design it is difficult to ascertain time of day or season. The few almost discernible open windows in the apartment building offer a slight clue that it is not in the dead of winter. |
| WHY (HOW) | This seems to be a play concerning a middle-class family struggling for survival, with the grown children still living at home. Given the skeletal walls and the openness of the downstage area, the audience has an opportunity to peer into the lives of the different characters as they move in and out of the defined spaces in a domestic drama. Given the paucity of amenities, this play may be a tragedy, and not a comedy. |

**Figure 6.2** Scenic Elements for *Death of a Salesman*

# LEARN MORE: SCENIC DESIGN EXERCISE 2

Now it's your turn to attempt an exercise with a production you might not know. The less familiar you are with a particular play the more fascinating this exercise becomes, since it is you alone who determines the success of a particular design in telling the story in a unified fashion. Pick out a few unrecognizable productions that are offered on our e-resources at the following link:

*"Theatrical Scenic Design"*

Make sure your choice has no actors present on the set. Try not to be led by the title of a play as you determine the Five Key Elements. Remember there are no incorrect answers for this exercise.

**weight**, or for our **movement** in it, revealed a change in our **attitude**. What we wore may have uncovered a mood, expressed an **emotion**, supported an imagined **role**, or transported us to another time **period**. For a costume designer fabric, color, texture, weight, movement, attitude, mood, emotion, role, and period are all integral components to a finalized costume worn on stage.

Historically, as we have previously noted, early Greek and Roman actors wore what fit their performance rituals. These included emotional masks for comedy or tragedy, and accompanying robes or period garments. In the Middle Ages, with the rise of religious plays, vestments and stylizations of court apparel found their way onto the stage. As scenic locales came to be later defined during Elizabethan times and thereafter, actors dressed closer to specific roles, such as kings, queens, or other stereotypes. They wore what was on hand, and added accessories, such as a crown to depict royalty or a cane to signify an elderly person.

Bear in mind that for centuries textiles were comprised of natural materials derived from animals (i.e. wool, fur, silk), from minerals (e.g. asbestos), or from plants (i.e. cotton, flax, sisal). Before these materials could be woven into fabric, each one of them went through long, arduous processing. It can be assumed that such a journey was not only labor intensive, but also expensive. Therefore, some of the first priorities for fabrics were clothing, sheltering materials such as tents, and rugs for additional warmth. The manufacturing of fabrics solely for theatrical costumes would have to be considered as a luxury.

One of the more striking periods in early costume design arose with a theatrical form known as **commedia dell'arte** (comedy performed by professional artists) in 16th-century northern Italy that spread throughout Europe over the next two centuries. Actors improvised their dialogue and donned colorful costumes associated with stock characters in various sketches. In particular, men would be identified with specific costumes and half masks, while women's costumes and those of their male lovers would be of particular coloring that would reveal social class and emotional state.

## LEARN MORE: COMMEDIA DELL'ARTE

For a peek at these multi-colored costumes worn by the various stock characters, go to the e-resources at the following link:

*"Commedia dell'arte"*

The advent of the Industrial Revolution in the 18th century provides a side-note to the history of costume design. New inventions such as the water-powered loom sped up the process of weaving, and mass production of cloth became a mainstream industry.

By 1801, with the invention of the **Jacquard loom** in France that operated through a system of punched cards (which was a harbinger for the computer industry), textiles could now be woven into complex patterns such as brocades and damask. It would naturally follow that, coinciding with the Duke of Saxe-Meiningen's unifying concepts, costumes would become authentic and specific for each character. Actors were no longer permitted to pick and choose from their own closet, which brings us closer to today's theatrical world. Therefore, once the director and scenic designer have unified their concept for the scenic elements of a production, it would follow that appropriately costumed actors would inhabit the environment.

## LEARN MORE: THE JACQUARD LOOM

A series of demonstration videos on how the Jacquard loom works may be viewed on our e-resources at the following link:

*"Jacquard loom"*

While viewing these videos you might notice that the way the loom works bears a resemblance to early computers. Thus, costumes might plausibly be made to order.

# COSTUME DESIGN

Ironically, the development of Jacquard loom and the burgeoning computer industry figure prominently in the design and fabrication of costumes. There are numerous software programs for designing theatrical costumes available on the internet. Starting with the Five Key Elements it all starts with the designer charting the play for Who, What, Where, When, Why (How) and then adapting the choices to the director's concept. The process is pretty much similar whether the production is a lavish musical, such as *The Lion King*, or the world premiere of Kate Benson's *Radium Now* at Brooklyn College. The costume designer, after thorough research germane to the Five Key Elements, presents a series of sketches befitting the concept.

For example, Jeannipher Pacheco's design for the character of Madame Marie Curie, the central character in *Radium Now* as depicted in Figures 6.3a–b, demonstrates a series of steps she undertook to realize a finished costume. From an initial sketch through a couple of renderings, in the last panel Pacheco details the resultant dress worn. Notice the difference between the first rendering and the construction rendering. Why do you think the changes came about?

One major addition to the second rendering is the amount of detail added for construction purposes. Included are sample color fabric swatches and actual instructions for all the costume elements. Of particular note is how the resultant costume will fit the director's concept for a production that reflects a contemporary twist on early 20th-century Madame Curie. In an

**Figure 6.3a** The Process of Costume Designing for *Radium Now*. (Credit: Used with permission of Jeannipher Pacheco, Brooklyn College)

**Figure 6.3b** The Process of Costume Designing for *Radium Now*. (Credit: Used with permission of Jeannipher Pacheco, Brooklyn College)

## LEARN MORE: COSTUME TECHNOLOGY

To see how a parallel existence is symbolically reflected by LED lights that are hidden and light up behind Madame Curie's necktie go to our e-resources at the following link:

*"Lightup Costume"*

What you should notice is the depiction of a period costume illuminated with 21st-century technology that attempts to reflect the director's concept.

attempt to illustrate a balance of reality between present-day humans who attract or repulse each other while intersecting each other's orbits, like atoms bounding around the periodic table, there is another reality lurking below the visible surface.

The Madame Curie costume is only an isolated examination of one costume. For a larger production or a musical on the scale of *The Phantom of the Opera* or *The Lion King* imagine the hundreds of sketches, renderings, and specialty items (masks, headdresses, puppetry stilts, etc.) that have to be designed in order to clothe and equip the sizeable casts. In Chapter 7 we will meet some of the other designers whose work contribute to the overall design.

Earlier we mentioned that fabric, color, texture, weight, movement, attitude, mood, emotion, role, and period are important considerations for designing a costume. Before finalizing these elements, the costume designer continually communicates with the director, the scenic designer, and the lighting designer, as well as with other designers, as we will soon see. On a practical level, some examples of communication between costume designer and scenic designer would be to determine issues such as:

- What would be the reasonable height for a plumage piled hat in a production of *Cyrano de Bergerac* that would not topple off when the actor had to enter through a doorway?

- What colors would best befit a costume that would not clash with the forestry scenery of *Into the Woods*?

- Would a choice of spike heels be appropriate for an actor who has to descend a grated metal staircase on the set of *Kiss Me Kate*?

Such considerations (and thousands more) have to be taken into account by designers. Communication, compromise, and change remain the bottom line. Try to think of other situations that mutually affect scenic and costume designers.

### COSTUME DESIGN EXERCISE

While you are working your imagination, the following exercise (similar in purpose to the scenic design exercise above) will help sharpen your skills as a costume designer. Figure 6.4

Gold Brocade
on Flat Fabric

Shiny Silver
Fabric

Silver Grid
on Pale Yellow
Sheer Fabric

Multi-Colored
Pattern on Soft Fabric

Dark Blue
Stiff Fabric

White Embroidery
on White Net

Figure 6.4 - Costume Swatches

Figure 6.4 Costume Swatches

presents six fabric swatches. As a costume designer you should select as many of the swatches as possible and come up with a character who might wear a costume item made of the material represented by each selected swatch. Brief descriptive information is provided below each swatch. However, it is up to you to decide what the fabric might be; then utilize the <u>Five Key Elements: Who, What, Where, When, Why (How)</u> to guide you in placing your character in a possible situation. Again, there are no incorrect answers for this exercise.

# A SHORT HISTORY OF LIGHTING DESIGN

Having examined scenic designers and costume designers we now turn our attention to the third member of the triumvirate of lead designers for a production: the lighting designer. For centuries lighting was merely illumination. Whether it was sunlight or torches that lit outdoor events by day or night, or candles and open-flame oil lamps that cast light when theatrical events moved indoors, there were few, if any, practical methods for controlling lighting. With the introduction of gas lighting in the early 19th century there arose some ability to control the distribution and intensity of lighting. For the first time, the German inventor Frederick Albert Winsor utilized gas to light the Lyceum stage in London (1806). In the United States, Philadelphia's Chestnut Street Theatre was the first to utilize gas (1816).

With the use of a **gas table** (a precursor to lighting switchboards) an operator could control a series of dimmer valves along the board to distribute gas to the various lamps across the stage. The gas arrived in the building through rubber tubing that was hooked into the gas table. The operator then regulated the dissemination of gas to the varied locations. Thus, bright lights, dull lights, and blackouts could be controlled by the operator. However, lighting remained as illumination for scenery and visibility, as well as bursts for effects.

One early innovation in lighting was the discovery that when a column of lime is heated by a flame produced by gas, oxygen, and hydrogen, it would produce a brilliant white glow. By placing the heated lime rod in front of a parabolic reflector that is contained in a pivoting apparatus, or **followspot**, the reflection could shine brightly on an actor. An operator, perched in the audience, could thus focus on the moving actor and keep the actor "in the limelight"— hence, the expression that today has grown to mean someone who is the focus of attention.

Another option for followspots was the utilization of the electrical arc light in place of heated lime. However, the major drawback to all forms of lighting was that fire had to be employed; thus creating a perpetual safety hazard. The big leap forward in lighting came with Nikola Tesla's discovery of alternating current (AC) in 1882 and Thomas Edison's invention of the incandescent light bulb in 1879. Fire no longer had to be employed for lighting.

The craft of lighting now fell into the hands of electricians. Ingenious technicians would provide various effects that artistic directors called for during the next century. Early 20th-century stage director and designer Edward Gordon Craig did away with traditional footlights and experimented with lighting from above the stage to unify all aspects of his productions.

He utilized light and color to convey intended moods and emotions, as well as adding shape and dimension to scenery such as trees, stones, and levels.

If one name were to stand out in theatrical lighting it would be the pioneer Jean Rosenthal, who in the 1930s set the template for modern lighting. With advances in the development of electronic control systems Rosenthal, who began her career lighting dance for choreographer/dancer Martha Graham, was able to manipulate light intensity, mix colors, and distribute light—and do it either quickly or slowly. Moving on to work with actor/producer John Houseman and eventually with Orson Welles's Mercury Theatre, Rosenthal initiated her objectives for stage lighting. These would include **visibility** by shifting cues to intensify light around the stage; additionally, she revealed **shape and form** instead of just flatly lighting an object. Painting the stage with light, she achieved a visual **composition** and finally contributed to creating **mood**.

Following in the footsteps of Rosenthal, Tharon Musser, who is generally considered the "Dean of American Lighting Designers," introduced a computer-controlled light system on the Broadway production of *A Chorus Line* (1975). Thereafter the technology in lighting control systems for programmable stationary and moving lighting instruments, as well as peripheral equipment, has grown exponentially. Increasingly, manufacturers are developing and introducing new components to the theatrical lighting industry. A quick survey of the **WEB RESOURCES** listed at the end of this chapter will provide you with great insight into the wide array of equipment available to lighting and sound designers.

## LIGHTING DESIGN

Practically every lighting designer (often abbreviated as **LD**) will tell you it all starts with the script. The emotional impact the LD derives from isolating the Five Key Elements: Who, What, Where, When, Why (How) has to be adapted in a non-tangible fashion in order to fulfill the director's concept.

Inasmuch as scenic and costume design begin with sketches of solid objects, lighting designers (and a sound designer, as we will shortly see) present their initial ideas on design at early production meetings in the form of theories. In support of their ideas they might present colored research photos to demonstrate a lighting effect referred to in the script. One example might be a reproduction of a Frederic Edwin Church painting of the aurora borealis that depicts shimmering light which might similarly be achieved through light onstage. A Claude Monet sunrise could also evoke the mood and the color tone that a lighting designer might be able to bring to a particular scenic moment. Ideally the LD strives to illuminate the actor, the scenery, and the costumes without calling attention to the lighting itself, except where a specific lighting effect is called for.

In doing so, it is somewhat difficult to get over the notion of lighting design as a craft, since so much of the design is the utilization and harnessing of a wide array of technical equipment to achieve the resultant design. A lighting designer has to understand the properties of electricity, the capabilities of different lighting consoles and types of instrument, the almost infinite palette of available colored **gels** (thin sheets of polycarbonate or polyester that project color when placed in front of lighting fixtures), as well as all possible hanging positions in a theatre. In addition, the LD has to be able to harness all this to provide distribution, illumination, shape, form, composition, mood, color, intensity, and tempo that support the director's overall concept.

Working closely with the scenic and costume designers, as well as observing the traffic patterns of actors during rehearsals, the LD will create reams of information and lighting plots for shop orders and installation in a theatre.

## LEARN MORE: LIGHTING DESIGN

The Theatrical Lighting Database provides many interesting illustrations and facts on the process of lighting design. To see Tharon Musser's handwritten information for the original *A Chorus Line* go to our e-resources at the following link:

*"A Chorus Line"*

Today, lighting designers' work for compiling, collating, and plotting is made easier by computers and computer-assisted drawing/design (**CAD**) or Vectorworks programs. A look at Figures 6.5a–b by former Brooklyn College student HaeJin Han provides a glimpse of her thorough paperwork and lighting plot.

The lighting plot depicts the position for every instrument that is either hung overhead or positioned on the floor to cast light on the cyclorama (**CYC**). The CYC serves as an ever-changing skyline surrounding the back of the scenery. The page of paperwork shown in Figure 6.5a (one of some thirteen) details the hookup for programmable dimming channels and information specific to a few of the instruments utilized to change the colors on the CYC. This is only a partial look at the intricate detail that a lighting designer has to think through before hanging and turning on lights in a theatre. Thereafter begins the actual process of lighting design: building programmable cues in which certain lighting instruments are turned on or off; or dimming at different rates of speed and intensity. It is within this process that HaeJin Han was able to "paint with light" the beautifully different western skylines that are exemplified by her production photos for *Flyin' West* (Figure 6.5b).

In larger theatres, hundreds of lighting instruments are utilized to light plays and the multiple scenes in musicals on Broadway and in the West End. Figure 6.6 shows both stationary lighting instruments and one that can be programmed to pan, tilt, and change colors on command.

### LIGHTING DESIGN EXERCISE

This exercise relies a bit on your ability to express emotions, moods, time, and perhaps place through colors. Specifically, you will need to choose particular colored gels to translate these

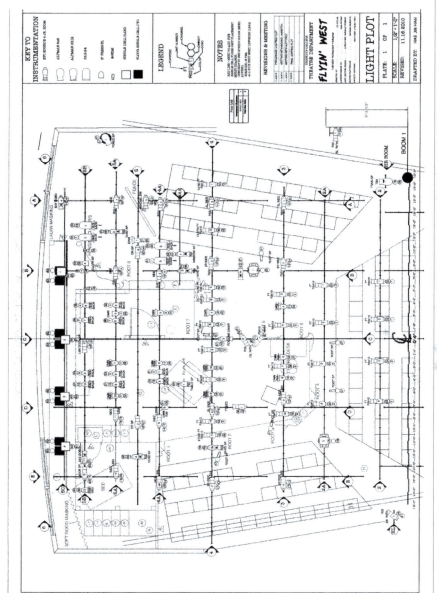

Figure 6.5a Lighting *Flyin' West*. (Credit: Used with permission of haejinhan.com)

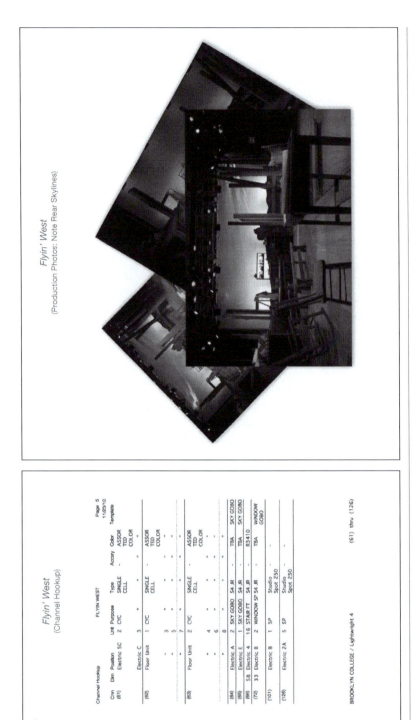

*Flyin' West*
(Production Photos: Note Rear Skylines)

*Flyin' West*
(Channel Hookup)

Channel Hookup

FLYIN WEST

Page 5
11/2/2010

| Chn | Dim | Position | Unit | Purpose | Type | Accsry | Color | Template |
|-----|-----|----------|------|---------|------|--------|-------|----------|
| (61) | | Electric 5C | 2 | CYC | SINGLE CELL | - | ASSOR TED COLOR | |
| | | Electric C | 3 | " | " | - | " | |
| (62) | | Floor Unit | 1 | CYC | SINGLE CELL | - | ASSOR TED COLOR | |
| | | " | 3 | " | " | - | " | |
| | | " | 5 | " | " | - | " | |
| | | " | 7 | " | " | - | " | |
| (63) | | Floor Unit | 2 | CYC | SINGLE CELL | - | ASSOR TED COLOR | |
| | | " | 4 | " | " | - | " | |
| | | " | 6 | " | " | - | " | |
| | | " | 8 | " | " | - | " | |
| (64) | | Electric A | 2 | SKY GOBO | S4 JR | - | TBA | SKY GOBO |
| (65) | | Electric E | 1 | SKY GOBO | S4 JR | - | TBA | SKY GOBO |
| (66) | 58 | Electric 4 | 16 | STAIR FT | S4 JR | - | R3410 | SKY GOBO |
| (72) | 33 | Electric B | 2 | WINDOW SP | S4 JR | - | TBA | WINDOW GOBO |
| (101) | | Electric B | 1 | SP | Studio Spot 250 | - | - | |
| (126) | | Electric 2A | 5 | SP | Studio Spot 250 | - | - | |

BROOKLYN COLLEGE / Lightwright 4

(61) thru (126)

**Figures 6.5** Lighting *Flyin' West*. (Credit: Used with permission of haejinhan.com)

**Figure 6.6** Various Lighting Instruments and Hanging Positions

various states of being, much like a lighting designer in support of the <u>Five Key Elements</u>. Although we will be working with LEE Colour Filters or gels, there are other manufacturers of lighting gels (e.g. Roscolux, Gam, Apollo, etc.) that you can use to complete a similar exercise while utilizing their accompanying **swatchbooks** that are generally obtainable for free at theatrical lighting conferences or from manufacturers at a nominal cost.

## *LEARN MORE: LIGHTING GELS EXERCISE*

For our purposes you will need to go online to the LEE Filters site by following the link listed on our e-resources. Figure 6.7 provides an **EXAMPLE** and a set of six different **PURPOSES/SITUATIONS** that require you to indicate what would be the appropriate **FILTER COLOUR** and its corresponding **LEE FILTER** #. Scrolling across the different colours on the LEE Filter site will provide you with the correct answers that match purpose/ situations provided in the left column of Figure 6.7.

Much of the joy of this exercise will be discovering how the different colors influence a variety of situations.

*"Lee Filters"*

An extension to this exercise is to shine a flashlight through gels of varying color and observe the effects for yourself. Participating in these exercises is an opportunity to experience how a lighting designer potentially "paints with light."

| LEE COLOUR EFFECT FILTERS | | |
|---|---|---|
| NOTE: The language in the examples below must exactly match the colour and Lee filter # | | |
| PURPOSE | COLOUR | LEE FILTER # |
| **EXAMPLE** | Rose Purple | 048 |
| Good for emulating evening. Great backlight | | |
| 1) Deep Moonlight. Great for colour mixing | | |
| 2) Good for sinister forest scenes, cyclorama, and backlighting | | |
| 3) To give a murky, dirty feel to tungsten. A darker, less pink chocolate | | |
| 4) A sunlight wash—use with gobos, disco, dark skin tones | | |
| 5) Great for sunsets, cyclorama lighting, and fire effects | | |
| 6) Great for dance sequences (useful for softening white costumes without affecting skin tones) | | |

**Figure 6.7** Lighting Gels Exercise

# A SHORT HISTORY OF SOUND DESIGN

Sound design is a recent addition to the triumvirate of designers. History prior to the transitional production of *A Chorus Line* (1975) was more about the amplification of a performer's voice and the presentation of live music and auditory effects. Since the ancient Greeks there has been much speculation on how the actors were heard in an amphitheater that seated 14,000. Varying reports included the contribution made by the shape of the mouthpieces on the masks worn; the way prevailing winds carried the actors' voices; or, more recently, how the actual composition of the limestone seats filtered out the low frequencies so that only high audible frequencies reached the audience's ears. In Shakespearean times the audiences were smaller, and the actors relied upon vocal projection and live musical interludes within a walled theatre. Throughout history various mechanical devices would be utilized to create special sound effects, such as the occasional offstage crashes, gunshots, thunder, or glass breaking.

As electricity developed, recordings were played back on phonographs (invented in 1877) and various sounds from real life could be heard from different stage locations. Toward the end of the 19th century and throughout the early 20th century audiences could be treated to the sound of a shrieking baby, raindrops falling on a roof, cows mooing in the distance, or ocean waves crashing in the wings. These effects were generally the responsibility of a stage manager and executed by an electrician. However, control of volume, tone, duration, or quality was still an issue.

With the development of analog audio tape and playback systems more control could be exercised for individual cues. Digital technology in the 1980s contributed to a rapid growth in sound technology. The use of all types of microphones grew increasingly. But it was on the aforementioned *A Chorus Line* that the pioneer Abe Jacob, oft considered the Godfather of Sound, collaborated with the design triumvirate to achieve a unified approach. This seamless achievement led to Jacob's distinct position of sound designer, with his introduction of a computerized sound control system. Since that time Jacob and his many disciples have exponentially refined the control of all aspects of sound, including the acoustical design of theatres; the placement and utilization of varying microphones; and sound reinforcement systems that practically place an audience's ears in close proximity to the actors and musicians.

# SOUND DESIGN

Examining the script for the <u>Five Key Elements: Who, What, Where, When, Why (How)</u> is the first order of business for a sound designer. This establishes:

- who will need various types of microphone (for performers and for musical instruments);

- what if any sound effects cues are designated by the script;

- where the performers, musicians, and special effects (**SFX**) cues will emanate from (i.e. where speakers might have to be placed in order to carry the sounds to the audience); and

- designated points in the script for mixing and amplification.

Finally, collaboration with all the designers and the director may determine whether additional sound cues might be needed to enhance the overall mood and tone of a production. With all these factors in mind, the sound designer will develop a sound score (a set of cues) designating which sounds reach an audience at any given time. Such cues might be Hamilton and Liza singing together, an alarm clock going off, or a solo guitar riff. Another such recurring element in a score might be Philip Glass's glacial, pulsing music that accompanies the stage action in Ivo van Hove's production of *The Crucible*. This is a design to get your heart rushing with heightened anxiety during key moments.

Along with the score, the sound designer would develop a diagram that basically details the technical specifications to track all sounds from their source to the inputs and subsequent outputs on a programmable computer mixing console. From there the signals are sent to amplifiers and on to the designated speakers.

On a production such as the musical *Hair* the design can be very elaborate. Much reduced for print purposes, Figure 6.8 illustrates this process. The left portion of the diagram itemizes close to sixty sources representing the various performers, musical instruments, and public address microphones, as well as their corresponding inputs/transmitters. In the middle is a complex process of receivers, amplifiers, various input processing stages, conversion devices, mixing consoles, output processing stages, and computer interfaces/programming consoles. On the right portion of the diagram are the loudspeakers that receive the programmed signals and ultimately transmit the sounds throughout the theatre.

Sound designers' work for enhancing productions is often immeasurable. However, as reward for their considerable contributions they were finally recognized with the first Tony Award for "Best Sound Design of a Play" and "Best Sound Design of a Musical" only in the 2007–2008 season. Unfortunately, this recognition was short-lived. Starting with the 2014–2015 season the sound design Tony Awards were eliminated. A probable excuse was that sound design was oft maligned as being purely technical. One of the most spectacular theatrical sound effects—that of the helicopter arriving and departing in the 1991 production of the musical *Miss Saigon*—makes a strong case for acknowledging the achievement of sound designers.

## THE DESIGN TEAM IN REHEARSAL AND BUDGETING

Rehearsals are significant for the entire design team. As they periodically drop into rehearsals, they allow designers opportunities to monitor the process of seeing the performers bring the script to life. In so doing, the actors' actions will reveal to each respective designer a

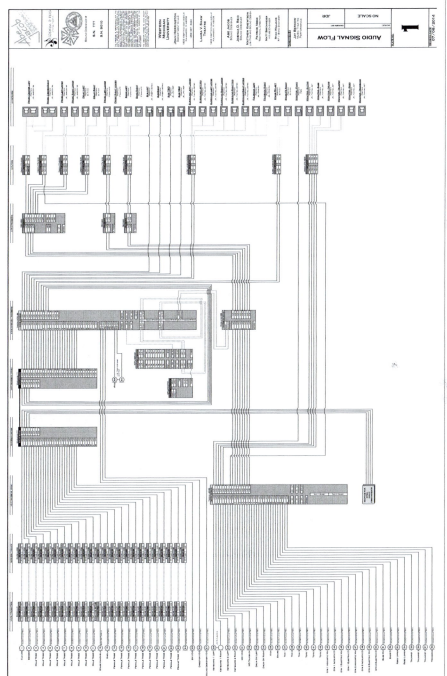

**Figure 6.8** Signal Line Diagram for *Hair*. (Credit: Used with permission of Abe Jacob and Joshua D. Reid, Sound Designers)

## LEARN MORE: SOUND EFFECTS

For an opportunity to hear how sound can envelop an audience and shake a theatre, go to the link below on our e-resources. Imagine the great impact of how the rumbling effect stirred the audience's emotions. For those that were in attendance bearing witness to such an event it revealed how transformative sound design can make a production.

*"Miss Saigon Helicopter"*

measurement of how successful original budgeted designs will be realized with actual production. Modifications to scenery and costumes that are under construction in shops, and equipment orders for both lighting and sound are less costly and easier to change prior to the actual load-in of the finished materials to a theatre.

Blocking rehearsals might reveal that a doorway as designed would be too narrow for actors to walk through two abreast. Originally intended dresses might be too full for a dancer's intended choreography. A potential lighting cue that fades the lights to darkness might be best served by adding more lighting instruments to bring down the lights gradually over a number of stage areas, rather than all at once. Or the director might decide that an approaching automobile from offstage needs to be heard before a group of actors enter. Reasonable changes can be handled with relative ease. However, any major changes (such as a brand new set for an already approved design) can be a sensitive matter and may involve considerable compromise, additional expense, and might even delay the opening of a production. Both the management and the creative team have to carefully consider not only cost factors, but also whether the requested changes will make for a successful production. Oversight for proposed modifications and safety initiatives within each design are generally handled by the production manager and the technical director, as we will see in **Chapter 8**.

## UNIONS

In the United States the United Scenic Artists Local USA 829 is the labor union and professional organization that collectively bargains forty different agreements with employers in shops and theatres for scenic, costume, lighting, and sound designers, etc. Payment for designs are determined by many factors, including where the venue is located (Broadway, Off Broadway, regional theatre, etc.), number of venue seats, and whether the production has a **unit set** (only one non-changing locale), multiple sets, numbers of costumes, etc.

Through the Society of British Designers, designers can find many useful links to representative associations and unions for different designers. British Equity not only represents performers, but also designers and directors.

# WHAT DID YOU LEARN?

1. Name the person who is generally credited with being "the Godfather of Sound." What did this person achieve in order to merit this recognition?

2. What is a gas table? Describe how it works.

3. What was the Jacquard loom, and what was its significance?

4. Name the ten integral components that go into finalizing a costume worn on stage. Explain each component.

5. What are the three major phases of any design before it is realized in production?

6. What do you call thin sheets of polycarbonate or polyester that project color, and why are they useful? Explain.

7. Explain what the following quotation means to a designer: "A stage space has two rules: (1) Anything can happen and (2) Something must happen."

## ANSWERS

1) Abe Jacob, who is considered the first Broadway sound designer, introduced the programmable computer sound console; 2) The first light console capable of mixing light cues by varying the amount of gas delivered to light flames; 3) A loom that could weave textiles in intricate patterns, operated using punched cards as a forerunner to today's computers; 4) Fabric, color, texture, weight, movement, attitude, mood, emotion, role, and period; 5) Design, fabrication, and installation; 6) Gels. They are useful for establishing mood, emotion, time, place, season, etc.; 7) A designer begins with an empty space and fills it according to the director's concept.

# ADDITIONAL RESOURCES

## BOOKS

*Collaboration and Design Background*

Peter Brook, *The Empty Space: A Book About the Theatre: Deadly, Holy, Rough, Immediate* (New York: Simon & Schuster), 1995.

Leah Hager Cohen, *The Stuff of Dreams: Behind the Scenes of an American Community Theater* (New York: Penguin), 2002.

Rob Roznowski and Kirk Domer, *Collaboration in Theatre: A Practical Guide for Designers and Directors* (New York: Palgrave Macmillan), 2009.

## Scenic Design

Arnold Aronson, *American Set Design* (New York: Theatre Communications Group), 1985.

Rob Napoli and Chuck Gloman, *Scenic Design and Lighting Techniques: A Basic Guide for Theatre* (London: Taylor & Francis), 2006.

W. Oren Parker and Harvey K. Smith, *Scene Design and Stage Lighting* (New York: Holt, Rinehart and Winston), 1974.

## Costume Design

Rebecca Cunningham, *The Magic Garment: Principles of Costume Design* (Long Grove, IL: Waveland Press), 2009.

## Lighting Design

Richard Pilbrow, *Stage Lighting Design: The Art, the Craft, the Life* (London: Nick Hearn Books), 2008.

Jean Rosenthal and Lael Wertenbaker, *The Magic of Light: The Craft and Career of Jean Rosenthal, Pioneer in Lighting for the Modern Stage* (Boston, MA: Little, Brown & Company), 1972.

Steven Louis Shelley, *A Practical Guide to Stage Lighting*, 3rd ed. (Burlington, MA: Focal Press), 2014.

Delbert Unruh, *The Designs of Tharon Musser* (Syracuse, NY: United States Institute for Theatre Technology, Inc.), 2007.

## Sound Design

Shannon Slaton, *Mixing a Musical: Broadway Theatrical Sound Techniques* (Burlington, MA: Focal Press), 2014.

Richard K. Thomas, *The Designs of Abe Jacob* (Syracuse, NY: United States Institute for Theatre Technology, Inc.), 2008.

## WEB RESOURCES

*Commedia dell'arte, Heilbrun: Timeline of Art History: The Met* ("accessed May 26, 2016"). www.metmuseum.org/toah/hd/comm/hd_comm.htm.

*FOH Online: People, Production, Gear, Gigs* ("accessed May 1, 2016"). www.fohonline.com/

*Lighting & Sound America* ("accessed May 1, 2016"). www.lightingandsoundamerica.com/

*PLSN: Projection, Lights and Staging News* ("accessed May 1, 2016"). http://plsn.com/

*Stage Directions: The Art and Technology of Theatre* ("accessed May 1, 2016"). http://stage-directions.com/

*td&t: Theatre Design & Technology* ("accessed May 1, 2016"). http://tdt.usitt.org/

### John Lee Beatty—Set Designer

Robin Pogrebin, "Lush, Plush or Seedy: Sets Filled with Power," *New York Times*, January 21, 2003, April 15, 2009, www.nytimes.com/2003/01/21/theater/lush-plush-or-seedy-sets-filled-with-power.html

### Costume Design

Whitney Blausen, "Theatrical Costume," Love to Know, http://fashion-history.lovetoknow.com/fashion-history-eras/theatrical-costume

### Lighting Design

"The Lighting Archive," http://thelightingarchive.org/

Larry Wild, "A Short Brief Outline of the History of Stage Lighting," Northern State University, September 14, 2015, www3.northern.edu/wild/LiteDes/ldhist.htm

### Abe Jacob—Sound Design

Jacob Coakley, "The Godfather of Sound," *Stage Directions*, March 2014, http://stage-directions.com/current-issue/5865-the-godfather-of-sound.html

### Unions and Related Organizations

British Equity, www.equity.org.uk/home

Society of British Designers, www.theatredesign.org.uk/about/links

United Scenic Artists Local USA 829, www.usa829.org

# Implementing the Designs

## *Crafting the Dream*

## ANCILLARY DESIGNERS

In Figure 5.9 we presented additional creative team members that included a number of specialty designers such as illusionist, aerial design, special effects, and climbing instructor. These positions fit the category of ancillary designers in that they are subsidiary to one of the four major designers presented in Chapter 6. In particular, the primary function of these specialty designers would be to coordinate their achievements with the scenic designer. There are many other types of specialty designers that might be requested to provide services, depending upon the nature of a production. For the moment though we will look at two of the more common ancillary design groups: properties, which falls under the aegis of the scenic designer; and a host of contributors to costume design.

## PROPERTIES OR PROP DESIGNER

For the actual scenic design to "come alive," it not only has to be occupied by performers who can carry or utilize every kind of object or device imaginable; the scenery itself has to include furnishings of every sort that define the place. Each property (prop) defined through the <u>Five Key Elements: Who, What, Where, When, Why (How)</u> should in large measure add to the personality of the show. Props can be intrinsic to telling the story. Sometimes, a prop will become the symbol of the show. Think of the iconic half-mask for *The Phantom of the Opera*, often paired with one red rose. In short, any physical object that exists in the world is fair game to be a prop in a theatre production, with one caveat: it has to fit onstage or be reasonably reproduced in facsimile to do so.

On a small production, such as one for community theatre or even Off-Broadway, generally the scenic designer will gather, borrow, or build their own props. As the scale of production increases, more likely there is a prop designer as well as subsidiary designers. The reason for this is that a broad view of properties yields a number of separate groupings. Designing items for each group could possibly befall one or more secondary designers. Ultimately all the subdividing will be determined by how much responsibility the scenic designer is able to shoulder alone, as well as whether a production's budget is capable of sustaining additional craftspeople.

Figure 7.1 provides a snapshot of what are generally regarded as the seven potential properties groups. In considering these groups, imagine any set before it is painted as being totally

| PROP CATEGORIES | INCLUDED PROPS |
|---|---|
| 1) Set Props | All items that touch the floor and are represented on the scale floor plan. Interior examples would include chairs, tables, various furniture, floor lamps, rugs, chests, etc. Exterior examples would include trash receptacles, traffic cones, bike stands, boulders, etc.<br><br>Set dressing might also include **practicals**, i.e. electrical props (lamps, chandeliers, wall sconces, and blinking signs) that actually work |
| 2) Trim Props | Anything that hangs on the walls. Items may be generic or help define a particular room or locale: i.e. venetian blinds, drapery, clocks, posters, kitchen racks, pictures, signage, etc. |
| 3) Set Dressing | Props that provide scenery with an environmental touch or insight into the occupants. These items are not utilized by actors, however; they seem to be possessed by the occupant. Examples might be trophies, sports equipment, books, a record collection, family photos, dirty dishes piled in a sink, etc. |
| 4) Hand Props | Anything the script indicates or a director chooses for actors to use during a play. Some choices might be a gun, knife, coffee service, luggage cart, etc. |
| 5) Personal Props | These items are intrinsic to an actor's character, called for by the script, or requested by an actor. They could be a wheelchair, cane, pipe, billfold, smartphone, cigarette lighter, etc. |
| 6) Floral & Fauna Props | Plant and wildlife such as real or artificial trees and other plants, or live animals such as parakeets, fish in a tank, etc. |
| 7) Live Sound Effects | These are props that produce sounds that are not recorded or do not emanate from the orchestra. They might include gunshots, thunder, offstage crashes, breakaway bottles, etc. Such sounds and effects are executed by actors or offstage crew members. |

**Figure 7.1** Properties Groups

blank. As it begins to be painted it takes on color, texture, place, period in time, and perhaps other defining elements. Into this process steps the props designer(s). As you examine the various properties groups you may notice there is possibility for items overlapping into more than one category. Hypothetically, a knife could be seen by the audience stuck into a wooden table as the curtain rises, and initially appears to be set dressing; but soon thereafter an actor enters and pulls the knife from the table. Now it is a hand prop. The actor then removes the knife and exits, only to return later with the knife tucked in his belt. At this point the knife becomes a personal prop. In the next scene, the knife is discarded into the wings in a large metal can, with accompanying offstage sound effects.

Can you think of other scenarios in which properties can be included in more than one category—or in all seven categories? By selecting from each of the properties categories the props designer contributes to the overall design and makes the scenery "come alive," as previously stated when we began this section.

Budget constraints and functionality, as well as the degree of realism, are further integral to what props will ultimately be included in a production. One director might spend hours choosing a single rocking chair that fulfills the production's concept, whereas another might simply go with any old rocking chair as a matter of expediency or budget. The selection process for scenic and properties designers can be very fulfilling when the correct prop is chosen, or fraught with harrowing anxiety and frustration until the exact desired prop is found, created, and/or selected.

Before leaving properties designers it is worth mentioning that with recurring frequency new products and methodology are constantly being developed to join the long list of tried and

## LEARN MORE: PROPERTIES DESIGN

Getting it right can be a richly rewarding experience, as exemplified in the two *New York Times* articles by Erik Piepenburg on budgeting and property design on our e-resources at the following links:

*"Off Broadway Mess"/"Good to See; Not to Eat"*

## LEARN MORE: PROP FOOD

To see how specialty food was prepared for the Broadway musical *Waitress* follow the link below on our e-resources.

*"Fresh Baked Pie"*

true blood-spurting effects, magic illusions and body wounds, armor design, flying effects, and automated objects, not to mention food preparation.

Let your imagination run wild and discover the next frontier for props design. If you happen to be employed in props work, take a cellphone with you as you go shopping for a particular prop, and snap a picture. By immediately sending a snapshot of your find back to the scenic designer and director in rehearsal you may gain instant purchase or rental approval for the exact treasured prop.

## COSTUME DESIGN CONTRIBUTORS

Arguably, when watching a production the primary focus is on the actors; thus the work of the costume designer receives much scrutiny from the viewing public. Subsequently a large network of ancillary designers contributes to the costume designer's final product. Figure 7.2 charts the lines of responsibility for those serving the costume designer.

Basically, Figure 7.2 is divided into three levels of responsibility. The first level is the costume designer and ancillary designers. The second and third levels (construction team and production running crew) will be discussed in Chapters 8 and 9 respectively. In order for

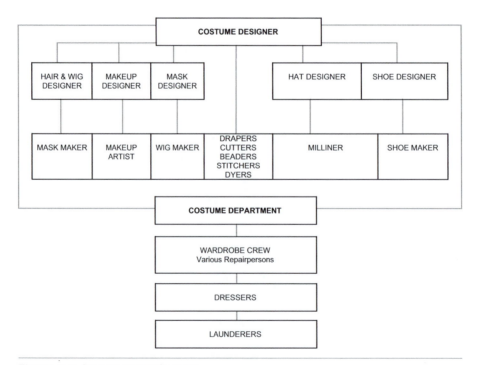

**Figure 7.2** Costume Design Overview

a production to take on specialty designers, some important determining factors include the skills of the costume designer, necessity, budget, and size of cast. A brief look at the five ancillary designers in Figure 7.2 follows.

## HAIR AND WIG DESIGNER

We have often heard the expression "Put a wig on him or her" when we want to achieve an older look or a change of personality, from amateur theatre all the way up to Broadway or the West End. From wretched off-the-rack hairpieces to high-quality designed wigs, any number of costume designers will easily reach for this solution to bring the overall design in line with the conceptual unity of the Five Key Elements: Who, What, Where, When, Why (How). Keeping in mind the production axiom in Figure 3.1—"Why can't you have all three?" (summarized as good, fast, cheap)—careful thought and purchasing have to be executed before a costume designer chooses a wig or engages a wig designer.

## LEARN MORE: HAIR AND WIG DESIGN

By looking at the broad range of productions designed by Paul Huntley, who is undoubtedly Broadway's most famous hair and wig designer, you should be able to see evidence of the central importance of supplemental, well-designed hair by following the link below on our e-resources.

*"Paul Huntley"*

## MAKEUP DESIGNER

For live theatre, unlike film or television, most actors apply their own basic makeup. Some are highly skilled at this craft: others may have taken one makeup course; or others may be able to apply rudimentary makeup since they have done so following their first brush with a tube of lipstick at an early age. Stage makeup is different. It has to hold up under glaring lights, read as intended (i.e. how an audience receives the look), and often not smudge. Then there is the specialty character makeup that might be necessary to age an actor, create scars, wounds, other disfigurements, prosthetics, or often transform someone into an animal, a monster, or a visitor from another world.

The makeup designer will be able to create with the actor a series of instructive photographs or sketches for each stage of makeup application, as well as advise on which products are cosmetically safe. Bringing in an expert at any level of theatre—for a single meeting or a series of sessions to teach an actor how to achieve the intended result—is money well spent.

## LEARN MORE: MAKEUP DESIGN

Shows in which makeup is an integral part of the costume design include *Cats*, *The Lion King*, *Tarzan*, and *Wicked*, and are revealed in the YouTube video by following the link below on our e-resources. Perhaps you can add other shows to this list.

*"Wicked Makeup"*

## MASK DESIGNER

Masks have been an integral part of theatre since ancient times. The convention of masks has been to assume a new identity, hide an identity, or to represent already accepted conventions for ancient gods in Western theatre and for Kabuki masks in Japanese theatre. The duality of personality with masks is used to great effect in Shakespearean roles that treat mistaken identity, recurrences in Eugene O'Neill's plays (especially *The Great God Brown*), and a central metaphor in Jean Genet's *The Blacks*. Additionally, Vermont's Bread and Puppet Theatre has been utilizing masks that are inspired by kneaded dough, almost exclusively in their productions for over fifty years.

## LEARN MORE: MASK DESIGN

A show in which masks range from the simplest ones that cover the top half of the face, with only the mouth revealed, is *Phantom of the Opera*. The masks designed for its "Masquerade" production number can be viewed in the YouTube video by following the link below on our e-resources. Perhaps you can add other shows to this.

*"Masquerade"*

## HAT DESIGNER (MILLINER)

There are many plays and musicals that include hats as memorable elements. In a play such as Regina Taylor's *Crowns*, the focus is on African American women's hats that are more than a fashion statement. Behind every hat worn is a story, which could be the outward expression of faith, a symbol of cultural continuity, or perhaps a badge of nobility. For such distinct expressions a costume designer not thoroughly versed in the significance of hats to the African American community might engage someone who could provide this special expertise.

*Crowns* and the more notable *My Fair Lady* include hats from African American traditions and early 20th-century London, England. Can you think of other productions in which hats importantly reveal the <u>Five Key Elements: Who, What, Where, When, Why (How)</u>?

## LEARN MORE: HAT DESIGN

The musical number "Ascot Gavotte" from *My Fair Lady* is a classic example of hats on parade. Memorably standing the test of time, costume and/or hat designers have primarily maintained artist Cecil Beaton's successful signature palette of blacks and whites for the many subsequent recreations of this musical number. An example follows in the YouTube video on our e-resources.

*"Ascot Gavotte"*

## SHOE DESIGNER

A look at shoe designers concludes our survey of ancillary designers supporting costume designers. Whether or not actors wear their own shoes, this costume element should also fit with the director's adherence to the Five Key Elements. A radical approach to not wearing shoes was employed in Ivo van Hove's *A View from the Bridge*, stripping away an expected element of well-behaved civilization. Breaking this convention occurs when Catherine appears in high heels, prancing about to reveal her emerging adult sexuality.

## LEARN MORE: SHOE DESIGN 1

We have been treated to a couple of musicals that feature shoes as centerpieces in their story-telling. *Kinky Boots*, the 2013 Tony Award winner for best musical, revolves around a shoe factory, a cabaret-performing drag queen, and a line of high-heeled boots. All of these elements made it a natural challenge for the costume designer/shoe designer to come up with something special that can be viewed in the following YouTube audio link on our e-resources.

*"Kinky Boots"*

# DESIGN ASSISTANTS

For the most part design assistants similarly function as administrative assistants, comparatively similar to positions in the corporate world. However, the design assistant in the theatre world is most apt to possess the same basic training and skills as the lead designer they assist. In the United States professional assistant designers work under the United Scenic Artists Local USA 829 agreement (as mentioned above). Likewise, in the United Kingdom lighting, video and projection designers work under the Association of Lighting Designers. In essence, most design assistants are designers-in-waiting.

## LEARN MORE: SHOE DESIGN 2

When the citizenry of the tiny fictional European town of Brachen launched into the musical number "Yellow Shoes" in the Broadway production *The Visit*, the central metaphor of greed and avarice was on full display. The impact of the frenzied characters showing off their brightly colored shoes highlighted the impact of new wealth to chilling dramatic effect. It was a testament to the designer's skill to capture the depth of inhumanity to which the townsfolk would eventually sink. By listening to "Yellow Shoes" you should hear a harrowing accompaniment to what was a visually startling number in the YouTube link on our e-resources.

*"Yellow Shoes"*

### ASSISTANT SCENIC DESIGNERS

Chapter 6 presented an overview of the process involved for the lead designers whereby many of the steps for fulfilling the final design would be passed to assistant designers should the size of production and budget warrant the hiring of assistants. Once the colors, textures, and dimensions of a final design are realized an assistant scenic designer might be responsible for constructing a scale model. The assistant might also oversee delivery of the model, scale drawings, and the floor plan(s) to the rehearsal studio. These materials are important to the director and performers for continued reference during the rehearsal period, and aid in the visualization of the actual scenery.

The acceptance of the design is only the initial step for the scenic designer and assistants. Along with the technical director (who oversees aspects of scenic construction), the team will develop plans for the fabrication and installation of the finished scenery in the theatre.

A common function of all assistants is that they are very often the eyes and ears of a designer who cannot be in two places at once. When a designer may be away at any one of the shops for consultation during construction or fabrication, the assistant might be monitoring rehearsals for both safety and eventual functionality of scenery, props, costumes, lighting, sound, etc. Reporting back to a designer on directorial changes that come up during rehearsals can also portend increased demands on the budget for more equipment or more time for construction and installation, as well as the potential for additional technical rehearsal time. An example might be that the director decides during the course of rehearsal to add a new piece of business which entails one of the performers flying. Perhaps a specialist from Flying by Foy or another group might be hired. Whether the designer or assistant notes this fact, a host of considerations may come into play before this feat can be achieved. Putting yourself in the designer or assistant's position for noting this possibility, Figure 7.3 summarizes some of the variables that impact the execution of such an idea.

| FLYING CONSIDERATIONS | |
|---|---|
| THEATRE ACCOMMODATIONS | Does the theatre structure need to be retrofitted to handle the necessary apparatus for carrying out the idea? |
| | Are there any local health and safety requirements covering such an act? |
| SCENIC ACCOMMODATIONS | Where would the performer enter? From above the existing scenery or flown in from the wings? |
| | Would there have to be any changes to the existing design to accommodate this action? |
| SUPERVISION | Would a flying specialist need to be hired? |
| | Would additional personnel need to be hired to oversee the action throughout the course of production? |
| PERFORMER ACCOMMODATIONS | How much additional time and training requirement would the performer need? |
| | When performing the act, how much time before and after the flight will the actor need to safely get into and out of the necessary rigging apparatus? |
| ADDITIONAL DESIGN ACCOMMODATIONS | Would there have to be alterations to costumes, lighting, and sound (e.g. micing the performer)? |
| SAFETY ACCOMMODATIONS | After considering all the above factors, is the act safe? |
| BUDGET | How do the above factors affect the budget? |
| | The need for additional supervision? |
| | The need for additional training and rehearsal time? |
| | The need for changes in design? Additional purchases? |
| WORTH | Only the producers can decide if the investment of time, energy, and money to achieve the flying effect will ultimately add to the success of the production. |

**Figure 7.3** Flying Considerations

Bear in mind that this might be an extreme directorial proposal; however, each and every designer and/or assistant designer has to be on alert for any change or modification to their design. As a cautionary word of wisdom for all designers in the theatre, there are only "solutions". "No" does not enter into the equation.

Very often a prop designer is as an assistant to the scenic designer. Logically this makes sense, since set props, set dressing, trim props, and floral props are intrinsic to the scenic design. Additionally, assistant scenic designers may supervise or even lend a hand in the construction and painting of the scenery in non-union productions. Other duties may include compiling track sheets that detail which pieces of scenery have to change during a scenic shift, as well as flying scenery cue sheets, and properties plots denoting where each prop is stored offstage and where it travels throughout a performance. Assistant scenic designers would also prepare paperwork for shop orders and timetables for delivery of set pieces to the theatre, as well as schedules for run-throughs of scenes, acts, scenic shifts, etc. in order for the scenic team to monitor the process leading to setup of the scenery in the theatre and the eventual smooth running of the production.

## ASSISTANT LIGHTING DESIGNERS

Continuing the practice of assistant scenic designers, assistant lighting designers similarly are responsible for tracking changes in rehearsals; assisting in the preparation of a lighting plot; preparing schedules; and coordinating bids and equipment orders with rental supply shops. Such a bid or order would be based on the accepted lighting plot. Basically, it could be a document that spells out the responsibilities of the bidding rental company and a complete equipment inventory that would be necessary in order to realize the design in a theatre. Figure 7.4 shows sample pages from a bid prepared by a Tony Award nominee for Lighting Design, Justin Townsend, and his associate lighting designer Sarah Johnston. The actual bid contains contact information for all parties, load-in, preview, and opening performance dates, as well as a table of contents for the entire document.

When setup occurs in a theatre the assistant lighting designer may cable, hang, focus, and program lighting instruments for non-union productions. For productions that occur under the jurisdiction of the International Alliance of Theatrical Stage Employees (**IATSE**, or **IA**) the work of the lighting designer and associates/assistants is primarily supervisory, and not hands-on. The physical handling of the lighting instruments and the attendant equipment is conducted by the IA stagehands, although the programming of cues may be conducted by designers. However, once a production is in actual running mode in a unionized theatre, an IA stagehand would be responsible for executing the cues. The next two chapters will cover the functioning of crews for both load-in and the running of productions. In addition, samples of the valuable documentation that lighting designers and their assistants prepare to keep the process running smoothly and accurately will be presented.

## ADDITIONAL ASSISTANT DESIGNERS

Depending upon the knowledge base of lead designers, various assistant designers would be delegated to tend to specialty areas. For instance, assistant scenic, lighting, and sound designers might oversee computer programming and cuing that complies with the overall intention of the director and lead designers.

INVISIBLE THREAD        GENERAL RESPONSIBILITY

The implementation of this lighting design must comply with the most stringent applicable federal and local safety and fire codes. All light plots, drawings, and this equipment list represent design intent and visual concepts and construction suggestions only. The lighting designer and his associates are unqualified to determine the structural appropriateness of this design and will not assume responsibility for improper engineering, construction, handling, or use of the lighting equipment that implements this design.

- Absolutely no substitutions or alterations in materials or methods will be acceptable, unless specifically approved by the designer and production electrician.
- Any revisions or substitutions must be disclosed at the time of the bid.
- Bidder assumes responsibility for any additional materials that are required on site due to rental shop  oversight or error.
- Entire package is to be made ready by supplier and is to include all lamps, connectors, cables, controls,  frames, etc. so as to comprise a complete working system.
- All equipment should be available on first day of shop prep unless alternate plans have been arranged with  Production Electrician.
- Bidder assumes responsibility for all trucking, shipping, and delivery of equipment to the venue.
- All cable and distribution requirements need to be specified by the electrician to be certain all set electrics  elements can be controlled via the lighting console.
- Please provide an appropriate number of spare units as determined by the lighting designer and the  production electrician.
- Any lighting fixtures to be provided by others will be so indicated.

GENERAL NOTES

- All units are to be supplied with appropriate lamp, gel frame, hanging hardware, and safety cable.
- All ellipsoidals are to be aligned.
- All TV Style equipment adapted to mount to theatrical pipe systems.
- All units, gel frames, mounting hardware, and safety cables should be painted flat black, front and back,  except where noted.
- All hardware and pipe to be painted flat black, except where noted.
- All hardware, perishables, cable lengths, and power distribution requirements as per Production  Electrician.
- All electronics are to have the latest software unless otherwise specified.
- All color changers to be supplied with face plates and appropriate top hat mounting hardware.

**Figure 7.4** Bid for *Invisible Thread* (Credit: Used with permission of Justin Townsend, Lighting Designer)

- All color scrolls to be made by Wybron and loaded by the shop.
- Use multi-cable and break-outs wherever possible. Spare lamps for all units.

## Equipment Summary

Dimming, Conventional Lighting Units, Accessories, Color Changers, Moving Lights, LED Units, FX & Atmospherics, Scenic Elements, Perishables

## Conventional Lighting Units

| Qty. | Instrument Type | Wattage Per Unit |
|---|---|---|
| 50 | ETC Source Four Leko LENS TBD | 575w |
| 50 | ETC Source Four 19° Lens Tubes | NA |
| 80 | ETC Source Four PARs with complete lens kits | 575w |
| 8 | ETC Source Four MultiPAR-4, MFL | 575w |
| 14 | 2kw Fresnel with barn doors | 2kw |
| 2 | 4.2kw HMI Fresnel with barn doors, scroller, and douser | 4.2kw |
| 20 | Mini-Tens with barn doors | 1kw |
| 2 | Lycian M2 Medium Lens Followspot | 1200w |

**+10% spare lamps for all lamp types.**

- All fixtures must come with appropriate color frames (painted flat black both sides), safety cables, and hanging hardware, unless noted.
- All Television equipment to be adapted for theatrical use.
- All fixtures to be painted flat black all sides.
- All fixtures to be tested and bench focused in the shop.

**Figure 7.4** Continued

It is not uncommon that there is a division of labor among the various assistant and associate designers. In the area of sound, an assistant designer might be responsible for the design, ordering, and eventual installation of all communication systems for the production once it is set up in the theatre. Scenic designers might call upon an assistant to work closely with a flying expert in order to avoid the risk of an actor becoming entangled in a piece of scenery. Similarly, assistant lighting designers would work with the same expert to prevent actors from bumping into lighting instruments, or to assist in the computer programming of the flying apparatus. Also, collaboration would be spread among assistant costume designers and assistant sound designers to insure functionality and safety regarding their design areas. In short, no one design area works alone. It is a collaborative effort involving all designers, their assistants, and the entire production team.

Before leaving this chapter it should be noted that major innovations continue to occur in the areas of lighting and scenic design. These changes include increased research/development in the use of projectors and light-emitting diode (**LED**) display screens. In the past, projection was generally handled by the lighting department, or in some cases the sound department. More recently, such usage has continued to enhance or even supplant the traditional use of physical scenery and lighting.

## *LEARN MORE: NEW DESIGN FRONTIERS*

The YouTube trailer on our e-resources for the London production of *The Curious Incident of the Dog in the Night-Time* provides a preview of this next design frontier.

*"LED Lighting"*

Breaking through the imagined fourth wall that separates the audience from the actors, the play *Privacy* encouraged the audience to keep their cellphones on during the performance. The production was an experiment in binding the audience with the action on the stage. What other technologic advances await audiences is something worth speculating.

## WHAT DID YOU LEARN?

Figure 7.5 is a portrayal of two people relaxing in a family den. For each of the five numbered items you are to determine which of the four design areas might be responsible for constructing, securing, or making the item operational. In addition, name all subgroupings or ancillary designers that could also play a part in completing the execution of each item.

**Figure 7.5** Is It Scenery, Lighting, Costumes, or Sound? (Credit: Roy and Martha Zurillo and children, 85 76th St., Bay Ridge, Brooklyn. July 26, 1978. The New York Public Library free digital collection, http://digitalcollections.nypl.org/items/510d47e2-cbbe-a3d9-e040-e00a18064a99)

# ADDITIONAL RESOURCES

## BOOKS

*Properties Design*

Susan Crabtree and Peter Beudert, *Scenic Art for the Theatre* (Burlington, MA: Focal Press), 2005.

Thurston James, *The Theater Props Handbook* (Betterway Publication, Inc.: White Hall: VA), 1987.

Harvey Sweet, *Handbook of Scenery, Properties, and Lighting: Volume I, Scenery and Properties* (2nd Edition) (Boston: Allyn and Bacon), 1995.

## Hair and Wig Design

Martha Ruskai and Allison Lowery, *Wig Making and Styling: A Complete Guide for Theatre and Film* (Burlington, MA: Focal Press), 2010.

Rosemarie Swinfield, *Hair and Wigs for the Stage: Step-by-Step* (London: A & C Black), 1999.

## Makeup Design

Gretchen Davis and Mindy Hall, *The Makeup Artist Handbook* (Burlington: MA: Focal Press), 2012.

## Mask Design

Irene Corey, *Mask of Reality: An Approach to Design for Theatre* (Anchorage, AK: Anchorage Press), 1988.

Thurston James, *The Mask-Making Handbook* (Studio City, CA: Players Press), 2008.

## Hat Design

Michael Cunningham, *Crowns: Portraits of Black Women in Church Hats* (New York: Doubleday), 2000.

Tim Dial, *Basic Millinery for the Stage* (Portsmouth, NH: Heinemann Drama), 2002.

## Shoe Design

Aki Choklat, *Footwear Design* (London: Laurence King Publishing), 2012.

Fashionary, *Fashionary Shoe Design: A Handbook for Footwear Designers* (Hong Kong: Fashionary), 2015.

## WEB RESOURCES

"B.H. Barry's Career: Long Fight to the Tony Award," *Playbill*, www.playbill.com/article/bh-barrys-career-long-fight-to-the-tony-award-com-191116 ("accessed July 23, 2016").

*Bread and Puppet Theatre*, http://breadandpuppet.org/ ("accessed July 7, 2016").

*Flying by Foy*, http://flybyfoy.com/ ("accessed July 23, 2016").

*PLSN: Projections, Lights, and Staging News*, http://plsn.com/ ("accessed July 23, 2016").

*The New York Public Library Theatrical Lighting Database*. http://lightingdb.nypl.org/ ("accessed July 12, 2016").

CHAPTER 8

# Production Supervisors

## Constructing the Dream

## THE TRANSITION TEAM

Depending upon the scale (varying from amateur to Broadway or West End), the complexity, cost factors, and safety needs for a production, a producer or general manager would assemble a transition team: **production manager**, **stage manager**, and **technical director**. This team would be responsible for shepherding the production from rehearsals and through **fabrication** (construction) to **installation** (load-in and set-up in a theatre). As a team they monitor all schedules and budgets. They act as facilitators between designers and shops; oversee every technical necessity; and finally integrate all these elements for the directorial staff, performers, and running crews to perform with.

### PRODUCTION MANAGERS

Every production needs someone to assume responsibility for the successful fabrication and installation of all technical elements in a theatre. Variously this person is referred to as a production manager, a production supervisor, or a technical director. The scale of production will determine whether one person or three people perform(s) these duties, either singularly or in combination. In smaller venues it is not uncommon for a production manager to double as technical director. No matter who fulfills these positions, that person must be highly organized, a skillful communicator, and knowledgeable about every technical detail that comprises a production.

In addition to a thorough understanding of the production through the <u>Five Key Elements: Who, What, Where, When, Why (How),</u> the production manager has to grasp the intention of each of the designers and all the elements in their respective designs. With this knowledge comes an understanding of the necessity for certain materials or equipment included in a bid, such as those referred to in Figure 7.4. Similarly, other designers would prepare bids that a production manager could send to specialty supply houses and construction shops for fulfillment.

All bids and construction costs have to be balanced against the total projected technical budget handed down by the producer and general manager. More than the lowest bid is taken into consideration. The reputation of a shop for fulfilling a quality order and delivering the finished product on schedule ranks high with production managers and designers. Continual communication among all parties is especially important. Therefore, reliance on familiar purveyors is a common occurrence.

The backbone for a successful production manager is a well-prepared production calendar, whether it is for a season of plays or a single production. Working backwards from opening night, the production manager—along with the production stage manager and general manager—would include benchmark dates for such items as dress rehearsals, technical rehearsals, scenery load-in, lighting setup (**LX**: abbreviation for electrics), sound installation, costume arrival, and various other equipment due dates. With such a calendar the production manager can keep the team moving forward in a timely and safe manner. Additionally, the calendar becomes essential for coordinating and tracking budgets, and pinpoints essential dates for hiring labor and other staff while all the technical elements are being assembled.

Figure 8.1 provides a snapshot of a month's scheduling for four productions taking place in two venues during the course of a semester. See if you can track the due dates for those four productions itemized as: (1) *Much Ado About Nothing*; (2) *DNA*; (3) *When We Wake Up Dead* (WWWUD); and (4) *Radium Now*.

An alternative method of presenting similar information is represented in Figure 8.2. In this matrix format for instance the lighting department could read across one line and determine on which dates they would start hanging lights for each production in the course of the school year. With these dates in hand the lighting department would then be able to set its own schedule for assembling shop orders for each production in order to be ready to install/hang on the aforementioned dates.

During the course of rehearsals, the production manager would remain in constant communication with the stage manager regarding any potential technical or schedule changes. This relationship allows the production manager to monitor any possible cost overrides and arrive at a realistic number of crew members that need be hired to run the show in performance. One rule of thumb for production managers in commercial theatre is that it is more cost effective to motorize moving pieces of scenery that have to be flown or brought in along the stage deck, rather than hire many union stagehands to do so.

## STAGE MANAGERS

Historically, it would be difficult to pinpoint exactly when the term "stage manager" came into vogue. However, the fact remains there was usually someone who took responsibility for gathering

collegeproductioncalendar@gmail.com

**Feb 2016 (Eastern Time)**

| Sun | Mon | Tue | Wed | Thu | Fri | Sat |
|---|---|---|---|---|---|---|
| **31** | **1**<br>(2) DNA Lx & Sound | **2**<br>8am - BCBC Rental-<br>12:30pm - Run Crew<br>3pm - Orch. reh | **3**<br>(1) Much Ado Lighting Install & Scenic | **4**<br>(3) WWUD Costume<br>12:30pm - (3)<br>12:30pm - Run Crew<br>1:30pm - (2) DNA | **5**<br>(1) Much Ado Install<br>Auditions for One- | **6** |
| **7** | **8**<br>(2) DNA - LX & Sound -<br>(4) Radium - SETS -<br>10am - (1) Much Ado<br>6:30pm - (3) First | **9**<br>(4) Radium - SETS -<br>Conversion day-<br>DNA reh. moves to<br>9am - (1) Much Ado<br>4pm - (1) Much Ado<br>6pm - (1) Much Ado | **10**<br>10am - (1) Much A | **11**<br>(3) WWWUD - LX &<br>9am - (1) Much Ado<br>12:30pm - (1) Much | **12**<br>Lincoln's B'day- CC<br>10am - (1) Much Ado<br>6pm - (1) Much Ado | **13**<br>10am - (1) Much Ado |
| **14**<br>3pm - (1) Tech Day 2 | **15**<br>President's Day- CC | **16**<br>12:30pm - (2) DNA<br>6pm - (1) Much Ado | **17**<br>12:30pm - (2) DNA<br>6pm - (1) Much Ado | **18**<br>9am - (4) Radium<br>12:30pm - (3)<br>1:30pm - (2) DNA<br>6pm - (1) Much Ado | **19**<br>7:30pm - (1) Much | **20**<br>2pm - (1) Much Ado<br>7:30pm - (1) Much |
| **21** | **22**<br>9:30am - (3) | **23**<br>9:30am - (3)<br>12:30pm - (2) DNA<br>7:30pm - (1) Much | **24**<br>(3) WWWUD Install Sets<br>12:30pm - (2) DNA<br>7:30pm - (1) Much | **25**<br>7:30pm - (1) Much | **26**<br>2:30pm - MFA<br>6pm - DNA crew run<br>7:30pm - (1) Much | **27**<br>2pm - (1) Much Ado<br>7:30pm - (1) Much |
| **28**<br>(1) Strike WW | **29**<br>(1) Strike WW day 2<br>6pm - (2) DNA Tech | **1**<br>6pm - (2)DNA Tech 2 | **2**<br>6pm - (2) DNA Dress | **3**<br>10:30am - (5) 1 AF<br>12:30pm - (3)<br>6pm - (2) DNA Dress | **4**<br>7:30pm - (2) DNA | **5**<br>2pm - (2) DNA Show<br>7:30pm - (2) DNA |

**Figure 8.1** College Production Calendar

| | Savage in Limbo | Mauritius | Top Girls | Bees in Honey | The Trojan Women | The Story | The Thugs | Pre-Thesis Festival |
|---|---|---|---|---|---|---|---|---|
| Preliminary Set Design due | | 28-Aug | 28-Aug | 9-Oct | | 15-Jan | 11-Feb | 11-Feb |
| Preliminary Costume Design due | | 28-Aug | 28-Aug | 9-Oct | | 15-Jan | 11-Feb | 11-Feb |
| Final Set Design due | | 4-Sep | 4-Sep | 16-Oct | | 22-Jan | 19-Feb | 19-Feb |
| Final Costume design due | | 4-Sep | 4-Sep | 16-Oct | | 22-Jan | 19-Feb | 19-Feb |
| First Production Meeting | 21-Aug | 11-Sep | 2-Oct | 23-Oct | | 29-Jan | 26-Feb | 26-Feb |
| First Rehearsal | 24-Aug | 14-Sep | 5-Oct | 29-Oct | 6-Jan | 1-Feb | 26-Feb | 26-Feb |
| Costume Preview | | | | | | | | |
| Preliminary Prop plot due from Dir/S | 21-Aug | 11-Sep | 2-Oct | 23-Oct | | 29-Jan | 26-Feb | 26-Feb |
| Preliminary Lighting Plot due | 2-Sep | 23-Sep | 14-Oct | 9-Nov | 13-Jan | 10-Feb | 17-Mar | 14-Apr |
| Final Lighting Plot due | 9-Sep | 30-Sep | 21-Oct | 16-Nov | 18-Jan | 17-Feb | 24-Mar | 21-Apr |
| Final Prop Plot due | | | | | | | | |
| Light Hang Starts | 16-Sep | 7-Oct | 28-Oct | 23-Nov | 25-Jan | 24-Feb | 31-Mar | 28-Apr |
| Light Focus Starts | 21-Sep | 9-Oct | 2-Nov | 30-Nov | 27-Jan | 1-Mar | 6-Apr | 3-May |
| Scenic Painting day | 23-Sep | 14-Oct | 4-Nov | 2-Dec | 1-Feb | 3-Mar | 8-Apr | 5-May |
| Last Production Meeting | 25-Sep | 16-Oct | 6-Nov | 4-Dec | 29-Jan | 5-Mar | 9-Apr | 7-May |
| Crew Run through | 25-Sep | 16-Oct | 6-Nov | 4-Dec | 3-Feb | 5-Mar | 9-Apr | 7-May |
| Technical rehearsal 1 | 26-Sep | 17-Oct | 7-Nov | 5-Dec | 4-Feb | 6-Mar | 10-Apr | 8-May |
| Technical Rehearsal 2 | 27-Sep | 18-Oct | 8-Nov | 6-Dec | 5-Feb | 7-Mar | 11-Apr | 9-May |
| Technical Rehearsal 3 | n/a | n/a | n/a | n/a | 6-Feb | n/a | n/a | n/a |
| Dress Rehearsal 1 | 28-Sep | 19-Oct | 9-Nov | 7-Dec | 7-Feb | 8-Mar | 12-Apr | 10-May |
| Dress Rehearsal 2 | 29-Sep | 20-Oct | 10-Nov | 8-Dec | 8-Feb | 9-Mar | 13-Apr | 11-May |
| Final Dress Rehearsal | 30-Sep | 21-Oct | 11-Nov | 9-Dec | 9-Feb | 10-Mar | 14-Apr | 12-May |
| Opening Night | 1-Oct | 22-Oct | 12-Nov | 10-Dec | 10-Feb | 11-Mar | 15-Apr | 13-May |
| Show Closes/Strike | 10-Oct | 25-Oct | 22-Nov | 13-Dec | 14-Feb | 14-Mar | 18-Apr | 16-May |
| Post Show Evaluation | 16-Oct | 30-Oct | 4-Dec | 15-Dec | 19-Feb | 19-Mar | 23-Apr | 21-May |

**Figure 8.2** Production Date Matrix

props, looking after costumes, organizing other backstage activities, and overseeing scheduling, as well as trouping a show from one town to the next. Whether it was the actor/manager in Shakespeare's day or theatre/manager or director/manager, a person who displayed outstanding qualities for being well **organized**, highly **responsible**, and adept at **leadership** could just as easily fulfill the role of a stage manager, whether given billing or not. Early mention of the title stage manager appears alongside an associate of Georg II, Duke of Saxe-Meiningen (1880s). In 1913 the Actors' Equity Association became the first professional union representing actors and stage managers in the United States. Similarly, Equity was founded in the United Kingdom in 1930.

Stage managers were invariably men, but a likely contender for the first woman stage manager is Maud Gill of the Birmingham Repertory Theatre in England. A shortage of men in wartime Britain elevated her to the position in 1920. A year later in the United States Maude T. Howell, assistant stage manager on *The Green Goddess*, became the first woman stage manager in New York theatre history after taking over when the show's manager (a Mr. A.) fell ill. You can find more on this in the ADDITIONAL RESOURCES at the end of the chapter.

## LEARN MORE: STAGE MANAGEMENT HISTORY

Some of the theories that trace the roots of stage management can be explored by going to the blog link on our e-resources.

*"SMNetwork"*

A refresher glance at Figure 0.1 (organization chart) and Figure 1.1 (production divisions) reveals the stage manager at or near the center of any production and straddling the management, creative, and technical divisions. Quite possibly the stage management staff are the prime practitioners for following the Five Key Elements: Who, What, Where, When, Why (How) on a conscious level for creating and organizing the many forms that facilitate communication links between all production personnel. The combining three qualities of organization, responsibility, and leadership keep the successful stage manager functioning at the nerve center of any production. By sharing continual communication with the production manager, both parties effectively ensure a seamless transition from rehearsals to performance, and thereafter.

Once contracted by the producer or general manager the stage manager immediately engages with the script and practically all personnel on the organization chart. The first order of business is the creation of a **contact sheet** as this opens the lines of communication for all personnel. Note that the confidential information has been purposely deleted in the sample shown in Figure 8.3a and 8.3b.

The stage manager would expand a contact sheet to include additional personnel such as all assistants, musicians, running crews, the general management and publicity teams, vendors,

## The Threepenny Opera
## CONFIDENTIAL
## PRODUCTION TEAM

| NAME | POSITION | CONTACT NUMBER | E-MAIL |
|------|----------|----------------|--------|
| Thomas Bullard | Director | | |
| Vincent Ingrisano | Assistant Director | | |
| Justin Sturges (2/27) | Stage Manager | | |
| Mana Fujikatsu (3/27) | Assistant Stage Manager | | |
| Ryad "Andy" Ali (11/22) | Assistant Stage Manager | | |
| Fred Tessler | Music Director | | |
| Liz Snyder | Rehearsal Pianist | | |
| Meghan Formwalt | Dramaturg | | |
| M. Louise McKay | Dramaturg | | |
| Lori Ann Laster | Dramaturg | | |
| John C. Scheffler | Scenic Designer | | |
| Jorge Dieppa | Assistant Scenic Designer | | |
| Rebecca Cunningham | Costume Designer | | |
| Kip Marsh | Lighting Designer | | |
| Mansik Kim | Properties Master | | |
| Amanda Schultze | Properties | | |

Figure 8.3a Sample Contact Sheet

## CAST

| NAME | CHARACTER | CONTACT # | E-MAIL |
|------|-----------|-----------|--------|
| Julia Amisano | Mrs. Peachum | | |
| Najat Arkadan 9/4 | Betty (and Beggar) | | |
| Dina Cataldi | Dolly (and Beggar) | | |
| Michael Fewx | Walt (and Beggar) | | |
| Christopher Gilkey | Filch (and Beggar) | | |
| Will Gozdziewski | Reverend Kimball (and Beggar) | | |
| Ava Jackson 10/2; ½ = 4/2 | Teaser (and Beggar) | | |
| Abigail Liddell 2/2 | Lucy Brown | | |
| Bryan Marshall *DEPUTY | Tiger Brown | | |
| Francis Mateo 3/6 | Matt (and Beggar) | | |
| Corydon Merritt 7/7 | Bob (and Beggar) | | |
| Vincent Ingrisano | Copper | | |
| Jonathan Job | Mr. Peachum | | |
| Larissa Laurel 4/1 | Coaxer (and Beggar) | | |
| Vanessa Parvin 11/30 | Jenny | | |
| Pablo Tufino 5/10 | Street Singer/ Jake | | |
| Sean Toohey 6/18 | Smith (and Beggar) | | |
| Valerie Vervoort 1/22 | Polly Peachum | | |
| Dirk Weiler 8/21 | Macheath | | |
| Jenn Whitman 10/9 | Molly | | |

**Figure 8.3b** Sample Contact Sheet

## LEARN MORE: CONTACT SHEETS

For other sample contact sheets follow the link on our e-resources.

*"Contact Sheet"*

etc. It would not be uncommon for a final contact sheet on a Broadway or West End production to run to over twenty pages. Coupling the production calendar with the contact sheet, both the production manager and the stage manager are equipped to embark upon their respective responsibilities through the four phases of production: **pre-production**, **rehearsals**, **performance**, and **post-production**.

### Pre-Production

The subject of stage management is exhaustively presented in various textbooks and educational courses today. However, it was not even a subject taught in schools until the 1970s. One of the key factors of a successful stage manager is to assume responsibility, as mentioned above.

## LEARN MORE: ACTORS' EQUITY ASSOCIATION STAGE MANAGEMENT

A look at Actors' Equity Association On-line Stage Manager Packet is a good place to begin to gather a sense of the type of paperwork a stage manager is responsible for organizing throughout the production process. Follow the link below on our e-resources to view the AEA Stage Management Packet.

*"SM Packet"*

Familiarization with the Stage Manager Packet, along with the creation of the scheduling calendar and contact sheet, is only the tip of the iceberg for the massive amount of organization the stage manager has to accomplish prior to heading into rehearsals. A thorough analysis of the script through the perspective of the Five Key Elements is mandatory for the stage manager.

An initial analysis that a stage manager might prepare is a scene breakdown by cast. Figure 8.4 for a unit set production of *The Laramie Project* details such Key Elements as Who (cast member); What (role in each scene); Where (defined by dialogue); When (act, scene, page number); and Why/How (note: 2nd Line or Moment Line on Chart).

Similarly, the stage manager would prepare a preliminary production analysis that tracks every element and potential change of scenery, lighting, costumes, sound, props, etc. In most

# Laramie Project

## SCENE BREAKDOWN BY CAST

| ACT-Moment/pg# | I-1/ pg21-24 | I-2/pg24-25 | I-3/pg25 | I-4/pg26-27 | I-5/pg27-28 | I-6/pg28-30 | I-7/pg30-32 | I-8/pg32-33 | I-9/pg33-34 |
|---|---|---|---|---|---|---|---|---|---|
| | Definition | Journal Entries | Rebecca Hilliker | Angels in America | Journal Entries | Alison&Marge | Matthew | Who's Getting What? | Easier Said Than Done |
| 1 Melanie | Eileen E./Reporter | Amanda G. | | | Narrator2 | Marge M. | Trish S. | | |
| 2 Valerie | N5/Rebecca H. | | Rebecca H. | | Waitress | | Narrator | | |
| 3 Emily | N4/April S. | Narrator1 | | | N1/Barbara P. | | | | Catherine C. |
| 4 Sarah | N3/Zackie S. | | | | Leigh F. | Alison S. | Romaine P. | | |
| 5 Ian | N5/Philip D. | Moisés K. | | | Moisés K. | | Jon P. | | |
| 6 Matthew | N2/Jedadiah | Andy P. | | Jedadiah S. | Narrator4 | | Andy P. | | Narrator |
| 7 Kent | Greg P. /Sgt. Hing | Narrator2 | | | Greg P. | Greg P. | | | |
| 8 Troy | N1/Doc O. | Stephen B | | | Narrator3 | | Doc O. | Doc O. | Jonas S. |

General Notes: Letter N stands for Narrator and number indicated after N is according to the order of appearance

| ACT-Moment/pg# | I-10/pg34 | I-11/pg34-36 | I-12/pg36-37 | I-13/pg37 | I-14/pg38-41 | I-15/pg41-42 | I-16/pg42-43 | I-17/pg43-46 |
|---|---|---|---|---|---|---|---|---|
| | Journal Entries | The Word | A Scarf | Lifestyle 1 | The Fireside | McKinney&Henderson | The Fence | Finding Matthew Shepard |
| 1 Melanie | Amanda G. | Bap. Minister | | Amanda G./Minister's wife | Shadow | | | Narrator |
| 2 Valerie | Narrator | | | | Narrator3 | | | Reggie F. |
| 3 Emily | | | Zubaida U. | | | | | |
| 4 Sarah | | | | | Barbara P./Kristin P. | N2/Sherry A. | | Aaron K. |
| 5 Ian | Moisés K. | Narrator | | | N2/Romaine P. | | Leigh F. | |
| 6 Matthew | | Stephen M. J. | | | Narrator1 | | Stephen M. | |
| 7 Kent | | Doug Laws | | | Matt. M | | Greg P. | Dr. Cantway |
| 8 Troy | | Father Roger | Stephen B. | | Phil L. | | | |
| | | | | | Matt G./Stephen B. | N1/Anonymous | Narrator | |

General Notes: Letter N stands for Narrator and number indicated after N is according to the order of appearance

| ACT-Moment/pg# | II-1/pg47-48 | II-2/pg49-50 | II-3/pg50 | II-4/pg51-53 | II-5/pg53-54 | II-6/pg54-57 | II-7/pg57 | II-8/pg58 | II-9/pg58 |
|---|---|---|---|---|---|---|---|---|---|
| | A Laramie Man | The Essential Facts | Live & Let Live | Gem City of the Plains | Medical Update | Seeing Matthew | E-Mail | Vigils | Medical Update |
| 1 Melanie | Trish S. | Newsperson | | NP#1/N2 | | Marge M. | | | |
| 2 Valerie | Narrator 3 | Judge | | NP#2/NP | | Reggie F. | Narrator | Narrator | |
| 3 Emily | Narrator 2&4 | Catherine C. | Catherine C. | NP#3 | NP#3 | Catherine C. | | | |
| 4 Sarah | Romanie P. | | | NP#4/N1/Tiffany/Eileen | NP#4 | Arron K. | Email Writer | | |
| 5 Ian | N1/Jon P. | | Jon P. | Jon P./ Gil E. | | Narrator 1 | | | |
| 6 Matthew | Matt M. | | N2/Jeffery L. | Gov. Geringer | | Narrator 2 | | | |
| 7 Kent | Rulon S. | | N1/Sgt. Hing | Sgt. Hing | Narrator/Rulon S. | Detective Sgt. Rob D. | Narrator/Philip D. | | Narrator/Rulon S. |
| 8 Troy | Matt G. | | | Bill M./Doc/ | | Matt G. | | | |

General Notes: Letter N stands for Narrator and number indicated after N is according to the order of appearance

Figure 8.4 Scene Breakdown by Cast

likelihood these change points will become actual cues that a stage manager will have to call in performance (discussed below). These track sheets would be incorporated into a **production book** that the stage manager assembles during the pre-production phase. The production book serves as the stage manager's "holy bible" throughout the entire production process.

Beside contact information, scheduling calendars for all production deadlines, and rehearsal schedules, the stage manager might include audition material, budget information, and sections that pertain to each individual technical element. This assemblage of material will prove invaluable during the various production meetings with the director, production manager, and the design team leading up to rehearsals.

A final act for the stage manager during pre-production is to prepare the rehearsal space(s). This could include securing tables, chairs, supplies, musical equipment, rehearsal props and scenic mock-ups, or other accommodations to insure a safe, comfortable, and productive rehearsal period. A chief responsibility for the stage manager is to **tape the floorplan** in each rehearsal space in actual scale for all scenery. This will enable the director and/or choreographer to block the actors in a space that has the same dimensions prior to moving onto the actual set.

## LEARN MORE: TAPING THE FLOORPLAN

For a video demonstration of stage management accomplishing the task of taping the floorplan, access the You Tube video by following the link below on our e-resources.

*"The Floorplan"*

### General Rehearsals

The initial day of rehearsal is generally the first opportunity for the entire company to meet one another. Up to that point actors may have met with the director and stage manager separately at auditions, or had chance encounters with designers and other personnel. On this first day the stage manager acts as a facilitator, pretty much introducing everyone and establishing the role of primary communicator.

It can be a day of excitement, nervous energy, and positive social interaction. How the director and stage manager present themselves in many ways sets the tone for the ensuing rehearsal process. Being communicative, firm, organized, and demonstrating a sense of humor while explaining any rehearsal rules and schedules, and answering questions directly will go a long way throughout the rehearsal process.

After the first rehearsal, management and design staff go their separate ways. As rehearsals proceed in the ensuing weeks the stage manager will record all the blocking and acting notes that a director extends to each actor for building a character. Such information will become important after the show has opened, the director has left, and the stage manager is left in charge to maintain the show and conduct **understudy** (backup cast) rehearsals.

Additionally, the stage manager will be held accountable for recording a host of other information and overseeing multiple aspects of rehearsal. Figure 8.5 itemizes many of these tasks.

1. Rehearsal Reports
2. Scheduling:
   - Daily
   - Weekly
   - Monthly
   - Production
   - Load-In/Load-Out Materials for Rehearsal Space
   - Off-Book
   - Fittings
   - Publicity/Photo Calls
   - Orchestra
   - Techs/Dress
   - Special Events
3. Rehearsal Rules/Breaks, etc.
4. Blocking
5. Script Changes
6. Line Notes:
   - Missed Words
   - Substituted Words
   - Paraphrasing
   - TBA (In-Performance)
   - TBA (In-Performance)
   - TBA (In-Performance)
7. Timings:
   - First Read-Thru
   - Subsequent Runs
   - Techs/Dress Rehearsals
   - Crew Importance
   - Directorial Importance
   - House Management Importance
8. Track Sheets
9. Program Information
10. Care & Morale of Company
    - Discipline & Order
    - Visitor Policy
11. The Golden Rule of Theatre Production: Good/Fast/Cheap
12. SAFETY

**Figure 8.5** Stage Management Rehearsal Responsibilities

After each rehearsal the stage manager distributes a report at the end of the day. This document is exceedingly important since it apprises the production staff what was accomplished at each rehearsal, whether schedules are being met, attendance or any disciplinary problems, if any changes or modifications need be addressed in any of the technical areas, and the possibility of budget alterations. Figure 8.6 is an example of one such report distributed via email to all production personnel.

### Technical Rehearsals

You might have noticed that the above report was filed for a technical rehearsal, or the second phase of rehearsals in the cycle of **general rehearsals**, **technical rehearsals**, and **dress rehearsals**. While general rehearsals are being conducted, the construction and assemblage of all the technical elements are being completed. Stage managers with input from designers will be noting in the production book where the various cues will occur. Once the production is assembled onstage and the cast moves from rehearsal studios to the theatre, technical rehearsals can begin.

In this second phase of rehearsal the stage managers become an instrumental force—particularly in the United States, England, France, and in Western productions imported to Japan and South Korea. In alternative situations we frequently see shows run by committee. The lighting designer runs the light board, sound people run their own cues, and stagehands move scenery on their own recognizance. However, much like directors unified their concepts, the organizing and calling of cues has been consolidated into one person: the stage manager. Operationally this makes complete sense and insures that all cues and personnel operate together.

Generally, one stage manager remains backstage to oversee the actors and the running crew while the production stage manager or calling stage manager sits in the auditorium to call cues. Tables in the theatre are usually set up to accommodate scenic designers, lighting designers, sound designers, costume designers, and any host of specialty designers and production personnel. Surrounded by tech-tables consisting of computers and communication apparatus, the production stage manager fields input over a headset and issues cues to the many members of the running crew.

Figure 8.7 provides an example of the lighting cues for Tony Award-nominated lighting design for *The Humans*. During technical rehearsals the stage manager would repeatedly call each cue until the exact selection of each instrument, intensity, placement, and timing was set by lighting designer Justin Townsend and associate lighting designer Sarah Johnston.

Constant repetition of cues to set lighting and sound levels to coincide with scenic moves can be a very arduous task. Remaining calm and exhibiting the highest quality of leadership are intrinsic to a stage manager's work at this point.

### Dress Rehearsals

Once most of the cues are set, or "frozen," the actors' interaction with the technical elements are assured; and if/when the production can be run pretty much without major interruption

# The Learned Ladies

| | | | | | | |
|---|---|---|---|---|---|---|
| | | | | | | **REHEARSAL** |
| | | | | | | 33 |
| | | | | | | **DATE** |
| | | | | | | 3/06/09 |
| **REHEARSAL START** | 10:00am | 11:30am | 2:00pm | 3:35pm | 4:30pm | **ELAPSED TIME** | **LOCATION** |
| **REHEARSAL BREAK** | 11:20am | 1:00pm | 3:25pm | 4:17pm | Etc... | 10 hours | Gershwin Stage |

*PLEASE READ ENTIRE REPORT AS NOTES MAY APPLY TO MULTIPLE AREAS*  **SM: Danielle Teague-Daniels ASM: Veronica Morgenstern**

**REHEARSAL NOTES**

This rehearsal:
Tech

Run Times:
Act I to Act III: N/A
Act IV to Act V: 40 minutes

Next rehearsal:
Tech

Attendance:
Laura Tesman, Chuja Seo , Danielle Teague-Daniels, Veronica Morgenstern, Kaila Pooler, Amy Miller, Jose Aranda, Stephanie Roy, John Isgro, Fernando Betancourt, Paula De Rose, Sarah Good, Jorge Luna, Justiin Davis, Arthur Kriklivy,, Annie Sumberg, Chris Hoyt, Kaitlyn Mulligan, Emmanuel Elpenord, Rekima Cummins, Jilan Byloun, Latoya Sampson, Robert Cohen, Michael Hariston and Ed Morril

Emmanuel Elpenord overslept this morning and was 20 minutes.

**STAGE MANAGEMENT:**

Again due to an issue with the sound we broke for a 30 minute break at 5:35 – 6:05pm (we only got as far as the transition from Act I to II). When we returned we resumed, paused for intermission, to the end of the play. Michael is looking into the sound problem.

**MISCELLANEOUS:**

- Due to a problem with the sound, we took a 30 break for repairs / dinner. We proceeded forward with the run when we return from break
- Tomorrow Cast and Crew are called for 6:00pm unless otherwise noted or on their own for their personal prep. We would like to start a run at 7:00pm.

**COSTUMES:**

- Veronica will be returning the rehearsal clothing tomorrow mid-day as stated on the release forms.
- Megan, Deb said that you would like to add your middle initial to the playbill, I will added it to the list of corrections.
- We very much look forward to the actors in costume tomorrow. Is it possible Deb, for you to send me the list of wig times?

**LIGHTS/ELECTRICS:**

Thank you for the magic this evening see you again tomorrow!

**SCENERY:**

- There are a few spots on the platform (on example on the DSL edge of the platform) where it`s starting to chip from the heels of the their shoes that may be touched up.
- Ed, are we wheel chair accessible?

**PROPERTIES:**
We will need the rest of the props by tomorrow including the mini croissants.

**SOUND:**

- Thank you for the magic this evening see you again tomorrow!
- Thank you Michael for working on the sound issue.

Distribute: Robert Cohen, Tom Bullard, Kip Marsh, Rose Bonczek, Christopher Hoyt, Andrea Stumpf, Melissa Tryn, Teresa Snider-Stein, Deborah Hertzberg, Jeanette Aultz Look, Michael Hairston, Jeff Stiefel, Judylee Vivier, Marybeth Easley, Diana Bayne, Niluka Hotaling, Kevin Sheynerman

**Figure 8.6** *The Learned Ladies* Rehearsal Report

THE HELEN HAYES THEATRE
240 W 44TH STREET
NEW YORK, NY 10036

LD: JUSTIN TOWNSEND
ALD: SARAH JOHNSTON
ME: CHRISTINA SEE

THE HUMANS

**CUE SHEET**

| CUE | PAGE | PLACEMENT | DESCRIPTION | ACTION | TIME |
|---|---|---|---|---|---|
| 100 | 3 | SM CALL | PRESET | | 2 |
| 105 | 3 | SM CALL | HOUSE TO HALF | | 5 |
| 110 | 3 | SM CALL | HOUSE OUT | | 8 |
| 120 | 3 | SM CALL | LIGHTS UP - ERIK @ C UPSTAIRS; RICH IN THE KITCHEN | ERIK **UPSTAIRS** | 26.6 |
| 122 | 3 | AS LADIES ENTER UC DOOR | SLIGHT BUILD DOWNSTAIRS FOR RICH TABLE BUSINESS | SHIFT TO RICH **DOWNSTAIRS** | 15 |
| 123 | 4 | DEIRDRE FLIPS OFF SWITCH | BATHROOM LIGHTS OFF | | 0 |
| 124 | 4 | MOMO SITS | LIFTING THE SL CHAIR FOR DEIRDRE & BRIGID **UPSTAIRS** | | 15 |
| 125 | 5 | SCENE SPREADS OUT UPSTAIRS | LIFT SR **UPSTAIRS** FOR ERIK @ WINDOW | | 25 |
| 126 | 5 | ALL CROSS TO MOMO | DIM DOWN ON THE SL CHAIR; AIMEE TOP OF STAIRCASE | CROSS TO MOMO **UPSTAIRS C** | 30 |
| 128 | 7 | ERIK FLIPS ON THE SWITCH | BATHROOM LIGHT ON FOR AIMEE | | 0 |
| 128.1 | 7 | FOLLOWS | LIFT ON THE SL CHAIR **UPSTAIRS** | ERIK TO SL CHAIR **UPSTAIRS** | 20 |
| 129 | 9 | BRIGID & DEIRDRE CROSS SR | DIM DOWN ON THE SL CHAIR | BRIGID/DEIRDRE TO MOMO | 20 |
| 130 | 10 | ERIK: "....NO, I'M GOOD." | RICH DRESSES THE TABLE LIFTING **DOWNSTAIRS** | BUILD ON RICH **DOWNSTAIRS** | 1:00 |
| 132 | 11 | AIMEE TURNS OFF BATHROOM LIGHT | BATHROOM LIGHT OUT | | 0 |
| 133 | 12 | ERIK'S CROSS TO DL CHAIR | BUILD ON THE SL CHAIR; 5 @TOP OF STAIRS FOR BRIGID | **UPSTAIRS** | 20 |
| 135 | 13 | BRIGID CROSSES TO STAIRS | BUILD ON THE STAIRCASE FOR BRIGID CROSS **DOWNSTAIRS** | BRIGID GOES **DOWNSTAIRS** | 40 |
| 135.5 | 13 | AFTER BRIGID CROSSES AWAY FROM THE STAIRS | DIM DOWN THE **UPSTAIRS** SR WALLS TOP OF STAIRCASE | BRIGID CROSS SL **UPSTAIRS** | 30 |
| 136 | 15 | BRIGID CROSSES BACK TO TOP OF STAIRS | LIFT ON TOP OF STAIRS | BRIGID CROSS SR **UPSTAIRS** | 20 |
| 137 | 17 | RICH EXITING THE KITCHEN | BUILDING **UPSTAIRS** FOR THE TOAST | RICH GOES **UPSTAIRS** | 15 |
| 138 | 18 | BRIGID STARTS TO SING | LIFT AT C ON THE FAMILY SINGING | 315 LIFT ON JAYNE **UPSTAIRS** | 40 |
| 140 | 20 | BRIGID - "GOOD IDEA, LET'S MOVE THE PARTY **DOWNSTAIRS** " | LIFTING **DOWNSTAIRS** & **DOWNSTAIRS** HALLWAY | RICH GOES **DOWNSTAIRS** | 1:30 |

7/14/16

CUE SHEET

PAGE 1

**Figure 8.7** *The Humans* Lighting Cue Sheet (Credit: Used with permission of Justin Townsend, Lighting Designer and Sarah Johnston, Associate Lighting Designer)

or stoppage, then the show can enter the final phase of rehearsal: dress rehearsals. Within this phase the final touches are put on the production, and all elements should be in place to run smoothly. Under the aegis of the stage manager it then becomes a matter of repetitive drilling for the company in preparation for an audience.

## LEARN MORE: STAGE MANAGER INTERVIEW

At this point it would be a good opportunity to review what you have learned about stage management. To do so it is suggested you view an interview with British-American stage manager Alan Hall on a YouTube video that you can see by following the link on our e-resources. The video should provide you with an opportunity to hear how a stage manager functions in performance.

*"Alan Hall Interview"*

## Performances

Following technical rehearsals, shows sometimes enter a period of preview performances, depending on the level of production. Preview performances for an audience paying full price or with reduced-price tickets allows further refinement and perhaps some tinkering before an actual opening. During this period the stage manager becomes more adept at calling cues, since audience reactions such as laughter or applause directly affects the pacing.

## LEARN MORE: STAGE MANAGER CALLING CUES

An example for hearing a stage manager calling cues for the Broadway musical *Hairspray* and seeing the cues executed can be viewed on a YouTube video by following the link on our e-resources.

*"Hairspray Cues"*

Once the show opens the actors become more comfortable in their roles, and sometimes tend to add "improvements" (changes to the director's original intentions). Since the stage manager is now in charge of maintaining the production as directed, it is their responsibility to give notes to actors to get back on track, keep the production fresh, and maintain the overall technical running of the show. To do so the stage manager also supervises brushup rehearsals, understudy rehearsals, and even replacement rehearsals

## LEARN MORE: MAINTAINING A PRODUCTION

Marybeth Abel, production stage manager for the Broadway musical *Wicked*, sheds light on the stage manager's duties during the course of a run in the YouTube video that can be seen by following the link below on our e-resources.

*"Wicked Stage Management"*

### Post Production

Depending on the level of success, failure, or profitability of a show, it will close, continue to run, go out on tour, or have duplicate companies mounted in other cities nationally or around the world. In these different situations the production stage manager becomes responsible for participating in overseeing the show's closure or supervising successive productions. Much of the paperwork the stage manager compiled from pre-production through all the modifications leading up to performance becomes valuable in order to accommodate a new mounting or touring of a production. In these situations, it is possible that the production stage manager will utilize the guidance of a previously well-compiled production book to oversee the installation of the many subsequent productions.

## TECHNICAL DIRECTORS

When the title "technical director" (TD) came into fashion is also a bit murky. However, somewhere around the late 1970s and early 1980s producers and directors grew bolder with production ideas and demands. With lighting and sound designers introducing computer methodology into production concepts it seemed natural that scenery should follow suit. For years carpenters with the International Alliance of Theatrical Stage Employees **(IATSE/IA)** took the lead and oversaw much of the building and/or installation of scenery in theatres. They followed traditional construction methods, utilizing lumber and steel for the most part. In the United States IA jobs were passed down from fathers to sons; but, the increasing scenic challenges could not be met by conventional means. The IA had to either retrain their members or extend membership to those equipped to meet a new surge in production.

Major changes happened on Broadway productions around the time that *Beatlemania* took up residence at the Winter Garden Theatre (1977). For this show projection screens mounted on steel arms were required to swing out over the audience from both sides of the proscenium. A few blocks away, the 1979 musical *Sweeny Todd* imported an iron foundry from Rhode Island to Broadway's Uris Theatre (now the Gershwin) in which an entire steel bridge had to move from upstage to downstage. With these productions it became more apparent that newer technologies would become requisite. Excited by these developments, sons and daughters of IATSE members in colleges learned architectural engineering, computer systems, and architectural technology, along with others taking courses in automation, robotics, and computer-assisted graphics. Many would pursue degrees in arts and technology design. This group of newly trained personnel stepped into the shoes of their elders and became today's technical directors.

Their expanded education paved the way for *Sunset Boulevard* at the Minskoff Theatre (1994) in which an entire stage was raised overhead to reveal a bungalow beneath it, making huge demands on the actual building structure to support such an architectural feat. Following suit would be such notable productions as *Les Misérables*, *Spider-Man: Turn off the Dark*, and *The Curious Incident of the Dog in the Night-Time*.

## LEARN MORE: LARGE TECHNICAL DEMANDS

For a look at the technical complexities of the musical *King Kong*, you can preview them in the YouTube video describing the making of the King Kong puppet for the 2013 Australian production by following the link below on our e-resources.

*"King Kong"*

The coordination and consolidation of responsibility for this technical wizardry is an ever-expanding job and requires someone who constantly keeps abreast of cutting-edge developments. However, it still comes down to the Five Key Elements for technical directors as they approach their job. No matter what massive piece of scenery they have to oversee the construction of, what effect they have to achieve, or how to safely achieve the desired result, it still comes down to Who is involved, What has to be integrated into the telling of the story, Where it takes place in the production, When it occurs, and Why it occurs within the director's concept. Otherwise, a technical director has created something that unfortunately does not propel the production forward, and winds up costing an inordinate amount of money—becoming an effect for effect's sake.

Upon thinking through the Five Key Elements following discussions with the director and various designers, the technical director would initially provide a set of technical drawings for every piece of scenery. Based upon these drawings the TD would then itemize the cost of all materials that would go into the construction of each piece of scenery, as well as project labor costs for their construction, delivery, and installation. An ancillary budget projection might be the operational/labor cost for running the piece over eight performances a week, e.g. the almost 20-foot high/1-ton King Kong puppet.

## TRANSITION TEAM ASSISTANTS

This chapter began by saying that, depending on the scale of a production, a production manager and technical director could very possibly be the same person. This is often the case in community theatre, regional theatres, and, to some extent, in academic settings when onsite resources are responsible for design and construction. When productions increase in scale and send out their production needs for bids to reputable shops, there will be more of a need for a production manager responsible for the production, as well as for a technical director to represent the shop's services. A look at the *Stage Directions' Theatre Resources Directory 2016–2017* listed in **WEB RESOURCES** at the end of this chapter will provide a wide variety of such services for involvement of both production managers and technical directors. Any number of scenic construction operations provide pre-production planning and budgeting to installation and maintenance in order to bring any project to life.

Once a shop or service is engaged, the production manager, the technical director, the designers, and their assistants play an important part in monitoring the progress of construction. Into this mix figure the production stage manager as well as their assistants, keeping everyone informed of possible modifications and schedule changes. It is a matter of keeping everyone on the same page for approaching deadlines for completion, installation, and technical rehearsals.

## ASSISTANT STAGE MANAGERS

The titles production stage manager (**PSM**) and stage manager (**SM**) are very often used interchangeably in the United States. Remember this is a result of production scale, amount of responsibility, or billing. The Actors' Equity Association, however, only recognizes the titles of stage manager and assistant stage manager in their contracts. In the United Kingdom a company stage manager (**CSM**) functions in the same capacity as the United States counterpart PSM.

PSMs or SMs, and even assistant stage managers (**ASMs**) in the United States may assume similar duties, such as calling cues for a production. In the United Kingdom the calling stage manager is referred to as a deputy stage manager (**DSM**), who may have a number of assistant managers. Nevertheless, however responsibilities and duties are divided, the major objective for the team is to run a show smoothly, efficiently, and with a vigilant eye on safety. Consulting both the Actors' Equity Association and the United Kingdom's Equity websites for particular information on stage management will provide great dividends on their similarities and differences (see **WEB RESOURCES**).

## PRODUCTION ASSISTANTS

Production assistants (**PAs**) or interns are commonplace in many theatrical productions. Working in this capacity—whether providing services to management, the creative team, designers, or the transition team—can be a positive learning opportunity. Diminutively, they may sometimes be called a **gopher** in the United States or a **dogsbody** in the United Kingdom.

Some of the tasks the production assistant may be called upon to carry out include: sharpening pencils, passing out scripts at rehearsals, and spending hours at a copying machine in order to distribute schedules, rewrites of the script, or any other notifications. The PA may also be in charge of making the coffee or setting up a refreshment table. Maintaining the cleanliness of the rehearsal space and securing rehearsal props are also common duties for the PA.

How this person will perform and whether they view their menial tasks as drudgery will often reflect on their ability to be recognized for a more permanent position in the future. The eager PA should think of their position as that of an intern and try to learn as much as possible from the stage management team above them. Moreover, in a business where networking is of utmost importance, an outstanding PA will be seen as a valued member for a successful production, and possibly in a position to be hired for a future production.

## WHAT DID YOU LEARN?

1. Name the three titles for the people who comprise the transitional team.

2. What are the four phases of production? Provide a short description of each phase.

3. What are the three qualities that make a stage manager outstanding? How would you apply these same qualities to a production manager?

4. Why is communication important between members of the transition team and others in the production process? What valuable tools aid in this communication?

5. What are the three major rehearsals a production might undergo before opening? Provide a short description of what occurs in each of these rehearsals.

1) Production manager, stage manager, technical director; 2) Pre-production, rehearsals, performance, post-production; 3) Organized, responsible, leadership; 4) Primarily to insure all parties remain on schedule and make any modifications warranted, on budget, and safely. Scheduling calendars, confidential contact lists, and rehearsal reports; 5) General, technical, and dress rehearsals.

## ADDITIONAL RESOURCES

### BOOKS

*Technical*

Association of Theatrical Artists and Craftspeople, *The Entertainment Sourcebook 2007* (New York: Applause Theatre and Cinema Books), 2007.

Paul Carter, *Backstage Handbook*: *An Illustrated Almanac of Technical Information*, 3rd edn (New York: Broadway Press, 1994).

Mike Lawlor, *Careers in Technical Theater* (New York: Allworth Press), 2007.

### Production Management

Peter Dean, *Production Management: Making Shows Happen: A Practical Guide* (Marlborough, UK: Crowood Press), 2002.

Cary Gillette and Jay Sheehan, *The Production Manager's Toolkit: Successful Production Management in Theatre and Performing Arts* (New York: Routledge), 2017.

### Stage Management

Claire Cochrane, *Twentieth-Century British Theatre: Industry, Art and Empire* (Cambridge: Cambridge University Press), 2011.

Larry Fazio, *Stage Manager: The Professional Experience* (Burlington, MA: Focal Press), 2013.

Maud Gill, *See the Players* (London: Hutchinson), 1938.

Thomas A. Kelly, *The Back Stage Guide to Stage Management*, 3rd edn (New York: Back Stage Books), 2009.

Baz Kershaw (ed.), *The Cambridge History of British Theatre: Volume 3, Since 1895* (Cambridge: Cambridge University Press), 2004.

Laurie Kincman, *The Stage Manager's Toolkit: Template and Communication Techniques to Guide Your Theatre Production from First Meeting to Final Performance* (Burlington, MA: Focal Press), 2013.

Peter Lawrence, *Production Stage Management for Broadway: From Idea to Opening Night and Beyond* (Los Angeles: Quite Specific Media Ltd.), 2015.

## WEB RESOURCES

"Maude T. Howell: Mr. A.'s Shadow," Arliss Archives, https://arlissarchives.com/2015/06/10/maude-t-howell-mr-as-shadow/

*Stage Directions' Theatre Resources Directory 2016–2017*, http://trd.stage-directions.com/ ("accessed August 14, 2016").

"Stage Management Association Career Guide," www.stagemanagementassociation.co.uk/sites/default/files/files/CareerGuidefinal.pdf ("accessed September 9, 2016").

Stage Management Association, www.stagemanagementassociation.co.uk/

Stage Managers' Association, www.stagemanagers.org/

"Stage Managers Document Library," Actors' Equity Association, www.actorsequity.org/library/library.asp?cat=34 ("accessed September 9, 2016").

# Production Crews

## *Assembling the Dream*

## STAGEHANDS

It would only be a matter of time before we came full circle in our theatre narrative in order to describe the assembly of a theatre production from its respective parts. In Chapter 1 we laid out the organizational chart (Figure 0.1). Thereafter we traced a path for the development of the dream. In one sense we have been placing the cart before the horse. The allusion is that we have been rehearsing, building, and gathering all the components to arrive at a moment of realization when we will soon see the script and/or score come to life in all its manifestations. Heretofore, we have been discussing the production in the abstract.

Now we are at the point where the producer's dream is ready to take shape in a theatre. Following all the labors of management, creators, creative teams, artists, transition teams, and constructors, the stagehands, or "grips," are poised at the loading doors ready to assemble and execute the dream.

Whether in a self-contained theatre plant in which the adjacent shops and equipment inventory were included (such as the Camelot Theatre examined in Chapter 1) or any variant of a freestanding theatre throughout history, human labor has had to provide the muscle to load in and set up the production. It may seem contradictory to say "Little has changed and much has changed over the course of time." In the world of theatre much of progress is marked by technology. The fact remains that scenery, lights, sound equipment, props, costumes, and computers—as well as any additional motorization or automation enhancements—have to be physically moved into a theatre and assembled there. All this work befalls the stagehands (the generic term for all who work backstage) who individually ply their trade in the various specialties that comprise a stage crew.

In non-unionized theatre—i.e. not under the jurisdiction of the International Alliance of Stage Employees (**IATSE**) in the United States—stagehands may cross departmental lines. That is to say all hands are able to do any job. A carpenter may perform the job of an electrician, or vice versa. Within the union, however, jobs fall into distinct departments: carpenters, electricians, properties, and wardrobe. These departments include as many as twenty different crafts. Our discussion on stagehands continues with a selection of these artisans from these four departments.

## CARPENTERS

Carpenters may be designated to load in the scenic pieces and all the various crates that contain every item that will be utilized in the production. Once an item enters the theatre building, other stagehands may take responsibility for their respective departmental materials.

Scenery and lighting equipment that hangs over the stage will generally be attended to first, clearing the way for people to work on the stage floor or stage **deck**. The term deck, as we shall shortly see, is one of the many designations that have been adopted by theatre practitioners from nautical terminology. Many of the early stagehands gained entry into theatrical jobs since their work resembled previous duties on ships. Cargo and heavy crates were loaded on deck. Flying painted scenic backdrops would not be much different than hoisting sails.

Eventually the carpenters, as a team of stagehands, will be responsible for moving scenery on- or offstage during the course of technical rehearsals, previews, and performances. Scenery can be brought onto the stage deck from a number of directions, both manually and automatically. Scenic items stored below stage level can be raised to the deck via elevators. Certain hard flats or cutouts (such as walls, two-dimensional trees, arches, etc.) may be suspended on overhead steel tracks (**travelers**) and stored in the wings on either side of the stage awaiting their cue to be rolled onto the stage.

In addition to flying scenery from above, elevating it from below, or traveling it on from the wings, there are various other methods of moving scenery along the stage deck:

- Physically **carrying** or **dragging** the scenery.
- Placing the scenery on a platform (in the United States a **wagon**; in the United Kingdom a **truck**) and either manually or through automation rolling it into position.
- Similarly, a piece of scenery can be placed on a sheet of plywood (sometimes called a **pallet**) and either manually or automatically moved into position. This method becomes practical for lighter pieces of scenery. From an audience's perspective the pallet would be low profile or barely discernible. Actors would only have to lift a foot ever so slightly (without breaking stride) to step onto a pallet, whereas they would actually have to raise a foot in full view of an audience in order to step onto a wagon.

- Whole sets can be positioned onstage with the use of a **turntable**. In practical terms you might think of a turntable as variant of a large revolving stage, or revolving platter. On the same turntable, hidden upstage by the wall facing away from the audience, the stagehands can be setting up another set. The turntable can be revolved manually or automatically on cue to reveal this second set to the audience. A theatre's turntable may be a round wagon that pivots on the deck in full view of the audience, or built such that the top is level with the deck. In the latter case, the workings are hidden below a false (or secondary) stage built on top of the permanent stage.

- Finally, a **slip stage** can be employed to bring an entire set onstage from the wings or from upstage in various directions. In essence a slip stage is a large wagon of varying size. Sometimes they can be as wide as the proscenium opening. Because its top is flush with the performance deck the apparatus for moving them on and offstage is below a false deck, much like the turntable above. When wheeled on from the wings one slip stage can displace another to the opposite wing. Cleverly, three slip stages can be placed on the same track, with two meeting to fill the proscenium space. The third slip stage that is in one of the offstage wings can be reset with an additional set. Constantly sliding slip stages on- and offstage can make for numerous set changes throughout a performance.

## LEARN MORE: SLIP STAGES

A visual reference for employing different slip stages can be found by following the link below on our e-resources.

*"Slip Stages"*

### FLYPERSONS

Certain carpenters are designated riggers or flypersons. They outfit or balance—using a series of pulleys, counterweights, ropes, and braking mechanisms—an entire system that extends from below the stage to an overhead iron grid for rigging the system. Their work enables equipment to fly in and out so scenery and lighting move smoothly and on cue. Figure 9.1 shows a floor view of the fly rail system and a close-up view of line-sets where a flyperson would pull ropes to operate such a system.

The steel handles on the locking rail have replaced the wooden pegs or pins used in earlier theatres. These pins were similar to the pegs where shipmen tied off the ropes that hoisted the sails. Also, see if you can locate the spiral staircase in the floor view that leads to the overhead grid depicted in Figure 9.1. Notice that the overhead grid includes two pipes of lighting equipment, as well as the cloth borders that hide this equipment from the audience.

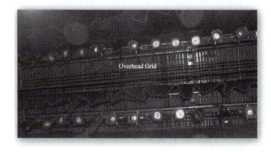

**Figure 9.1** Various components of Rigging or Fly Systems (Credit: All photos © Robert I. Sutherland-Cohen)

Once, all the scenery has been fully assembled and flying pieces are completely hung, the head carpenter and head flyperson are presented with track sheets for all moving and flying scenery. The various entries on all these sheets adhere to the Five Key Elements.

As you look at Figure 9.2, which includes three rail cues (RQ3–RQ5) for a production of the opera *Capulets and Montagues*, see if you can determine which entries represent each of the Five Key Elements. As an additional point of information, rail cues are generally signaled to the flypersons with colored lightbulbs placed near the fly floor. In our case, **RED** and **BLUE** lights are indicated. When a light is turned on by the calling stage manager, the flypersons are signaled to be in a warning mode. When a colored light goes off then the flyperson must execute the cue.

| RAIL CUES | | | CAPULETS MONTAGUES 2001 | | | revised 8/20/01 |
|---|---|---|---|---|---|---|
| CUE # | | LINE SET | PIECE | SPEED | ↓ ↑ | TRIM |
| | | | | | | |
| | | | **SCENE SHIFT TO I-3:** | | | |
| **RQ 3** | | 26 | CLARENDON COLUMN    **6 ft.** | very slow | ↑ | |
| 50/4/3 | | 42 | CLARENDON COL FLAT    2" | very slow | ↑ | "float" |
| **26:30mins** | | | | | | |
| **RED** | | | | | | |
| | | | | | | |
| | | | | | | |
| | | | | | | |
| **RQ 4** | | 14 | SL CURTAIN FLAT | medium | ↓ | |
| 51/1/1 | | | | | ↓ | |
| **26:45mins** | | | | | | |
| **BLUE** | | | **autofollow with:** | | | |
| | | 26 | CLARENDON COLUMN | very slow | ↓ | |
| | | 42 | CLARENDON COLUMN FLAT | very slow | ↓ | |
| | | | | | | |
| | | | | | | |
| | | | | | | |
| | | | | | | |
| **RQ 5** | | 24 | DESK LAMP | med/fast | ↓ | |
| 51/1/5 | | | | | ↓ | |
| **26:55mins** | | | | | | |
| **2ND RED** | | | | | | |
| | | | | | | |
| | | | | | | |
| | | | | | | |
| | | | | | | |

Page 3

**Figure 9.2** Rail Cues

Although they may wear headsets, often taking their cues from a head flyperson or from cue lights, flypersons work best when they have memorized their cue sheets. This enables them to be hands-free, without fear of being encumbered by headsets.

Additionally, since our representative cue sheet is for an opera, there are a number of references to the music score, minutes, and colors under each RQ in the Cue # column. What do you think these mean?

## LEARN MORE: STAGEHANDS RESEMBLING SHIPS' CREWS

Overall, you might have begun to develop a better picture of how functioning stagehands resemble the aforementioned ships' crews. For a quaint look at theatrical operations in 1960s' Washington, D.C., see the YouTube video on our e-resources, that provides a historical perspective.

*"Stagehands"*

Although hemp and cloth drops still exist in many theatres, much has been replaced by steel cables, solid scenery, and computer-operated flying and scenic moving systems on Broadway and in the West End. Although certain jobs may appear obsolete and made new by technology, the human element is still very much present. Stagehands will continue to make productions run smoothly under the guidance and cueing of stage managers throughout technical rehearsals and performances.

## PROPERTIES (PROP) PERSONS

The properties crew are very often grouped under stagehands, since much of their work is on a stage deck and integral to the scenic elements. However, in many instances they are a department unto their selves.

During load-ins and scenic setups, they are active participants in dressing the set, organizing offstage prop storage areas, and arranging quick-change areas for the wardrobe crew. Their offstage duties extend to preparing and furnishing all dressing rooms for performers in accordance with the stage manager's assignments.

In preparation for technical rehearsals prop persons will assist in the setup of tech tables, as well as provide chairs, music stands, and lights for musicians (whether in a pit or onstage). Similarly, the props crew provide the needs for the orchestra and performers' **sitzprobe** (a German term applied to the first rehearsal in which the singers and orchestra sit in order to explore the score together). Such a rehearsal might happen in a space away from the stage.

Onstage and offstage cleanliness as it relates to the production is a large part of the prop department's duties. Prop persons are responsible for sweeping, mopping, and vacuuming the stage continually throughout the setup process and prior to every rehearsal and/or performance. The IATSE contract has included a provision for a mopping hour prior to the half hour when the rest of the crew is due in the theatre. Additional responsibilities might include repairing broken auditorium seats, minor maintenance, and maintaining the guardrails and ramps that keep the building in compliance for assisting people with disabilities.

Prior to each performance members of the prop crew would prepare any food items, blood capsules, firearms, or special effects, etc. as needed. During the running of a production the prop crew also sets and strikes (takes down) all properties during scenic shifts, as well as providing designated spaces where props can be picked up or discarded by performers making entrances or exits.

Figure 9.3a and 9.3b provide a compressed glimpse of the top-of-show activity and preset list for a New York City Opera production of *The Ballad of Baby Doe*. You should note that

NEW YORK CITY OPERA                                BALLAD OF BABY DOE 2001
PROP RUNNING SHEETS                                   DATE: 3/21/01
                                                       **REVISED: 4/18/01**

PRESET:       Stage Empty
              OPERA HOUSE preset SR on Slipstage #1
              SALOON preset offstage on SL Slipstage #2
              LEADVILLE preset in SL-4  (telescope section IN)
              HOTEL STAIRS with ESCAPES preset in SL-3

**PROPS:**

    **STAGE LEFT:**      **PRESET HOTEL DESK PROPS**
                   PIANO SET-UP Standing by (for Slipstage 1)

    **STAGE RIGHT:**      **ASHTRAY SET ON OPERA UNIT** (on Slipstage 1)
                   POUF Standing by (for Slipstage 2)

NEW YORK CITY OPERA                                BALLAD OF BABY DOE 2001
PROP RUNNING SHEETS                                   DATE: 3/21/01

**ACT ONE, SCENE 2 (Clarendon Hotel Lobby)**
Running Time: 11 minutes

14:15     LEADVILLE OFF UL and TELESCOPE IN (same time)
          SLIPSTAGE #2 ON – SR to SL (Pouf ON / Saloon OFF)

14:30     HOTEL STAIRS ON SL-3

15:00     SLIPSTAGE #1 ON – SL to SR (Opera House OFF / Piano ON)
          RQ 1 – Hotel Columns IN

          STRIKE Saloon to Slave Wagon / RESET Slipstage #2

**PROPS PRESET:   AFTER SALOON and OPERA HOUSE STRUCK**

    **STAGE LEFT:**      **ROLLTOP DESK SET-UP on Slipstage #2**  (after Saloon struck)
                   Rolltop Desk <u>SEE DIAGRAM,</u> Desk Chair, Waste Basket

    **STAGE RIGHT:**      **SOFA SET-UP on Slipstage #1** (after Opera House struck)
                   Sofa, Armchair, Rug, Small Round Table, 3-Fold Screen

NEW YORK CITY OPERA                                BALLAD OF BABY DOE 2001
PROP RUNNING SHEETS                                   DATE: 3/21/01
                                                       **REVISED: 4/18/01**

**Figures 9.3a and 9.3b** Prop Running Sheet and Hand Prop List

NEW YORK CITY OPERA
HANDPROP LIST
Date: 2/14/01
**Revised: 4/18/2001**

**OPERA: BABY DOE**
**ACT: I**
**SCENE: ALL**
Running Time: 70:00

## STAGE LEFT

| | |
|---|---|
| Pistol (non practical) | Old Miner |
| Bag of silver ore | Old Miner |
| Back pack | Old Miner |
| Check Register | Augusta |
| Aria Letter + envelope | Baby Doe |
| 5 letters without stamps | Augusta |
| Black Parasol w/ carved handle | Augusta |
| 3 Pink Chairs (Wedding) | Super Lackey |
| 1 Jardiniere | Super Lackey |
| Folding Chair for Crew Costumes in Hallway | |

### PRESET ON HAMPER FOR 1-6

| | |
|---|---|
| 2 Silver Trays | Super Lackey |
| - 1 with 6 champagne flutes | |
| - 1 with 10 champagne flutes | |
|   - filled with sparkling water | |
| 1 Empty Bottle of Champagne in white cloth | Super Lackey |
| 1 Silver Tray w/ 5 Champagne Flutes w/ sparkling water | Super Lackey |
| Champagne Flutes - 5  (filled , not on tray) | |
| Dust pan + Brush | Super Lackey |

## STAGE LEFT (continued)

### TOP OF ACT PRESET ON STAIR UNIT
Clerk's desk w/
- Register Book **(on shelf)**
- Postage Stamp Book with
        1 Loose Sticky Stamp  **(on shelf)**
- Postage Paste pot w/ brush
- Stationery
- Steel pen and inkwell  (pen in inkwell)
- Room Key on hook
- Desk Bell
- Fancy Letter Holder
- Keys, Letters, Newspapers set in various
  pigeonholes

### Act I, Sc 2 & 4 (HOTEL) for slipstage #1

| | |
|---|---|
| Piano w/ stool w/: | **Act I, Sc. 2 & 4** |
| - Piano shawl | |
| - Willow song (5 pages) | Scene 2 only |
| - Colorful Sheet Music - 3 | Scene 2 only |
| Potted Palm on stand | **Act I, Sc. 2 & 4** |

### Act I, Sc 3 (APARTMENT) for slipstage #2

| | |
|---|---|
| Rolltop Desk (lid 1/2 closed) | **Act I, Sc.3** |
| - Loose papers (messy) | |
|   - government documents | |
|   - letters | |
|   - newspaper clippings | |
| Lg brown Book with | |
| - 1 Check to Jack Sands - inserted between pages of book, sticking out bottom edge | |
| - 4-fold Note to Baby Doe | |
|   - preset under prop Lace Gloves | |
|   - Note & Gloves wrapped in tissue paper | |
| - 3 Books (on top of desk) | |
| - Large accordian ledger (on top of desk) | |
| - Brown letter holder w/ letters (on top of desk) | |
| Desk chair | **Act I, Sc.3** |
| Waste Basket (w/ filling) | **Act I, Sc.3** |

**Figures 9.3a and 9.3b** Continued

this production utilized two slip stages which the prop crew had to set up and strike for the scene change going from Act 1, Scene 1 to Act 2, Scene 2. Once again, as you look at these sheets, see if you can identify the entries that represent each of the Five Key Elements.

## ELECTRICIANS AND SOUND ENGINEERS

During the load-in process, as crates come off trucks or are rolled into the theatre, electricians and sound engineers stand ready to identify which boxes containing cables and instruments should be wheeled onto the stage for hanging first. Other containers are sent to the auditorium and front of house, nearest to positions of installation. Additional crates may also be sent to a basement or other areas for the many positions from which a computer lighting board operator may actually run the production. Working alongside electricians, sound engineers apply the same instructions for their incoming containers, certain of which containing computerized sound consoles will often be sent to the rear of the audience seating area. From there the sound operators can hear and mix the sound at balanced levels and volumes for an audience to enjoy.

Throughout the theatre there is a beehive of activity as scenic pieces, lighting equipment, and speakers are flown concurrently or simultaneously. Miles of electrical and sound cables seem to be running throughout the theatre. In order to keep track of all this equipment the lighting designer and associate lighting designers would prepare track sheets similar to Figure 9.4a and 9.4b. Guided by these sheets, a head electrician and/or master electrician would be able to instruct the crew as to where particular instruments are positioned, cabled to particular dimmers, and onward to designated computer channels, as well as which gel colors would be specified for every instrument.

In addition, electricians would install all running lights backstage, cue lights, and electrical hookups for various special effects, and also assist in the electrical portions associated with automation.

Working alongside electricians, the sound crew runs cables throughout the theatre. Their hookups would be to speakers hung in the auditorium, as well as at monitoring positions backstage and throughout dressing rooms. This network would include amplification systems, video, and means for communication. Eventually when all amplifiers, mixers, and computer consoles are integrated into the system, the sound engineer will "ring out the system." This is to make sure that all microphones and other sources are properly hooked up and appear at the correct channels at the computerized mixing boards. At this point the actual process of sound designing can begin. This would include equalization, sound balancing, setting of volumes, timings, etc. for the production.

When all electrical and sound equipment has been positioned or hung throughout the theatre, and when all manual and automated moving scenery has been assembled, technical rehearsals can begin. It is during this period that the actual lighting and sound designs are realized.

# 10 OUT OF 12

## CHANNEL HOOKUP

SOHO REP.
46 WALKER STREET
NEW YORK, NY 10013

LD: JUSTIN TOWNSEND
ALD: SARAH JOHNSTON
ME: TIM PARRISH

| Channel | Dm | Position | U# | Purpose | Inst Type & Access & Watt | Color |
|---|---|---|---|---|---|---|
| **(1)** | 18 | HR TAIL DOWN 1 | 3 | LOW FRONT L | ETC S4 36°+12" SIDE ARM+ SHORT HAT 575w | L202+R119 |
| **(2)** | 19 | HR TAIL DOWN 2 | 3 | LOW FRONT L | ETC S4 50°+12" SIDE ARM+ SHORT HAT 575w | L202+R119 |
| **(3)** | 60 | HL TAIL DOWN 1 | 3 | LOW FRONT R | ETC S4 36°+12" SIDE ARM+ SHORT HAT 575w | L202+R119 |
| **(4)** | 68 | HL TAIL DOWN 2 | 3 | LOW FRONT R | ETC S4 50°+12" SIDE ARM+ SHORT HAT 575w | L202+R119 |
| **(5)** | 1 | HR TAIL DOWN 1 | 2 | SHAPES L | ETC S4 26°+12" SIDE ARM+TOP HAT 575w | L202+R119 |
| **(6)** | 9 | HR TAIL DOWN 2 | 2 | SHAPES L | ETC S4 26°+12" SIDE ARM+TOP HAT 575w | L202+R119 |
| **(7)** | 61 | HL TAIL DOWN 2 | 2 | SHAPES R | ETC S4 26°+12" SIDE ARM+TOP HAT 575w | L202+R119 |
| **(8)** | 53 | HL TAIL DOWN 1 | 2 | SHAPES R | ETC S4 26°+12" SIDE ARM+TOP HAT 575w | L202+R119 |
| **(11)** | 10 | HR TAIL DOWN 1 | 3a | COLOR FILL L | ETC S4 36°+12" SIDE ARM+ SHORT HAT 575w | R119 |
|  |  | " | 3a.1 | " | WYBRON CXI SCROLLER 6 1/4" |  |
| **(12)** | 2 | HR TAIL DOWN 1 | 1 | COLOR FILL L | ETC S4 26°+12" SIDE ARM+TOP HAT 575w | R119 |
|  |  | " | 1.1 | " | WYBRON CXI SCROLLER 6 1/4" |  |
| **(13)** | 17 | 4A PIPE | 0a | COLOR FILL L | ETC S4 19°+12" SIDE ARM+TOP HAT 575w | R119 |
|  |  | " | 0a.1 | " | WYBRON CXI SCROLLER 6 1/4" |  |
| **(16)** | 54 | HL TAIL DOWN 2 | 1 | COLOR FILL R | ETC S4 36°+12" SIDE ARM+ SHORT HAT 575w | R119 |
|  |  | " | 1.1 | " | WYBRON CXI SCROLLER 6 1/4" |  |
| **(17)** | 69 | HL TAIL DOWN 1 | 1 | COLOR FILL R | ETC S4 26°+12" SIDE ARM+TOP HAT 575w | R119 |
|  |  | " | 1.1 | " | WYBRON CXI SCROLLER 6 1/4" |  |

Sarah Johnston / Lightwright 5

(1) thru (17)

**Figures 9.4a and 9.4b** *10 Out of 12* Channel Hookup and *Mother Courage* Instrument Schedule (Credit: Used with permission of Justin Townsend, Lighting Designer and Sarah Johnston, Associate Lighting Designer)

# INSTRUMENT SCHEDULE

CLASSIC STAGE COMPANY
136 E 13TH STREET
NEW YORK, NY 10003

LD: JUSTIN TOWNSEND
ALD: SARAH JOHNSTON
ME: DAVE POLATO

## 1 PIPE

| U# | Purpose | Inst Type & Access & Watt | Ckt | C# | Color | Gobo | Gsiz | Dim | Chan |
|---|---|---|---|---|---|---|---|---|---|
| 1 | HOUSE LIGHTS | ETC PARNEL 550w | B | 5a | R104+ R104 | | | 36a | (602) |
| 2 | HOUSE LIGHTS | ETC PARNEL 550w | B | 5a | R104+ R104 | | | 36a | (602) |

## 2 PIPE

| U# | Purpose | Inst Type & Access & Watt | Ckt | C# | Color | Gobo | Gsiz | Dim | Chan |
|---|---|---|---|---|---|---|---|---|---|
| 1 | FRONTS | ETC S4 26°+TOP HAT 550w | C | 5b | R119 | | | 30b | (101) |
| 2 | FRONTS COOL | ETC S4 19°+TOP HAT 550w | C | 4a | L201 | | | 45a | (225) |
| 3 | FRONTS | ETC S4 26°+TOP HAT 550w | C | 4b | R119 | | | 45b | (102) |
| 4 | FRONTS COOL | ETC S4 19°+TOP HAT 550w | C | 3a | L201 | | | 37a | (226) |
| 5 | CENTER AISLE | ETC S4 50° 550w | C | 3b | | | | 37b | (507) |
| 6 | FRONTS | ETC S4 26°+TOP HAT 550w | B | 3b | R119 | | | 43b | (103) |
| 7 | FRONTS COOL | ETC S4 19°+TOP HAT 550w | B | 3a | L201 | | | 43a | (227) |
| 8 | FRONTS | ETC S4 26°+TOP HAT 550w | B | 4b | R119 | | | 28b | (104) |
| 9 | FRONTS COOL | ETC S4 19°+TOP HAT 550w | B | 4a | L201 | | | 28a | (228) |
| 10 | FRONTS | ETC S4 26°+TOP HAT 550w | B | 5b | R119 | | | 36b | (105) |

**Figures 9.4a and 9.4b** Continued

The process of loading in and assembling the elements of scenery, properties, electrics, sound, and costumes requires the production manager, the technical director, stage managers, and the various crew departmental heads to carefully schedule and carry out the entire operation in almost military fashion. Depending upon the scale of a production, the whole progression might take days or even months. Getting it right and safely executed is in the best interest of all members of a production.

## FOLLOWSPOT OPERATORS

Followspot (or spotlight) operators manually operate a specialized lighting instrument to track actors in a beam of light moving around the stage. Refinement of their cues occurs during technical rehearsals, as noted above.

Similarly, productions might include special effects (SFX) that require specialized operators. These could possibly include projectionists, laser operators, aerialists, pyrotechnicians, etc. Each of these technicians would be guided by their own track sheets and would iron out any kinks in their respective operations. As operators they may execute cues on their own recognizance; i.e. the stage manager may not call cues directly to them through a headset. The reason is that with a headset they might not be as hands-free to operate their equipment efficiently and safely.

Sound engineers and followspot operators are two such examples who follow this technique. For a sound operator, hearing clearly and distinctly out of both ears is essential. A headset could hamper efficiency, so instead they may memorize their cue sheets. Should a sound cue need to be executed in conjunction with a lighting cue or scenic move for instance, the engineer could be cued with a light similar to flypersons backstage.

Since followspot operators need to focus on stage movement, they will memorize their cue sheets and generally execute their cues upon command of a head flyperson speaking to them through headsets. Figure 9.4c is one such example of a cue sheet that a followspot operator would memorize. See if you can isolate the Five Key Elements on this sheet.

# COSTUME DEPARTMENT

While stagehands and electricians are tending to the scenic and electrical elements, the members of the costume department or wardrobe crew are busy setting up their shop(s) backstage, in dressing rooms, and determining quick-change logistics. Organizing all the costumes, in addition to any masks, wigs, hats, shoes, makeup, and accessories—and many other costume elements that are delivered to the theatre by the assistant designers (as depicted in Figure 7.2)—requires painstaking detail on the part of the crew.

Imagine how much time you might spend organizing apparel in your own bureau, drawers, and closets so that you can easily access any items when you need them. Then think of all the

# AMERICAN PSYCHO
FOLLOWSPOT CUE SHEET

LD: JUSTIN TOWNSEND
ALD: JOEL SHIER
ALD: SARAH JOHNSTON

**SPOT 3** | **SPOT 2** | **SPOT 1**

## 12.2 REQUIEM - CLEAN REPRISE

**LQ VIS**

| SPOT 3 | SPOT 2 | SPOT 1 |
|---|---|---|
| OFF | Fade Out 0% — PATRICK BATEMAN — 1+2 / HB / 3s — CC — VIS - HE GOES DOWN THE TRAP | OFF |

## 14.1 "DON'T YOU WANT ME"

| SPOT 3 | SPOT 2 | SPOT 1 | LQ |
|---|---|---|---|
| OFF | OFF | Bump Up 50% — PAUL OWEN — 1+2 / Head / 0s — UC — "YOU WERE WORKING...." | 1 |
| Bump Up 50% — LUIS CARRUTHERS — 1+2 / Head / 0s — SR — ANTICIPATE LUIS SINGING | OFF | Fade Out 0% — PAUL OWEN — 1+2 / Head / 1s — UC — ANTICIPATE LUIS SINGING | 2 |
| Fade Out 0% — LUIS CARRUTHERS — 1+2 / Head / 1s — SR — ANTICIPATE SEAN SINGING | Bump Up 50% — SEAN BATEMAN — 1+2 / Head / 0s — SL — ANTICIPATE SEAN SINGING | OFF | 3 |
| OFF | Fade Out 0% — SEAN BATEMAN — 1+2 / Head / 1s — SL — ANTICIPATE PAUL SINGING | Bump Up 50% — PAUL OWEN — 1+2 / Head / 0s — UC — ANTICIPATE PAUL SINGING | 4 |
| OFF | Fade Up 50% — PATRICK BATEMAN — 1+2 / Head / 2s — CC — ANTICIPATE THE CHORUS "DON'T YOU.." | | 5 |
| Pick Up 50% — DETECTIVE KIMBALL — 1+2 / H&S / 3s — DR — WHEN PATRICK NOTICES KIMBALL | OFF | Fade Out 0% — PAUL OWEN — 1+2 / Head / 2s — VIS - AS HE PASSES PATRICK (VIS) | 5.1 |
| | | OFF | 6 |

Figure 9.4C *American Psycho* Followspot Cue Sheet (Credit: Used with permission of Justin Townsend, Lighting Designer and Sarah Johnston, Associate Lighting Designer)

spaces in the backstage area of a theatre, with its many rooms or cubicles. A similar task has to be considered by a wardrobe department head on how to accommodate outfitting a small cast or the many members of a large musical. There has to be room for repairing and laundering costumes, and for donning wigs, and equitable dressing-room space for all performers. In addition, consideration has to be given to the traffic patterns and optimal locations for the numerous quick changes that might take place in the wings during a fast-paced musical or a complex play.

Utilizing a scene breakdown prepared in collaboration with the stage manager, the head of the wardrobe department would create a master template composed of the <u>Five Key Elements</u> in order to track the costume requirements for each cast member. The template would list the cast member, costume elements for each of their character(s), when changes occur in the course of performance, where (side of stage, quick-change booth, vista backstage, or even in a dressing room), and which **dresser** has to assist a performer. Where timing is a matter of essence, each change has to be rehearsed down to the order in which garment portion of the costume has to be removed and replaced. Actors often have to be underdressed (i.e. wearing one costume under another) so that the quick change really can take place rapidly. The scene backstage to a casual observer can be seen as organized chaos. However, when a flurry of performers enters a quick-change booth in an orderly fashion, execute their changes, and exit in similar fashion, activity occurs in drill precision, similar to a pit stop at a major auto race.

---

### LEARN MORE: BACKSTAGE AT THE LION KING

For a glimpse of the quick-change bunker, wig room, makeup room, various dressing rooms, and other backstage rooms, take a YouTube tour of *The Lion King* with Kissy Overall that you can find by following the link on our e-resources.

*"The Lion King"*

---

The world of the dresser is not only one of quick snaps, zippers, Velcro, and emergency repairs. Since they work in such close proximity with actors, they are also there to lend a soothing hand or offer a cajoling word or a soothing lozenge, and often provide a sympathetic ear to many an actor's life problems.

## THE DREAM ASSEMBLED

By now you should be close to a fully formed understanding of the many people it takes to assemble any type of production and bring the dream to fruition. This chapter has presented a number of backstage personnel. Perhaps you know of many more.

## LEARN MORE: STAGEHANDS AT WORK

*Sing Faster: The Stagehands' Ring Cycle* is a behind-the-scenes spirited and sometimes comical look at the San Francisco Opera company's production of Richard Wagner's *Ring Cycle: Das Rheingold, Die Walküre, Siegfried*, and *Götterdämmerung*. Viewing all six video segments by following the link on our e-resources will enrich your understanding and appreciation for the stagehands' and stage managers' participation in putting together such a production.

*"Sing Faster"*

Beginning with YouTube segment 1 of 6 in the "Sing Faster" video above, take note of the different skills and concerns that the stagehands have to call upon in order to perform their jobs throughout the course of the condensed one-hour video version of the 17-hour production. As you watch the video, make a list of the different types of backstage personnel (not the performers) that you encounter during the production. Also note how stagehands relax between cues. What other jobs do you think might bear similarities to the stagehands' work?

Your notes on the video may be entered on a chart such as Figure 9.5, which itemizes the different backstage job positions that were portrayed in the various videos. Also, note some of the different functions performed by each of these positions that were demonstrated in the six videos.

The early task of "rolling a wall unit into place" performed by the grips is the first demonstration of that functioning position. Your job is to come up with more functions as well as the many other positions, and demonstrations of the tasks involved. **In essence you are creating your own study guide for the various backstage positions and how they function in putting together any production.**

SCORE YOURSELF ON HOW MANY DIFFERENT JOBS YOU OBSERVED:

16 or above Reward yourself with a career in theatre

14–15 Give serious thought to working in the theatre

12–13 Perhaps you might want to volunteer for a community theatre production

12 or below Congratulations for exposing yourself to theatre production opportunities

## STAGE MANAGERS

At this point the stage management team would prepare cast and crew to move into "performance mode" (i.e. to run the show with all lines and cues executed in actual time—without stopping).

| BACKSTAGE POSITION | DEMONSTRATION OF FUNCTION |
|---|---|
| GRIPS | 1. ROLLED WALL UNITS INTO PLACE<br>2. Etc. |
|  |  |
|  |  |
|  |  |
|  |  |
|  |  |
|  |  |
|  |  |
|  |  |
|  |  |

**Figure 9.5** The Dream Assemblers: Backstage Personnel

A stage manager readies everyone with verbal calls that follow a customary protocol, such as: "½ hour, please" (the time when practically all personnel have to "sign in"—i.e. signify on a posted sheet that they are in attendance for a performance). The next call would be "15 minutes, please" (generally signaling that stage management will collect performers' valuables for safekeeping during performance). Subsequent calls would be, "5 minutes, please" and "Places, please" (a rallying call for "all hands to be on deck")—figuratively, "ready to set sail." The performance is about to begin. If there was an intermission the stage manager would repeat those 15-minute, 5-minute, and places calls as needed.

In addition to calling cues for a performance, a stage manager notates timings and acting notes regarding blocking, volume, pacing, and any deviations from the director's intentions. Also, technical mishaps or damaged scenery, burnt-out lamps or gels in need of replacement, instruments that dropped focus, costumes requiring repair, and anything else necessitating maintenance would be duly noted by the stage manager. Figure 9.8 provides a template for such a report that would be filled in and distributed following every performance. With such a report the intended parties are alerted to make corrections or repairs for the following performance.

Stage managers traditionally give notes to actors during the ½-hour preceding each performance. Additionally, during the course of a run three types of rehearsals may be called and run by a stage manager:

- **brush-up** rehearsals (to clean up pieces of business, choreography, or make vocal adjustments);
- **understudy** rehearsals (to prepare understudies to go on in case of emergencies or illness); and
- **replacement** rehearsals (to actually replace a star or another member of the cast).

Stage managers should also be aware of any behavioral issues that might arise or of illnesses, and should observe the possibility of boredom setting in during long runs, or any deviations from the director's original intention.

As captains of the ship, field generals, or leaders entrusted with the operation of a well-oiled machine, theirs is a highly responsible position. Above all else, stage managers must remain vigilant for the **safety** concerns of everyone involved in the performance, as well as those in attendance.

**As It Is In Heaven**

| DATE | |
|---|---|
| PERFORMANCE # | |
| LOCATION | |

Distribute: TBullard, RCohen, RCunningham, MHairston, DHertzberg, RKearney, MKisner, Tun-Wei Lee, SLeiter, TRust NSamarasekera, JScheffler, Hwa-Soo Son

*PLEASE READ ENTIRE REPORT AS NOTES MAY APPLY TO MULTIPLE AREAS – STAGE MANAGER:BRAD L. STRICKLER*

**NOTES:**
❏

| ACT I | | | INTER. TOTAL | | ACT II | |
|---|---|---|---|---|---|---|
| END | | | | | END | |
| TOTAL | | | | | TOTAL | |

| TOTAL RUN TIME | |
|---|---|

**WEATHER / AUDIENCE / FOH:**
❏

**ABSENT / LATE / ILL / ACCIDENT:**
❏

## T E C H N I C A L   R E P A I R S   /   N O T E S   /   S C H E D U L I N G

**SCENERY:**
❏

**COSTUMES:**
❏

**PROPERTIES:**
❏

**LIGHTS / ELECTRICS:**
❏

**SOUND:**
❏

**STAGE MANAGEMENT:**
❏

**Figure 9.6** Performance Report

# ADDITIONAL RESOURCES

## BOOKS

R.W. (Rick) Boychuk, *Nobody Looks Up: The History of the Counterweight Rigging System: 1500 to 1925* (Toronto, Ontario, Canada: Grid Well Press), 2015.

William H. Lord, *Stagecraft 1: A Complete Guide to Backstage Work*, 3rd edn (Colorado Springs: Meriwether Publishing), 2000.

Warren C. Lounsbury and Norman C. Boulanger, *Theatre Backstage from A to Z*, 4th edn (Seattle: University of Washington Press), 2000.

Monona Rossol, *The Health and Safety Guide for Film, TV and Theater*, 2nd edn (New York: Allworth Press), 2011.

Monona Rossol, *Stage Fright: Health and Safety in the Theater* (New York: Allworth Press), 1991.

## WEB RESOURCES

*IATSE 470 Stagehand Basics*, www.ia470.com/basics/stagebasics.html ("accessed September 20, 2016").

*10 Questions for a Broadway Pro: A Local 1 Stagehand Talks Props*, www.theproducersperspective.com/my_weblog/2011/01/10-questions-for-a-broadway-pro-a-local-1-stagehand-talks-props.html ("accessed September 20, 2016").

# FRONT OF HOUSE

## *Caring for the Dream*

## HOUSE MANAGEMENT

Congratulations to the production team, the performers, and you the reader who are now ready to face an opening night—or, for that matter, any performance. Not only will stage management and company management be responsible for the everyday running of a show; there is also a whole range of front-of-house (**FOH**) staff that will be attending to the audience and carrying out the behind-the-scenes care of the production, and of the building itself. This staff is headed by a **house manager** (theatre manager) or, in some cases, a facilities manager at a performing arts center. Again, it all depends upon scale—whether the production takes place in a stand-alone theatre or in a venue that is included in a larger theatre complex. The job positions that report to a house manager or an overall facilities manager are represented in Figure 10.1.

In a small theatre, whether operated by a producer or run by a house manager, one person may combine the duties of security, custodian, box office ticket seller (sometimes referred to as treasurer), usher, and maintenance individual. Ultimately, a house manager is responsible for all **creature comforts of an audience** from the moment an individual enters the lobby, purchases a ticket at the box office, attends a performance, and has a positive viewing experience, to the moment they safely depart the theatre following the show. In addition, the house manager supervises the **upkeep of the venue** and is responsible **for a production** during the entire process of load-in, running, and load-out.

House managers and company managers working on Broadway and touring productions of musicals and straight plays in the United States, Canada, and internationally must do so under the union auspices of the Association of Theatrical Press Agents and Managers

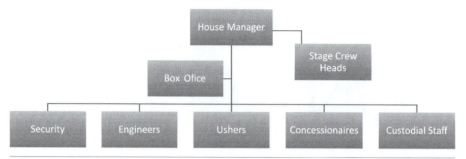

**Figure 10.1** House Management Team

(**ATPAM**). This governance was negotiated between the League of American Theater Owners and Producers (**the League**) through a Minimum Basic Agreement (**MBA**) between ATPAM and the League. ATPAM may individually negotiate agreements outside of the MBA to cover various institutional or regional facilities, such as the Washington, D.C. Kennedy Center, New York's Lincoln Center, and the Brooklyn Academy of Music, to name a few. Additionally, ATPAM has a Memorandum of Agreement (**MOA**) that was negotiated with the League and is administered jointly by IATSE and ATPAM. Under such an agreement, heads of house crews could be designated to perform duties within the theatre for which they have become resident crew heads, as we will see shortly.

## HOUSE MANAGEMENT AND THE PRODUCTION

No matter the venue, but particularly more so in union-regulated situations, the house manager acts as the facilitator and/or advisor to many city agencies that must become involved during the production process. Strict coordination of dates and times are gone over thoroughly with the production management, stage management, and technical director prior to the first load-in. This is because the house manager often has to deal with many city or state agencies and comply with plenty of legal codes before a single truck can pull up to the loading door.

Whether it is a street in the heart of midtown Manhattan's Broadway district or London's West End, or other locations, permits may have to be secured for parking and street closures. Tying up traffic is disruptive to residents and merchants in the area; therefore, prior scheduling with production management and stage management strive to keep such situations to a minimum. This keeps production load-in moving efficiently and on time.

Also, notification to the local fire department has to be considered. It is the wise production manager along with the house manager that begin this process as early as possible. Upfront opening of the doors of communication with the fire department in preparation for the required visits by the Fire Marshall (or chief) will eventually facilitate approval of any pyrotechnical aspects of the production.

Dialogue between the production manager, the house manager, and fire department can begin as early as final designs and construction plans are approved by the production manager and/or technical director. Should the fire department note the need for any foreseeable modifications in materials and/or potential fire code violations, then this would be the point to implement changes before actual construction begins.

Depending on the complexity and number of pyrotechnical effects, it might also be prudent to arrange for the Fire Marshall to witness a series of such effects under full performance conditions on a day separate from the final dress rehearsal. No matter the size of the venue, these ongoing open lines of communication with the fire department will prove beneficial to help ward off any citations on that final day of dress rehearsal when the production is run in real time, under performance conditions with the Fire Marshall present. It would follow that it would be very costly to have to postpone an opening performance should the Fire Marshall cite the production for violations on this final dress rehearsal day.

## FURTHER DISCUSSION: ADDITIONAL AGENCIES

The traffic and fire departments are only two examples of agencies that must be notified prior to load-in. Others might include:

Actors' Equity Association

Department of Buildings

Department of Education

Health and Safety

Immigration Affairs

Police Department

Department of Transportation

What duties do you think they would perform in conjunction with a production? Can you think of other agencies that might need notification?

From videos that you have viewed of stagehands loading-in and setting up productions in various venues you may have also noted that cables, production desks, steel lighting trusses, and speakers are hung throughout theatres. Any number of these items might impinge upon the integrity of a theatre's structure.

The house manager, facilities manager, or even a house engineer possibly possesses the building's plans. Such detailed drawings ultimately will reveal to a production manager and design team which locations are safest to best avoid damage to a landmarked ceiling or how not to obstruct an audience's view when hanging heavy sound and lighting equipment.

Theatre seating plans also have to be consulted. These will help determine which locations are available to the sound engineers that will minimize the permanent appropriation of seats for the installation of sound consoles, or for that matter lighting control systems.

The acquisition of such seats means less income for a production and acquiring a minimum amount, as well as optimal location, has to be worked out among all levels of management. If certain seats have to be "pulled" (removed from future sales) not only the box office, but all ticket selling agencies have to be notified not to show these seats for sale on seating charts. Additionally, obstructed views may also be duly noted and perhaps sold at lower prices to make up for this audience inconvenience.

Storage space in most theatres is always at a premium. Therefore, house management has to carefully work out with the production where empty crates and spare equipment can be safely stored or permanently removed from the premises.

Part of a house manager's preparation to accommodate a production also entails making sure that the physical venue is ready to receive the production. Outside engineers or specialty service persons may need to be brought in to ensure that all systems are in order, e.g. that **HIVAC** (air-control systems), hot and cold running water, and all electrical power systems are up to standard. In short, the house manager, acting in a supervisory capacity, must fully prepare the venue and adjacent loading areas to receive all equipment and personages in a timely and safe manner. This responsibility extends throughout the production's residency.

## HOUSE MANAGEMENT AND THE HOUSE CREW

Included in the preparation for a production's arrival the house manager would supervise the **house crew heads** (those employed by a particular venue) to carry out various maintenance duties. These heads would work alongside the **production crew heads** (those employed by the incoming production).

Again, depending on scale of a venue, the in-house duties might befall one jack-of-all trades in smaller venues, an IATSE house crew head in a Broadway theatre, or similar person in a West End Theatre who has been hired by the theatre owner. The number of permanent crew heads required at a particular union-regulated theatre varies through prior negotiation with IATSE. In some Off-Broadway houses, the requirement may only be a carpenter and/ or electrician. On Broadway the numbers go up, with a basic minimum of house crew heads counted as carpenter, electrician, properties, and flyperson.

## LEARN MORE: HIRING CREW

In order to learn more about crew-hiring practices and the required numbers, follow the link below on our e-resources.

*"Crew Hiring"*

In preparation for the load-in, house crew heads would hire any additional stagehands as needed. Carpentry would make necessary repairs to doors, ramps, and stage deck; and, along with the fly crew and electricians, strip out any drapery or lighting instruments that might be in the air. Basically, they are preparing the theatre for a "**four-wall-rental**"—i.e. the conditions that exist when a production rents a theatre, needing nothing more than an actually stripped stage devoid of all soft goods (borders, legs, traveling curtains, etc.) and electrical equipment. All that remains would be the four walls and the theatre's fly system. Thereafter, a production would bring everything required by the designers and supplied by various vendors for a particular production.

The properties crew would pull the aforementioned seats to accommodate sound and/or lighting consoles. Additionally, they would prepare dressing rooms, painting, installing counters and mirrors as needed, or obtaining any furnishings that might be specified within certain actors' contracts.

During a performance the house crew heads' duties may vary. This could easily be in reverse proportion to the actual scale of a production. In smaller venues, the fewest crew members generally would perform the most duties. On Broadway, where the crews can be quite sizable, the crew heads might mainly operate in a supervisory capacity over larger crews and just operate house lights or a house curtain prior to the performance, during the intermission, or at the conclusion of a performance. A chief duty for the properties crew is the sweeping and mopping of the stage from day one of the load-in and throughout the entire performance schedule.

In the hours when not performing show-related duties, the house crew heads are under the aegis of the house manager and may be called upon for various maintenance duties. These can range from repairing broken seats, house drapery, music stands, etc., to replacing burnt-out light bulbs. After load-out, the house crew heads reverse their load-in duties, and restore the theatre to its previous state.

House crew hours and payroll are submitted by the house manager. Various submissions for other crew members will go through the company manager as well as the house manager.

## HOUSE MANAGEMENT AND THE BOX OFFICE

On Broadway and other high-profile entertainment venues where the stakes are high and productions are budgeted in millions of dollars, box office personnel (commonly referred to as treasurers and ticket sellers) are represented by Union Local 751, IATSE in New York City. Other major cities also provide union representation for ticket sellers. With such fiduciary responsibility for handling sales and large amounts of money, they are also highly bonded against financial mismanagement in many venues.

Reportage and reconciliation of ticket sales and attendance records are entered on various statements for each performance, as well as through weekly summaries. There are any number

## LEARN MORE: TICKET SELLERS' UNION

In order to learn more about treasurers and ticket sellers, follow the link below on our e-resources.

*"751, IATSE"*

of checks and balances that theatres of all sizes institute to counter potential theft, fraud, or deception. These may include multiple signatories such as a house manager, a company manager, and a treasurer to verify a box office statement. Those theatres that utilize bar-coded tickets that are scanned by ushers upon entry help streamline this process. The accounting procedures and forms that treasurers file with company managers and producers is beyond the scope of this book, but additional material can be found in some of the books listed at the end of this chapter.

Following union guidelines, box office treasurers and assistants are scheduled by the house manager. Their hours reflect performance schedules and optimal times for the ticket-buying public making purchases. Additionally, tickets are sold on the internet through any number of ticketing agencies, outlets, and brokers.

## DISCOUNT TICKETS

TKTS Discount Booths, www.tdf.org/nyc/7TKTS-ticket-booths

TKTS: Leicester Square Ticket Booth, ww.tkts.co.uk/leicester-square

Box office personnel have little interaction with the actual production beyond selling tickets and dispensing **house seats** (those set aside for purchase by the producers, cast members, creative teams, and others directly involved in the production) or complimentary seats. However, as they are in the front line for meeting potential audience members their attitude and tone for dealing with the public could possibly reflect how an audience member is predisposed to view a performance.

## LEARN MORE: HOW NOT TO BUY TICKETS

In order to learn more about ticket buying, follow the link below on our e-resources.

*"Ticketing"*

Being among the first front-of-house staff to converse with potential audience members, box office personnel might possibly benefit the most from reading the script. Familiarizing themselves with the script's Five Key Elements could become a valuable sales tool when ticket buyers ask any number of questions concerning the play for which they are to purchase tickets. An informed enthusiasm for the play may help close a sale and possibly contribute to the buyer's eagerness for the performance.

The one major effect the box office has on a production is how efficiently and rapidly the treasurers are able to transact sales and/or ticket pickup ("will call") as the announced performance time approaches. The house manager acts as a go-between for the box office and stage management, actively communicating if there is a slowdown at the box office and to hold the curtain, or that all is going smoothly and proceed to start the show.

## HOUSE MANAGEMENT AND SECURITY

Where large numbers of people gather, tightened security assumes a larger role. Incoming audience members are routinely screened for hazardous materials and contraband that could potentially do harm. It is no longer enough to have a doorperson administer the comings and goings of performers, crew, and visitors at a backstage door. House managers along with hired security staff participate in the scheduling, coordination, and training of front line personnel. Stage managers, ushers, and doorpersons become active participants in ensuring the safety of both audience and performance personnel in times of emergencies.

Scheduled through the house manager, security personnel are generally the first to arrive at a venue and the last to leave, so that they are able to inspect the building for anything suspicious. Setting themselves up at key entry and exit points around the theatre, they are able to monitor who enters and leaves prior to, during, and following all activity that takes place on the premises.

Through house management, the security team would be able to communicate rapidly with police, fire, medical, or other responders to emergencies. An evacuation plan and the training of key personnel would have previously been put in place by the house manager. Coordinating such a plan with stage management is essential in order to publicly address both the audience and stage personnel to exit the theatre in a safe, orderly, and non-panicked fashion.

Evacuation notwithstanding, there are other situations that may involve security. Someone in the audience or backstage may require emergency medical attention. A technical mishap might occur and the show might be stopped temporarily or suspended. A fire might break out. House management, along with security, ushers, and stage management, would have to react in a fashion that is least disruptive to the performance or participate in the halting of it.

## HOUSE MANAGEMENT AND ENGINEERING

Larger theatres and entertainment venues generally employ an engineer or staff of engineers. Although they might not be directly scheduled by the house manager, their hours would be coordinated between house management and the theatre's owner. Theatre engineers employed in the United States very often belong to a local union branch under the jurisdiction of the International Union of Operating Engineers (**IUOE**).

## *LEARN MORE: OPERATING ENGINEERS*

To learn more about operating engineers, follow the link below on our e-resources.

*"IUOE"*

Once the theatre has been opened, an engineer might arrive on the scene to perform the routine of turning on air-conditioning, heating, or hot water systems. Their duties may also include checking any fire alarms and/or smoke-detectors, and dealing with any plumbing issues, electrical outages, marquee malfunctions, or other equipment that the house manager may deem as needing engineering attention.

On Broadway, all house managers and numerous operating engineers and/or crew members possess fire-guard certificates. Before each performance, the house manager has to sign a log book confirming that all fire procedures have been met prior to curtain up (beginning of the performance).

In the West End and other theatres, prior to the beginning of a performance, if a fire curtain is part of the theatre structure it must be lowered in full view of the audience. Both in the United States and the United Kingdom theatres may also be subject to a surprise visit by a member of the fire department just prior to the start of a performance in order to confirm that all regulations are being met.

Perhaps torrential overnight rain or a snow storm has occurred. Engineers might have to repair leaks or possible other damage in preparation for both the audience and all other occupants' arrival at the building.

During performances, engineers might have to monitor temperature settings due to irregularity during cold or hot spells. With productions that have many flying pieces, air flow can be problematic. Since soft goods tend to billow like sails, engineers may have to constantly adjust the intakes and outtakes on air-flow equipment in order to alleviate any fluttering during a performance.

## HOUSE MANAGEMENT AND USHERS

The front-of-house personnel that are most visible to an audience are the **ushers**. From the smallest of venues to the largest, ticket takers and ushers initially greet and direct patrons to their seats, and possibly hand out programs. In union-regulated theatres in larger cities, ticket takers and ushers generally belong to a local union under IATSE jurisdiction. On Broadway such an organization is Local 306, IATSE.

Ushers directly report to the house manager, who not only schedules their hours but also assigns them their stations in a theatre. Whether a theatre is general seating or assigned

## *LEARN MORE: TICKET TAKERS AND USHERS*

In order to learn more about ticket takers and ushers, please follow the link below on our e-resources.

*"306, IATSE"*

locations, ushers are responsible for accommodating patrons in a pleasant and timely manner in order to avoid any delays to the start of a performance. Bearing the responsibility for seating dignitaries, famous personalities, and a wide spectrum of the public requires a high level of respect among all parties. Ushers very often instruct patrons to turn off cellphones, and not to take pictures or record videos during the forthcoming performance. In case of medical emergencies, they communicate the situation to the house manager. Should evacuation be necessary, they would direct people to the nearest exit.

Their full staff generally remains on duty for the first half hour of a performance to seat late-comers with minimal disruption. Certain ushers may be assigned to distribute assisted listening devices or to oversee the seating of patrons with disabilities.

Following an intermission the staff of ushers is partially dismissed. Thereafter a skeletal crew remains for the duration of a performance. Following the performance, they are available to accept the return of assisted listening devices and guide the audience to exits.

In some theatres interested parties may serve as ushers in exchange for seats. On the surface ushering seems a simple task. However, ushers need to memorize seating plans, read the seat location for each ticket, and conduct each individual to their designated seat. However, that is not always the case.

## *LEARN MORE: USHERING*

Ushers have had many interesting encounters in their line of work and one person shares experiences in an article, "Confessions of a Broadway Usher" that may be found by following the link below on our e-resources.

*"Ushering"*

## HOUSE MANAGEMENT AND CONCESSIONAIRES

As the cost of putting on a production continues to grow daily, it is incumbent on producers to generate ancillary income. One method is to sell show-related merchandise (**concessions**). Practically every Broadway and West End theatre has an omnipresent concession stand or kiosk. Smaller theatres have also taken up the practice; even if it is a simple table selling refreshments and perhaps books or authorized script(s) by that evening's playwright. Both in the United States and in the United Kingdom lavish souvenir books studded with the actors' pictures, production photos, and interesting facts are often on sale. Branding a show's logo on mugs, t-shirts, CDs, DVDS, key chains, or refrigerator magnets, or selling books and other items related to a show are just a few of the merchandising possibilities patrons will find at a production's concession stand. Bars sometimes sell premium drinks in show-branded mugs to boost income.

Allocating space and scheduling **concessionaires** can be an additional duty for house managers. Since bars and concessions are primarily on-the-spot cash or credit enterprises, a system to prevent theft has to be in place. Reconciling sales with inventory and reporting the figures to general management goes through a series of checks and balances that mirror box office reportage in many ways. A house manager very often figures prominently in the oversight of such reportage. Additionally, a house manager can often be the center of a dissatisfied customer's dispute with a concessionaire or bartender.

## HOUSE MANAGEMENT AND CUSTODIANS

Keeping restrooms stocked with toilet tissue and paper towels, and unclogging toilets and sinks is a common responsibility for house managers, no matter the size of a theatre. If fortunate enough to be working in a larger theatre that includes a custodial staff, then a house manager can schedule, assign, and supervise the staff to perform these tasks. The astute house manager will realize that a theatregoer's experience can easily be marred by a less than sanitary restroom or an unclean theatre.

Following each performance, custodians ready the theatre by picking up lost items and litter, sweeping, vacuuming, disposing of trash, and polishing brass railings according to house manager scheduling. And, should a production have special effects that might engulf an audience in confetti, streamers, or balloons, the cleanup usually befalls the custodians. Exceptions might occur if such intrusions on the audience have to be recycled for the next performance. Then the prop crew might have to assume this responsibility.

Daily operations for custodians extend to the lobby and sidewalks outside of a theatre. Should a snow storm occur, then the crew would also be called upon to shovel and de-ice walkways. In preparation for imminent weather conditions, a house manager would monitor forecasts and adjust custodial schedules as conditions warrant.

## WHAT DID YOU LEARN?

1. What does the abbreviation FOH stand for?
2. What job position involves oversight of a theatrical venue, and which union would they need to belong to in a Broadway theatre?

3. Name the seven areas of personnel that those with oversight of the venue would supervise.

4. Explain what is meant by "house seats."

5. Which job position discussed in this chapter would derive most value in reading the script for the <u>Five Key Elements: Who, What, Where, When, Why (How)?</u> What benefit would this serve?

6. Explain a "four-wall-rental."

7. Along what three lines of responsibility would a house manager execute their duties? Explain.

---

1) Front of house; 2) House manager, ATPAM; 3) Box office, stage crew heads (house crew), security, engineers, ushers, concessionaires, custodians; 4) Those set aside for purchase by producers, cast members, creative teams, and others directly involved in the production; 5) Box office; inform potential ticket buyers; 6) The conditions that exist when a production rents a theatre, with nothing more than a stripped theatre, devoid of all soft goods and electrical equipment; 7) The physical theatre facility, audience comfort and safety, and the production.

---

## ADDITIONAL RESOURCES

### BOOKS

Suzanne Carmack Celentano and Kevin Marshall, *Theatre Management: A Successful Guide to Producing Plays on Commercial and Non-Profit Stages* (Studio City, CA: Players Press, Inc.), 1998.

David M. Conte and Stephen Langley, *Theatre Management: Producing and Managing the Performing Arts* (Hollywood, CA: Quite Specific Media Group, Ltd), 2007.

Donald C. Farber, *Producing Theatre: A Comprehensive and Legal Business Guide*, 3rd revised edn (Pompton Plains, NJ: Limelight Editions), 2006.

Richard E. Schneider and Mary Jo Ford, *The Well-Run Theatre: Forms and Systems for Daily Operations* (New York: Drama Book Publishers), 1993.

Jim Volz, *How to Run a Theater: A Witty, Practical, and Fun Guide to Arts Management*, 2nd edn (London: Bloomsbury), 2010.

Mitch Weiss and Perri Gaffney, *The Business of Broadway: An Insider's Guide to Working, Producing, and Investing in the World's Greatest Theatre Community* (New York: Allworth Press), 2015.

## WEB RESOURCES

Association of Theatrical Press Agents and Managers (ATPAM), www.atpam.com/

"Life Behind the Curtain: The Show Couldn't Go On Without Them," *Playbill*, www.playbill.com/article/life-behind-the-curtainthe-show-couldnt-go-on-without-them ("accessed September 27, 2016").

# The Performers/ Afterwords

## *Such Stuff as Dreams are Made On*

### THE PERFORMERS

Hopefully this book has provided an opportunity to peer behind the veil of creating wonderful performances with enlightening stories—the exploration of primary factors in theatre creation. Actors performing a well-constructed story occupy a central position in any theatrical organization. Surrounded by a supportive production team, this mutual collaboration can lift our spirits, enliven our dreams, and whisk us to other worlds. If the combination of story (the addition of song in a musical) and performance falls short, then no matter how astounding the production elements, an audience will not "walk out humming the scenery." Ultimately, audience applause and critical acclaim come from how well the performers and the production team deliver a story.

With many well-regarded training institutions for actors, dancers, and musicians—as well as an inexhaustible list of research materials for such performers—these subjects are beyond the limits of this book. Therefore, in bringing this book to its conclusion it is only natural to summarize how each position within Figure 0.1 serves the performers and how performers might avail themselves of each service to realize the best production.

### THE PRODUCER

Often productions are chosen around the availability of a particular actor and/or, in the case of commercial theatre, a star. Starting with the producer choosing such a performer, a close bond and working relationship could likely be formed. The combination of an agreed-upon fee and the willingness of the star to promote the production are determinants of a performer's value to a production.

The goals for the producer in choosing actor(s) are that they be the best to perform the script, receive critical acclaim for doing so, and ultimately transform the production into a success; financially or critically. Choice of a particular actor may come from a pool of friends engaged in the development of a play, through auditions or agent submissions, as well as inquiries by performers who would like to undertake a particular project. Generally speaking, stars will contact producers through their agents (intermediaries). In all events a producer will have to determine if the undertaking is worthwhile artistically or if a particular star has bankability (is able to attract potential investors), which ultimately may result in profitable gain. This is where the services of a general manager would come in if the production is of suitable scale.

## THE GENERAL MANAGER

It is one thing for an actor and/or their agent to be excited by a project, as well as to agree in principle to a role; it is another to come to contractual terms. Considering all the elements that comprise the budget, the financial package that would be allocated to a star should not jeopardize the quality represented by the other budget lines. Although it might be just a shake of a hand for a non-union theatre, when contracts are involved this business aspect involves negotiations between agents and general management.

The general manager needs to know how much money the producer has allocated for all salaries and to understand how to accommodate demands in order to balance the overall budget. Also, the general manager has complete command of the schedule and would be able to determine any potential conflicts that might arise if an actor has other commitments during the span of production. Such conflicts could be a movie shoot, a television series, the filming of a commercial, a concert appearance, etc. The actor's availability and fee requests are major determinants for hiring.

Once a fee and a clearance of dates are agreed upon in principle, then the general manager and the agent would negotiate the various **riders** (additions made without rewriting the entire contract). Riders could include provisions for a limousine service to be provided for the actor, certain dressing room accommodations, the hiring of a special assistant to the actor, etc. Since these are additional budget items that would need to be added to an actor's complete money package, negotiations for these additions can become very sensitive.

It is not an exact science to figure out how bankable one actor is over another. A producer's excitement can often be outweighed by a trustworthy general manager's opinion given all the other factors that would be feasible or necessary for a successful production. How well the producer and general manager successfully come to terms with the actor (and/or agent) and positively treat their actors can go a long way in the development for a successful production.

## THE COMPANY MANAGER

Similarly, the company manager's day-to-day treatment of an actor would have to reinforce the positive tone set by the producer and general manager. If a company manager is receptive to an actor's needs and reacts accordingly, that actor would, in all likelihood, bring positive energy to their work on a daily basis.

It is the company manager who has to follow through in satisfying all contractual riders such as arranging a limousine, providing the properties crew head with details for setting up a dressing room, fulfilling the special assistant's requests, etc.

While serving the star actor, the company manager also has to answer the needs of all the performers with reasonable equality. Such responsibilities would include: ensuring that dressing areas and stage areas are suitably climate controlled; that showers, plumbing, and sanitary issues are fixed; that guest ticketing is arranged equitably, and that all payroll questions or discrepancies are resolved fairly, as well as ensuring that all transportation and housing arrangements are thoroughly organized when the production is touring, etc. Additionally, the company manager would become involved in scheduling publicity appearances.

## THE PUBLICITY DEPARTMENT

It would follow that the publicity department would want to avail itself of every possible opportunity to publicize the production and optimize sales. However, this would have to be accomplished with coordination between the actor (and/or agent), along with stage management and publicity departments. Consideration must be made so that publicity appearances do not impinge on the actor's work or proper rest periods. Actors' Equity Association restricts differing amounts of hours through its various contracts that actors might devote to such appearances during work weeks. However, stars with drawing power tend to exempt themselves from such restrictions, and have to have their stamina and productivity carefully monitored by the company manager and stage manager. It is a delicate balance weighing the actor's obligations to provide their best performance against the need to sell tickets.

In choosing publicity appearances, the **publicist** also has to be aware of an actor's tendencies. Some actors might do well in front of a camera and be able to field questions extemporaneously when not speaking lines from a script. Others might fare better in press interviews. Still others react well in publicity stunts such as throwing out the first pitch at a baseball game, making appearances at charity events, or serving as a judge at a country fair, etc. Whatever angle a publicist could potentially involve an actor in has to be approved by the actor along with their agent so as not to tarnish the actor's reputation, but at the same time increase audience potential.

Timing for such appearances during a rehearsal period is another factor. Early on, everyone tends to be a bit more relaxed and possibly more generous with their time for publicity. Directors are inculcating everyone, including the actors with the play/musical's concept. Inherently the actors are absorbing their own Five Key Elements: Who, What, Where, When, Why (How) and using this information to address the public eager for information on the forthcoming production. Publicity demands have to be weighed against an actor's further rehearsal requirements.

## THE CREATIVE AND ARTISTIC TEAMS

The real work for the actor/performer is to build their character around all the intentions of the writer and director, as well as those of a choreographer and composer for a musical, who interpret the words, lyrics, and music of the creative team. The individual talents, skills, training, and methodology performers utilize to complete their role, as previously mentioned, are beyond scope of this book. The day-to-day relationships between these parties have to be built along the lines of mutual respect, belief in the concept, complete understanding of the goals, and extreme trust for any chance for a successful production.

With members of the creative team present in these situations there often arises the need for an actor to seek out answers regarding background, word choices, demographics, and perhaps the feeling to be evoked through song. Informative answers delivered with encouragement, tact, and clarity in response to all performers' questions become very helpful for building their characters throughout the rehearsal process. Additionally, the artistic team could offer advice to actors regarding particular questions that might arise during rehearsals concerning scenic details, lighting situations, or costume issues for instance.

As the production strides toward technical rehearsals, the situation grows more urgent. The actors are made more aware of the technical elements they will encounter; particularly scenery and, perhaps more personally, costumes. How much time and how much importance the artistic team allots during rehearsals to build an actor's familiarity and confidence with such elements becomes an integral part of building a character as well. Interacting with the creative artists during the rehearsal period helps allay many actors' fears. The performers will become comfortable facing a new scenic element, realize that they are being shown in the best light, and that they will be unencumbered by their costumes.

## THE CREATIVE ARTISTS AND ASSISTANTS

Very often with a scenery model visible in the rehearsal space an actor can relate to any number of moves that the artistic team might impose upon them. Perhaps an actor might be called upon to run up or down a flight of stairs; exit or enter rapidly through a doorway; or execute a pirouette on a raked stage, etc. With the model serving as a reference, the actor might question the scenic designer or assistants on the steepness of the stairs; or whether an additional railing could be added; or perhaps the swing of the door be moved to the opposite side; or to clarify the composition of the stage surface for safety reasons, etc. Addressing such concerns with an actor during rehearsals will save a lot of angst, time, and money prior to actually taking the stage.

Similarly, actors may be most concerned with how they look and move in costume. Therefore, their relationship with the costume designers and/or assistants can often be the most delicate of all the designers. Also important, though, is how an actor will relate to the set in character: will their costume allow them this same ease of relationship? Tackling stairs or a raked stage wearing a hooped skirt and high heels is very different than doing the same in

| ACTOR CONCERNS | CREATIVE ARTIST |
|---|---|
| The script calls for me to eat a peanut butter sandwich. How will I be able to speak my lines if the peanut butter sticks to the roof of my mouth? | Prop designer |
| | |
| | |
| | |
| | |
| | |
| | |
| | |
| | |
| | |
| | |
| | |

**Figure 11.1** Actor/Creative Artist Concerns

a straight skirt and flat shoes. Or, how would a mask or wig hamper facial or head gestures? With a costume designer or assistant attending rehearsals on occasion a large measure of adjustments could be made to a costume well ahead of technical rehearsals.

These are only a few examples of actor/creative artist concerns that might be shared during rehearsals. Can you include examples of other such concerns that might arise in a rehearsal situation between actors and any number of creative artists on the chart in Figure 11.1? While a creative artist could address an actor's concerns on the spot, a stage manager who is present at all rehearsals is the communicating link to all production members.

## THE STAGE MANAGEMENT TEAM

Whereas a company manager is beholden to the actors for all concerns business related and is said to be responsible for matters "in front of the curtain," the stage manager is responsible for all matters of the production "behind the curtain." From the moment an actor reports for rehearsals, many of their actions are noted by the stage manager. Whether it is recording attendance incidents, scheduling (rehearsals, public appearances, fittings), blocking notations, deviations from the director's intentions, assigning dressing rooms, transmitting an actor's concerns to company management or designers, and all-around support for an actor's efforts, the stage manager is the front-line, go-to person for an actor. How well a stage manager executes those duties that affect an actor and how receptive the stage manager is to an actor's concerns go a long way toward peace and harmony throughout the entire production process. Displays of humor, tact, and positive reinforcement for an actor's work makes for a pleasant work situation. Likewise, a stage manager's respect and treatment of an actor carries over to how a crew reacts to actors.

## THE PRODUCTION CREW

Although an actor may not come in contact with all members of a large production crew, there are a few interactions that can bear considerable weight on the attitude of the entire crew. How the actors react to lighting designers during technical rehearsals when requested to repeat movements and stand where expected is observed by all crew members. The actor who does so with a gracious and obliging attitude is easily recognized as one who supports the technical efforts of the crew.

Actors most commonly come in contact with dressers, properties personnel, and, to some extent, those moving scenery on the deck. Cordial exchanges among them all makes for a smoother production. How the actor treats their costumes, utilizes and disposes of props as requested, and offers "thank yous" to every stagehand who assists throughout the course of a production truly demonstrates that sincere collaboration is the desired norm for every production.

## FRONT-OF-HOUSE PERSONNEL

Although seldom in contact with actors, the front-of-house personnel can really make a difference in the treatment of actors' guests as well as other attendees. Depending on a theatre's layout, actors come to work entering through the auditorium or through a backstage entry, and thus interact with FOH staff.

It should be very easy for an actor entering through the auditorium to greet any personnel present with a cheery "Hello." This could extend to the box office staff, the house manager, the ushers, and other support personnel. All FOH staff wishes a positive theatregoing experience for the audience, and congenial support from the actors always enhances the experience. Pleasant exchanges between actors and FOH posits a willingness to please any of the actors' guests.

Likewise, an actor's pleasantries toward a backstage doorperson practically insures favorable service throughout the run, for it is the doorperson who receives and distributes letters, packages, flowers, and gifts that have been sent backstage. Additionally, the doorperson greets guests and is the gatekeeper for who gets backstage. These courtesies are all part of theatrical cooperation.

# AFTERWORDS

Addressing <u>collaboration</u> and closing on a note of <u>cooperation</u>, this book concludes its presentation of crucial relationships among production team members. As a further stimulus for assimilating the theatrical concepts, new terminology, and additional research you have brought to your studies, Figure 11.2 offers a challenging review of some of the key points covered in this book. If the answers prove elusive at first, seek them out in the book before turning to the answers in Figure 11.3 at the end of this chapter.

Upon completion of the crossword puzzle, unscramble the nine letters in the blocks containing stars to spell out a good-luck phrase frequently offered before performances:

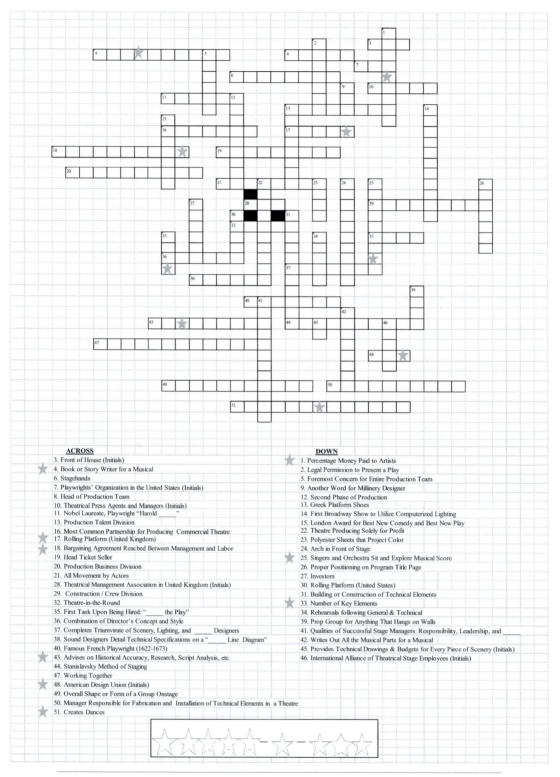

**ACROSS**

3. Front of House (Initials)
4. Book or Story Writer for a Musical
6. Stagehands
7. Playwrights' Organization in the United States (Initials)
8. Head of Production Team
10. Theatrical Press Agents and Managers (Initials)
11. Nobel Laureate, Playwright "Harold ____"
13. Production Talent Division
16. Most Common Partnership for Producing Commercial Theatre
17. Rolling Platform (United Kingdom)
18. Bargaining Agreement Reached Between Management and Labor
19. Head Ticket Seller
20. Production Business Division
21. All Movement by Actors
28. Theatrical Management Association in United Kingdom (Initials)
29. Construction / Crew Division
32. Theatre-in-the-Round
35. First Task Upon Being Hired: "____ the Play"
36. Combination of Director's Concept and Style
37. Completes Triumvirate of Scenery, Lighting, and ____ Designers
38. Sound Designers Detail Technical Specifications on a "____ Line Diagram"
40. Famous French Playwright (1622-1673)
43. Advises on Historical Accuracy, Research, Script Analysis, etc.
44. Stanislavsky Method of Staging
47. Working Together
48. American Design Union (Initials)
49. Overall Shape or Form of a Group Onstage
50. Manager Responsible for Fabrication and Installation of Technical Elements in a Theatre
51. Creates Dances

**DOWN**

1. Percentage Money Paid to Artists
2. Legal Permission to Present a Play
5. Foremost Concern for Entire Production Team
9. Another Word for Millinery Designer
12. Second Phase of Production
13. Greek Platform Shoes
14. First Broadway Show to Utilize Computerized Lighting
15. London Award for Best New Comedy and Best New Play
22. Theatre Producing Solely for Profit
23. Polyester Sheets that Project Color
24. Arch in Front of Stage
25. Singers and Orchestra Sit and Explore Musical Score
26. Proper Positioning on Program Title Page
27. Investors
30. Rolling Platform (United States)
31. Building or Construction of Technical Elements
33. Number of Key Elements
34. Rehearsals following General & Technical
39. Prop Group for Anything That Hangs on Walls
41. Qualities of Successful Stage Managers: Responsibility, Leadership, and ____
42. Writes Out All the Musical Parts for a Musical
45. Provides Technical Drawings & Budgets for Every Piece of Scenery (Initials)
46. International Alliance of Theatrical Stage Employees (Initials)

**Figure 11.2** Theatre Production Crossword Puzzle

# WHAT DID YOU LEARN?

Congratulations on the knowledge that you have gained from reading this book. It is now time to attend a theatrical performance of a play or musical. There is no substitute for live theatre. It can move you to tears. Provide you with joyous laughter. Lift your spirits. Enlighten you beyond belief. Entertain like no other art form!

So stick around until the last musical note is sounded and/or the final applause has subsided. Take a few moments to gather your thoughts. Now is the opportunity to apply your own critical eye to what you have just witnessed.

1. Ask yourself, did the production successfully meet or not meet the demands of the <u>Five Key Elements: Who, What, Where, When, Why (How)</u> in its portrayal of the story? Explain.

2. Did the three divisions of production—management team, creative team, technical team—properly execute their contributions to the performance? Explain based upon what you have just witnessed with reasoning that you have learned from this book.

   a. Management Team?

   b. Creative Team?

   c. Technical Team?

3. Examine the production you have attended through the lens of the axiom that weighs the benefits of the outcome being good, fast, or cheap. Upon reviewing the axiom, you will realize that only two out of the three options are possible. It is impossible to obtain all three outcomes at the same time. Which of the two outcomes do you think were achieved in the production you witnessed? Explain.

4. What elements of the production would you have liked to see added or subtracted? How would your choices have improved its success or lack of success? Explain.

5. How did the front-of-house staff contribute to or detract from your enjoyment of the production?

6. Were you stimulated to attend future performances following the production you just witnessed, knowing what you now know from reading this book? Explain.

7. Do you consider yourself a business person, someone who is talented or in possession of technical skills? Explain your reasoning.

8. Is there any particular production position you might consider pursuing? Explain.

9. What courses would you study in your pursuit of such a position?

10. Upon further reflection, what other information would you have added to this book that would have enriched your understanding of the production you witnessed?

# ADDITIONAL RESOURCES

## BOOKS

### Acting

Richard Boleslavsky, *Acting: The First Six Lessons* (New York: Routledge), 1933, 2005.

Uta Hagan, *Respect for Acting* (Hoboken, NJ: Wiley), 1973, 2008.

Sanford Meisner, *Sanford Meisner on Acting* (New York: Random House), 1987.

Viola Spolin, *Improvisation for the Theater*, 3rd edn (Evanston, IL: Northwestern University Press), 1999.

Constantin Stanislavski, *An Actor Prepares* (New York: Routledge), 1936, 2003.

### Dance

Kara Anne Gardner, *Agnes de Mille: Telling Stories in Broadway Dance* (New York: Oxford University Press), 2016.

Tina Paul, *So You Want to Dance on Broadway?* (Boston, MA: Heinemann), 2003.

### Music

Aaron Frankel, *Writing the Broadway Musical* (New York: Da Capo Press), 2009.

Joseph P. Swain, *The Broadway Musical: A Critical and Musical Survey*. 2nd edn (Lanham, MD: Scarecrow Press), 2002.

### General

John Caird, *Theatre Craft: A Director's Practical Companion from A to Z* (New York: Farrar, Straus & Giroux), 2010.

Gill Foreman, *A Practical Guide to Working in Theatre* (London: Bloomsbury), 2009.

GIZ GmbH (ed.), *Cooperation Management for Practitioners: Managing Social Change with Capacity WORKS* (Wiesbaden, Germany: Springer Gabler), 2015.

## WEB RESOURCES

*Playwrights Welcome* (offers tickets to professional playwrights across the United States on the day of a performance, free of charge), www.samuelfrench.com/playwrightswelcome

*Who Works in a Theatre?* www.theatrestrust.org.uk/resources/exploring-theatres/who-works-in-a-theatre

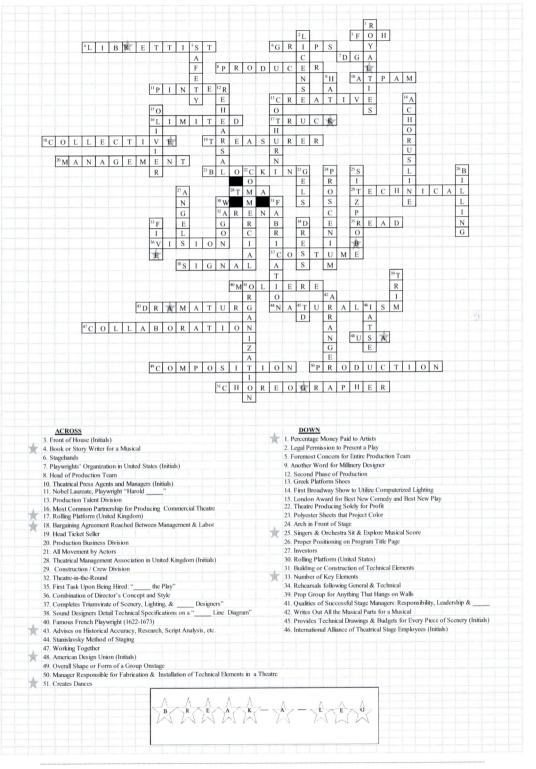

**ACROSS**

3. Front of House (Initials)
4. Book or Story Writer for a Musical
6. Stagehands
7. Playwrights' Organization in United States (Initials)
8. Head of Production Team
10. Theatrical Press Agents and Managers (Initials)
11. Nobel Laureate, Playwright "Harold _____"
13. Production Talent Division
16. Most Common Partnership for Producing Commercial Theatre
17. Rolling Platform (United Kingdom)
18. Bargaining Agreement Reached Between Management & Labor
19. Head Ticket Seller
20. Production Business Division
21. All Movement by Actors
28. Theatrical Management Association in United Kingdom (Initials)
29. Construction / Crew Division
32. Theatre-in-the-Round
35. First Task Upon Being Hired: "_____ the Play"
36. Combination of Director's Concept and Style
37. Completes Triumvirate of Scenery, Lighting, & _____ Designers"
38. Sound Designers Detail Technical Specifications on a "_____ Line Diagram"
40. Famous French Playwright (1622-1673)
43. Advises on Historical Accuracy, Research, Script Analysis, etc.
44. Stanislavsky Method of Staging
47. Working Together
48. American Design Union (Initials)
49. Overall Shape or Form of a Group Onstage
50. Manager Responsible for Fabrication & Installation of Technical Elements in a Theatre
51. Creates Dances

**DOWN**

1. Percentage Money Paid to Artists
2. Legal Permission to Present a Play
5. Foremost Concern for Entire Production Team
9. Another Word for Millinery Designer
12. Second Phase of Production
13. Greek Platform Shoes
14. First Broadway Show to Utilize Computerized Lighting
15. London Award for Best New Comedy and Best New Play
22. Theatre Producing Solely for Profit
23. Polyester Sheets that Project Color
24. Arch in Front of Stage
25. Singers & Orchestra Sit & Explore Musical Score
26. Proper Positioning on Program Title Page
27. Investors
30. Rolling Platform (United States)
31. Building or Construction of Technical Elements
33. Number of Key Elements
34. Rehearsals following General & Technical
39. Prop Group for Anything That Hangs on Walls
41. Qualities of Successful Stage Managers: Responsibility, Leadership & _____
42. Writes Out All the Musical Parts for a Musical
45. Provides Technical Drawings & Budgets for Every Piece of Scenery (Initials)
46. International Alliance of Theatrical Stage Employees (Initials)

**Figure 11.3** Theatre Production Crossword Puzzle Answers

# Index

Page numbers in **bold** type refer to **figures**